D0836073

The
Relational
Way

The
Relational
Way

From small group structures to holistic life connections

M. SCOTT BOREN

TOUCH® PUBLICATIONS
Houston, Texas, U.S.A.

Published by TOUCH® Publications
P.O. Box 7847
Houston, Texas, 77270, U.S.A.
1-800-735-5865

International Standard Book Number: 0-9788779-0-X

TOUCH® Publications is the book-publishing division
of TOUCH® Outreach Ministries, a resource and consulting ministry for churches with a vision for a holistic
small group-based local church structure.

Find us on the World Wide Web at
http://www.touch®usa.org

Dedication

In the movie *As Good as It Gets*, Jack Nicholson plays a reclusive writer. As he gets to know the character portrayed by Helen Hunt, he says to her, "You make me want to be a better man."

This book is dedicated to my wife, Shawna, who makes me want to come out of the writer's cave and be the love that Jesus displayed. Your beauty both inside and out challenges me to become a better man. I thank God for you every day and the beauty you have brought into my life.

Table of Contents

Foreword

by ALAN J. ROXBURGH

This is an important book. Read it slowly, prepared to have your view of small groups in the church reoriented. If you are a church leader wrestling with a desire to form God's people, then you're holding a book that can be incredibly important for your future.

I have known Scott for more than a dozen years. I have had the immense privilege of watching him wrestle with big questions about the church and small groups. What fascinates me about Scott is his constant desire to figure things out. He's a very practical individual, concerned about how to make ideas land in ways that people can understand and apply them to their context.

Small group ministry in the local church has been at the heart of Scott's wrestling. What Scott has written in this book is far more than theory or nice ideas garnered from books, conferences and programs. This book distills his practical wisdom in working with many kinds of churches over an extended period of time. However, the book is far more than an incredibly helpful guide into small group ministry. Let me explain.

I have worked with small group ministry for many years as a pastor in three local churches. The renewal movements of the 1960s placed the small group at the center of its strategies. But so often the shape of these groups was something like 'encounter groups lite' where suburban, expressive individualism could find a religious version of its search for identity and experience. When people like Ralph Neighbour tried to address these captivities, their voices were hardly heard. As a result, most small group ministry remained simply a mechanism for integrating and supporting individuals within a church.

I have grown tired and suspicious of most small group processes I've seen over the years. In fact, there is this part of me that wants to run away from most of the small groups I see functioning in churches today. This is where Scott's book makes a difference. He understands that North American culture is in the midst of massive shifts, especially in relationship to structures, programs, and their use to get individuals to do things. Scott knows that one more program or another list of steps and 'how-to's' will not address the deep malaise of Christian life in our churches.

If you are looking for a theological framework linked to a practical way of cultivating a missionary people, this book will take you on that journey. I urge you to be clear about one thing before you read further. Scott is inviting you to consider changing some of your most basic frameworks and understanding of small group ministry in the church. He wants you to think theologically and biblically before all else. He wants you to change the culture of your local church with a set of convictions that go far beyond making small groups 'work.' This book is about the formation of local churches which are infecting their communities with Jesus' life and message. It's not just a new set of ideas but a radically re-oriented way of life.

Read on, read slowly, and hear an invitation to become a different kind of church.

Alan J. Roxburgh
Pastor, Author and Consultant

Foreword

by RANDY FRAZEE

The Christian conversation on community begins with the very nature of God. The one true God of the *Shema* of Deuteronomy 6 is a relational God. The Father, Son and Holy Spirit are three distinct persons but share an essence or oneness. We cannot fully understand one person of the Godhead without looking at them as a single community.

We were made in the image of God. Genesis 1:26 is not a statement directed at our individuality as much as it towards our nature as a community. It was not just Adam who was made in the image of God, but Adam and Eve. This is why God said it was not good for the Adam to be alone in the garden. The image of God is not completely manifested in us without community.

Of course, as a result of sin, community is greatly damaged if not destroyed in Genesis 3. This is the birth of death and of individualism. "What causes fights and quarrels among you?" James asks. He answers his own question straightforwardly, "You desire but you do not have, so you kill. You covet but you cannot get what you want, so you quarrel and fight" (James 4:2; cf. Genesis 4). This is the story of our life.

Christ came to change this condition. The gospel is not merely the redemption of the individual into an eternal relationship with God; it is the restoration of community or the image of God in us. This New Community is called "The Church." Without the presence and practice of community in Christ there is no church. What you have instead is a collection of individuals who happen to gather in the same room. There is a fundamental difference.

Many of us who are church leaders are just now coming to terms with the negative impact of the last 50 years has had on the church, particularly in modern, high-tech societies. The United States has been dubbed by many sociologists as the most individualized society in human history. Our lives are severely fragmented by planes, trains and automobiles; by excessive activity and just enough discretionary money to pay for it. We are a society that only asks *can* we do something, not *should* we do something.

It is in this context that church leaders must form authentic, Christ-centered community. Most leaders were born into isolation and individualism and "do not know that they do not know" that there is a fundamental problem. Other leaders see the vision of Christ and try to do what they can, but at times it seems nearly impossible. It is easy to give up and many do.

This is where *The Relational Way* comes to our rescue. Scott has devoted his life to the cause of community. Here are a couple of things among many that I think you will like about this book. First, Scott gets it. He understands the ancient biblical mandate for the church to be a community of oneness laid out so clearly by Jesus in John 17 and Paul in the book of Ephesians. Second, he doesn't just pontificate on lofty theological ideals, but addresses our contemporary problem of fragmentation head on. It is imperative that every church leader and parishioner understand the "pickle" we've gotten ourselves into as a society and church. Scott does a fine job of helping us grasp this dilemma. Third, Scott is not going to give us a "one size fits all" proposal for a relational church, but peruses several worthy models and invites us to think for ourselves. All models must be contextualized and localized. Scott not only believes this but encourages it in his writing.

Most of all, a fellow practitioner, Scott is rooting for you to succeed all throughout the book. Success for Scott is your success in building a strong relational church that God the Father envisioned when he sent the Son and the Holy Spirit to us.

Randy Frazee
Teaching Pastor, Willow Creek Community Church

Fast-food, Bones and the Way of God

In the early 1950s, two brothers became frustrated with the costs involved with running their car-hop restaurant in San Bernardino, California. To save money, they experimented with a simplified menu, a streamlined food preparation process and inexpensive food, and they fired all of the servers on roller skates. Very quickly, the McDonald brothers became rich off of this experiment.

Ray Kroc sold milk-shake mixers, and he inquired as to why the McDonald's® restaurant had purchased eight mixers as opposed to one or two like most of his other customers. Immediately, he saw the potential to take this method of serving food across the country. He bought the rights to franchise, and the rest is history.[1] From that model came many other fast-food providers, thus shaping an industry that feeds 25 percent of America every day.[2] With the promise of speed, service, and somewhat appealing taste, the world can eat three filling meals per day without focusing on the act of eating itself. In addition, the innovation of the drive-thru window created a scenario where eating can serve as a subsidiary function of the driving process.

The fast-food industry and the drive-thru experience serve as metaphors for how life works today. The pace of life, the demands on time and the expectations of efficiency and production rule our lives. The fast-food way of life also acts as a kind of parable for modern spirituality. It paints a picture for how many people approach God and the church. For instance, some people treat God as if he is the voice coming through the speaker at a drive-thru sign. As a result, instead of sitting down with God and communing with him, they only set forth their requests of him. They drive thru whenever they need God to meet some pressing need, usually in the form of financial burdens, emotional problems, physical ailments, or the need to discover God's will. God has been reshaped into the image of a provider of spiritual goods and services to meet individual needs. As a result, the Bible serves as a book for quick answers to modern-day problems.

In the same vein, this way of doing life has infiltrated the church. Pastors and church leaders find themselves under intense pressure to meet the expectations of people who are looking for the drive-thru God experience. Spiritual shoppers are looking for the "God-made-easy" church, and if one church does not provide the right goods and services, then the spiritual shopper drives down the road to another church. The authors of the book *Stormfront* state, "What we, as discriminating shoppers of spiritual goods and services, finally want to know is, How will believing in this god improve my quality of life? Bottom line, what does this deity do for me?"[3] Low-cost spirituality, prepackaged words from God, limited time commitment and non-invasive programming will always attract a crowd because the crowd has been shaped by the fast-food life.

The Marginalization of the Church

In addition to the pressure to meet the expectation of spiritual consumers, pastors and church leaders feel an overwhelming pressure from another source. This pressure is felt but often left unidentified. We don't know how to talk about it. It is a nagging pain with unknown origins. Alan Roxburgh helps us identify its source. He writes, "North American Christians are in an 'in-between' place. A certain world has come to an end but there is, as yet, no clarity on what is emerging."[4] This in-between place sits after the period labeled as modernity, a time when the role of the church was clear. However, in this world of the "in-between," the role of the church is far from obvious. The church has become marginalized in what has been labeled a "post-Christian" society, and most church leaders—at least the honest ones—are looking for answers and direction with regard to the future of the church.

The church as we know it was built upon the idea of attracting people to attend spiritual events and services. In other words, people "go to church" and church leaders spend their efforts on developing ways to get people to "come to church." Church is a spiritual service that occurs at a specific spiritual time, at a specific spiritual place, led by spiritual people, for people with spiritual interests.

This model is founded upon the Constantinian assumptions about the role of spirituality in culture. When Constantine became the Roman Emperor, the church shifted from a gathering of radical subversives who chose to participate in a counter movement to a gathering of people who were being good Roman citizens by participating in the new religion of the Emperor. Roxburgh goes on to write that the church has developed since the fourth century at, or near, the center of culture, resulting in a level of congruence "between the overarching values and frameworks of the wider culture and the churches. Culture and church reflected congruence rather than contrast. The public square had room for both the church building and the town hall."[5]

On this side of the world, the role of the church took on a slightly different form than the European version. While there was no official link between church and state in North America, the church remained at the center of our culture. As the western church has developed through its various manifestations and denominations, the purpose of the church has morphed into an organization that attracts people and meets their spiritual needs. The center of the church has become the Sunday morning event with the goal of making that event attractive enough to draw in observers from the culture.

While I am in no way castigating excellence in worship services or preaching, the goal of attracting people has a limited return on its investment. The church faces a crisis unique to our times. Church leaders are becoming aware of the massive transition within our culture. Accelerated change, uncertainty about the future, and instability dominate the social landscape. As such, this unprecedented cultural change is also changing the location of the church within the cultural mindset. The church finds itself in the midst of a culture that it is no longer equipped to understand or reach. It calls people to Jesus by trying to attract them to events and services, but those very people now view the church as increasingly marginalized, irrelevant, and even unattractive.

The Small Group Alternative

In the midst of these pressures, church leaders have discovered alternative ways of organizing and leading the people of God. Many have adopted small group strategies as a way to connect people and to counteract some of these pressures.

I found hope in small groups while reading David Yongii Cho's book *Successful Home Cell Groups*. Through it, my imagination was captured by a radical way of being the church. This vision for the church disturbed me as much as it excited me. Because I was reading about a relational way of being the church, I could no longer settle for doing church the way I knew. Through his stories about small groups of people loving one another, along with the testimonies of idol worshippers who were led to Jesus through the love of these groups, God captured my imagination of what the church could be. I wanted to—no, I had to—live in this kind of church, even if the investment took the rest of my life.

As I dialog with pastors and church leaders across North America, I hear many stories that resemble that of my own. They read a book, attend a conference, or start a 40-day small-group campaign. The conclusion usually is, we need small groups to generate community. The leaders imagine that a small-group structure will address the challenges that churches face in the midst of the fast-food culture.

However, more often than not, the groups serve as another structure for attracting people to another spiritual meeting. This spiritual meeting is forced to compete with all the other spiritual offerings on the market. Fast-food spirituality doesn't die easily. Small-group structures can organize people into groups and even promote church growth, but they don't necessarily challenge the fast-food life that people bring to church. While looking upon the landscape of small-group experiments over the last few decades in North America, one pastor has observed, "Small groups simply became a part of an individual's personal 'do-it-yourself' religion that reinforced 'individualized faith.'"[6]

The Breath and the Bones

I have been helping churches develop small group systems since the early 1990s. Throughout these years, I have observed churches that have experimented with many different small-group models. Some have failed while others have entered into the land of great success. Most have wandered in the land of mediocrity, searching for ways to develop their groups. The difference between success and failure doesn't correlate with a particular model or specific structure. In fact, one church could copy the exact structure and procedures that another church used successfully with drastically different results.

If the structure was not the key to success, what was? If small groups alone did not help a church enter into a radical lifestyle for God's kingdom, what did? As I asked these questions, I reflected on Ezekiel 37. In this chapter, God led the prophet into the valley where he saw piles of dry bones. Ezekiel wrote, *"He (the Spirit) led me back and forth among them, and I saw a great many bones on the floor of the valley, bones that were very dry."* Today, many churches have a lot in common with these bones. People attend and some churches are even growing. But most only gather the people in one place without helping them connect with one another. The people sit together, but they are not connected in such a way as to form a connected body.

First, Ezekiel spoke to the bones, *"And as I was prophesying, there was a noise, a rattling sound, and the bones came together, bone to bone. I looked, and tendons and flesh appeared on them and skin covered them, but there was no breath in them."* The church needs practical structures and methods for connecting individuals so as to form a body. We also need prophets today who will confront practices that promote the values of independence and individualism of the culture. It is time to re-think church so that it might become more than a gathering of like-minded individuals.

After the bones came together, Ezekiel observed, *"There is no breath in them."* Many churches find themselves making the same observations about their church structures. They know how to do small groups. They know how to organize small group oversight (coaching). Some even know how to develop curriculum and grow their groups. But they don't see the life they desire within them. God told Ezekiel to prophesy to the breath. Ezekiel reported, *"So I prophesied as he commanded me, and breath entered them; they came to life and stood up on their feet—a vast army."*

Churches require structures. All breath and no structure results in church blobs, not church bodies. God's army requires efficient and flexible structures. Most churches stop at the search for church structure and settle for connected bones, failing to discover what God wants to do within these structures. As a result, they miss out on the way of God.

Identifying the Breath

The breath could be called relational kingdom living. Such would be defined as a way of living with others that fits with the coming of the kingdom of God. It is a relational paradigm for life, a mode of living that defines the nature of the relational way.

The relational way is founded upon the God of relationality. Father, Son, and Holy Spirit share life together perfectly, relating in such a way that each is fully available to the others. The mystery of God lies in how the three are one and the one are three. However, the Father, Son, and Holy Spirit do not horde their relational sharing. The community shared by the godhead is missional in nature, self-giving in such a way that God invites people to participate in the God life, sharing in the community in which God exists. As the church enters into this communion with God, sitting at his table with him, the people share community with one another. As the church practices life as community it becomes contagious, sharing life with those who have yet to participate in communion with God.

Communion with God, community with one another, and contagion of life overflowing from the nature of the relational God comprise the three aspects of what it means to live as a relational way of being the church.

Evidently, this is what was transpiring in the churches of the New Testament. In fact, the early church was often referred to as The Way. In one of the stories Luke records, he writes, *"Paul entered the synagogue and spoke boldly there for three months, arguing persuasively about the kingdom of God. But some of them became obstinate; they refused to believe and publicly maligned the Way"* (Acts 19:8-9). Jesus referred to himself as The Way (John 14:6). The way of kingdom living in the early church was distinctive and missional. By referring to the church as The Way, it denotes that the people of God are called to action, a mode of interacting with the world that infects it with the life of God.

This model stands in stark contrast to the attractional approach to church. The attractional model assumes that people will come to God when they need him. It is true that he waits patiently for us, but God's sending nature is the model of God that we see in Jesus. God is a sending God. If the church today is to participate in the life of the Trinity, the people of God must learn to shift from a "come and observe" approach to a "go and demonstrate" approach. It must set aside the need to preserve the church as we know it—whether through small groups or through any number of other strategies—and give up our status to be on mission with God. In his excellent book *Transforming Mission*, David Bosch states, "God is a missionary God. ... Mission is thereby seen as a movement from God to the world; the church is viewed as an instrument for that mission. There is a church because there is mission, not vice versa. To participate in mission is to participate in the movement of God's love toward people, since God is a fountain of sending love."[7]

The foundational question, then, is not "How do we create more small groups?" or "How do we grow the church through small groups?" or "What model of small groups works the best?" These are structural questions and you must learn to ask contrary questions about being a church on The Way: "How do we become a people that live in community that stands in contrast to the social structures of this world?" or "What are the practices of a people on the way with God?" or "What ways of living would manifest in being a church on mission with God?"

A Few Notes About This Book

To address this question, I have identified ten assumptions that church leaders often make when they embark on the small-group journey. They are structural myths that have quietly crept into small-group strategies, myths that logically coincide with the attractional church model. Because they cause church leaders to focus on the bones, there is some truth to them. This is what makes believing them so tempting. If they were obviously wrong, then this book would not be necessary. At some point on my small-group journey, I have believed each one of these to be true. As you read these myths, you may think that they are obviously errant. They are intentionally stated in black and white terms, but while working through the chapters you will discover the subtleties that make them so easy to believe.

To expose these myths, each chapter proposes a constructive alternative that I call a relational truth. These alternatives are presented through a unique approach. Rather than identifying specific churches or models for implementing specific practices, I have steered clear of pointing you to churches that are doing what I am talking about. There are enough books in print that do this. My goal is not to point you to easy answers or quick fixes that other churches have developed. When we depend upon models and methods developed elsewhere, we can easily miss out on God's activity in the midst of our own church. While emulating another church promises immediate results, I have discovered that I overlook how God is reshaping me and my church when I focus on following a model. Today is a day that God is reforming the church. He is calling the church from one place to another, much like he called the Israelite slaves out of Egypt to the Promised Land. The call is not to new programs or even to new ways of doing small groups. The call is to a new way of being the people of God. This requires transformative reshaping of both the corporate church and individual lives.

This book aims to stir your imagination rather than provide answers. To do this, I have woven theology together with practical application. Most books are written either theologically or practically. Few works merge these two worlds, which has always concerned me. Good theology is often left disconnected from church strategies. As well, applied or practical theology is often presented in isolation from good theology. The first half of each chapter offers a dialogue with the Word of God and theology that is meant to call church leaders out of the world of pragmatic answers to urgent problems. It is my attempt to move back into the rhythm of listening to the Spirit first. The second half offers guidelines that are connected to the theological dialogue, which follow the subtitle, "What does this mean … practically?" These suggestions are meant to be read as conversation starters rather than definitive methods so that we can imagine how this might look. If you are practically-minded by nature, feel free to start with the practical half and then work back through the theological foundation. However, my hope is that you will work through each chapter from the beginning and allow the broad guidelines to stimulate your imagination.

I offer the theology and the practical parts as an invitation for further dialogue. Set aside your preconceived notions, assumptions, or rules about small groups and church and wrestle with the content. Argue with the points and figure out what each means in your context. If you extend the limits to your imagination, you will be surprised at what the Spirit of God speaks to you.

A Prayer

I long for the day when God fulfills the vision of the valley of dry bones in North America. It is happening in pockets, but for the most part we have yet to see what God has for us. In this "in-between" time, the church has the opportunity to walk with God in new ways. Because we can no longer depend upon the methods and strategies of the past, we must depend upon God's life in us. Today is a day of great opportunity for the church if we have the courage to enter honestly into this "in-between" time.

An experienced small-group pastor reviewed this book for me prior to publication. He commented, "I wonder if American church leadership can wait on God long enough to achieve the picture you are painting." For sure, this book calls for imaginative thinking. As a result, some may conclude that it is impractical. I pray that you will find it compelling, a vision that will capture your heart and even mess with your expectations of God and the church. As I have written it, God has captured my imagination again, and he has messed with me to the point that I cannot be satisfied with a nice small group program in a growing church. He has implanted a call for a vision that will require a lifelong battle.

I will fight for a relational way of being the church even if it never comes to fruition in my lifetime. My imagination can now envision that which I have not completely seen. I am seeking God for a vision for the church that I can pass to my sons who are now toddlers. I want to start something that they will experience in a way than I may never know in my life and ministry. I hope and pray I get to experience it fully, but my guess is that we are embarking on a new way of being God's people that will only be realized by future generations, which excites me.

I believe this is how the prophets of the Old Testament felt about God's work in the world. At the end of Ezekiel's vision, God said, *"O my people, I am going to open your graves and bring you up from them; I will bring you back to the land of Israel. Then you, my people, will know that I am the Lord, when I open your graves and bring you up from them. I will put my Spirit in you and you will live, and I will settle you in your land. Then you will know that I the Lord have spoken, and I have done it, declares the Lord."*

Lord, stir our imaginations that we might again see the relational kingdom that you have for us. Let this imagination renew hope. Let this hope stimulate faith. And let this faith produce endurance. May we realize the reality of the Spirit living through us that we might participate in mission with you to settle this land as a kingdom people. You have spoken, you are faithful, and we trust that you will fulfill. By your grace we will participate in this calling. Amen!

CHAPTER 1

Prioritize the Way of Relationality

At a small group conference, a pastor was talking with one of the speakers. The speaker asked the pastor, "Do you have small groups?"

"No, we don't," he responded.

"Why not?" the speaker interjected. "Get small groups going and your church will grow like ours. There is no other way to expand your church."

I used to say the same thing to pastors, assuming that all a pastor needed was a new vision for small groups. However, the school of hard knocks as a pastor and volunteer leader in three different churches in vastly different cities in North America has changed my perspective.

In addition, I have seen too many pastors attend a small group conference, purchase all the available material, return home to start groups, and then disband the group enterprise in less than three years. It is too simplistic to argue that small groups are the key to success in the twenty-first century church. On the other hand, it is hard to argue against them. Groups are right. (By the way, the conference speaker mentioned above leads a very large church with lots of small groups.) So what is the real issue?

I falsely made the assumption that small group growth is a product of the small group structure. Groups might be the right thing to do, but they only produce the desired fruit when you do them the right way. Doing the right thing the wrong way won't produce a relational way experience. Jesus said that he is the *way, the truth and the life*" (John 14:6). It is not enough to embrace the truth of small group community. His way of doing his ministry is more important than an efficient church organization. If a church plans to develop effective small groups, it must adopt Jesus' way of relationships, as opposed to the way of programmatic small groups.

Structural Myth #1:
Doing the right thing (a small group program) without consideration of the right way (the relational way) will produce community.

The Relational Truth:
God's relational kingdom is a product of leaders who establish a way of living that stands in contrast to the culture.

Small Groups Built as a Program

Two patterns are found in churches that multiply small groups consistently. Whether you go to Korea, Singapore, Colombia, El Salvador, South Africa or the Ivory Coast, you will observe both. First, they pray ... and they pray a lot. Prayer has become a way of life for them as a church. Second, they have a singular focus on small groups. In these churches, the groups are the priority. Yet for some reason, this prioritization of small groups has not translated well into the church of North America.

Part of the problem stems from the terms used to discuss the strategy: cell church, small group-based church, cell-driven church, or church of small groups. Small group experts use titles as a short-hand way to communicate the activities that lie behind the words. These titles focus on the small group structure because it is the easiest and most tangible component to communicate. The New Testament is used to support this use of titles, again focusing on the most accessible component, the small group structure.

However, small groups were never the focus of the New Testament church. Yes, the first century church met in small groups in homes (see Acts 2:42-6, 5:42, 20:20), but they did not treat small groups as a strategy to grow the church or reach the lost. The first century church was a fledgling movement that did not have official buildings or recognized status. Where else would they have met but in homes? The New Testament never instructs the church to meet in small groups. Instead, the New Testament authors write without thinking about the structures of church meetings. The small group house church was the paradigm that shaped how they thought about church, but structural direction itself is strikingly absent from the inspired canon.

What is not lacking in the New Testament are the overt commands concerning how members of the church should relate to one another: love one another, serve one another, edify one another, and consider others more important than self. Instead of instructions about being a "cell-based church" or "church *of* small groups," the authors of the biblical text were extremely concerned about how members of the church related to one another. The relationality of people in the groups is what provides the base of life from which ministry occurs. Groups are only a means to the end of a relational life.

The Air We Breath

When traveling along Interstate 10 from El Paso, Texas to Los Cruces, New Mexico, it is impossible to miss a remarkable olfactory experience. Adjacent to the highway is a series of dairy farms that produce an infiltrating smell. As we passed the dairy farms, the driver of the car in which I was riding told of a friend who worked on one of these dairy farms. Apparently, he grew so accustomed to the odor that breathing city air was an odd experience. The smell of dairy cow manure became a way of life for him.

When we grow so accustomed to living a certain way, it is impossible to see how that way affects our lives. It becomes the glasses through which we see life, a reality that shapes us. We don't have to study this or even know how it works. It is just the way things are and we just accept it as a given way of life.

In America, one of the primary ways of living that shapes us is called programmatic living. We are a people who breathe the air of the programmatic life. We live each day according to a set of predetermined and proven steps that promise greater success. To lose weight, we follow a diet program. To improve a marriage, a couple will follow a communication program. For financial freedom, there are books that spell out proven methods. We have programs for learning how to cook, becoming an executive, raising a healthy family, and retiring early. If you want simple how-to steps for living life, just go to the bookstore.

Why do we use these programs? As one who is currently following a diet program as I write this book, I can tell you why I follow them. They promise results without requiring research on my part, and are easy to initially embrace.

The McDonald's Corporation has developed a program with detailed procedures on how to perform all the duties and functions within each McDonald's franchise. Such a program allows franchise owners to start-up quickly without having to become hamburger experts. As a result of this program, inexperienced teenagers can cook and package hamburgers and French fries just like every other McDonald's employee around the world.

Pastors have the option of taking the programmatic approach to small groups. They can purchase all of the manuals and follow the user-friendly steps that have been developed, tested and proven by another church, which has taken the time to figure out all of the underlying details. Such an approach is quite attractive because it allows for a quick start-up and promises the results of the church that developed the program. Church leaders don't have to think; they only need to follow the instructions of the literature developed at the model church. Plus, pastors don't have to attain a clear sense of the church's mission during this present age of chaotic transition. They only need to find the program that is working and purchase it.

We are so accustomed to the programmatic air we breathe that many pastors immediately raise arguments. "But it works!" a pastor might retort. Others would say, "Our church grew and our people became committed. We even have more groups." Such arguments reveal one of the unseen roots of the programmatic approach to church: pragmatism. The test of what works determines what program a church should do, and the key variable to the test of what works is numbers. "Big" equals success in our programmatic world. We must not fall to the temptation of pragmatism, merely focusing on numbers, growth ratios, and evangelism statistics. An imbalanced focus on the pragmatic questions of church growth can lead the church down a path of attracting people and starting new groups, while sacrificing the people within those groups.

The programmatic drive to produce fruit (numbers) undermines the very essence that causes fruit to grow in the first place (relationships). It might produce short-term results, but the long-term impact will be negative. Growing up a farm, I saw this short-term focus taken by some of the farmers in my area. Because they knew that their fields would soon be purchased by housing developers, they did not worry about erosion or overusing the land. They just plowed and fertilized and planted and harvested as much as they could and as quickly as they could. But if this land were to be farmland for the next 50 years, then such an approach would be counter-productive. The long-term approach to farming does not sacrifice future productivity of the land for short-term yield.

Focusing on Relationships

Small-group expert Joel Comiskey and I are good friends. A few years ago, I joined him during his four-hour layover at the Houston airport. At that time, he was serving as a missionary pastor in Ecuador. We talked about family, personal interests, ministry, God, and the projects we were working on together. As we drank coffee, he said, "In Ecuador, the people do what we have been doing the last three hours nearly every day. They spend extended time relating to one another. We just use small groups to connect them together with God." In America, people don't relate to one another this way. Therefore, the American church has to learn not only how to do small groups but also how to do relationships.

Small groups are flourishing in Third World countries in South America, Asia, and Africa. These cultures breathe a different air than we do in North America. They never learned to breathe the air of pragmatism. They never learned to measure their lives by what they produce (although this is changing rapidly in some places). Instead, they measure their lives by the life they live with others.

American Christians must learn how to do relationships on top of learning how to do small groups. We are relational neophytes compared to most other cultures of the world. Life in America is one that lacks "refrigerator rights." This is the argument of Will Miller in his book by the same title. He writes, "I've slowly come to the conclusion that the core emotional problem of modern life is this: a pervasive personal detachment and aloofness from other people."[1] He challenges his readers to analyze their lives because his research has revealed a direct link between personal detachment or isolation and personal anxiety. One psychologist he quotes writes, "Our greater autonomy may lead to increased challenge and excitement, but it also leads to greater isolation from others, more threats to our bodies and minds, and thus higher levels of free-floating anxiety."[2]

Miller asks his readers, "How many people in your life right now have refrigerator rights in your home? How many of the people you encounter every day see you unshaven or without makeup? How many people hear you express yourself in that blunt, unguarded way you do with your family? How many can you talk to at a genuine, deep, intimate level? And how many people grant you refrigerator rights? How many people confide in you—tell you about the things that really matter to them?"[3]

The lack of refrigerator rights is a by-product of the pragmatic myth that every individual is entitled to pursue his or her dreams to become as successful as possible. Statements like, "You can do whatever you set your mind to," and "Be all that you can be," cause people to believe that personal fulfillment is primarily found through one's profession. This drive to find "my" personal field of success compels me to focus on my needs, my dreams, and me. Relationships, then, serve my goals. There is little intrinsic value in just relating. In other words, refrigerator rights are not deemed necessary.

While writing this chapter, my family received some difficult news. My aunt and uncle (her brother) died within 30 hours of one another. While my aunt's death was expected, my uncle's passing came suddenly and as a surprise to our family. While attending the funerals, God spoke to me in ways that I never expected. My aunt had experienced a series of strokes over the last eight years, making her homebound and requiring the constant care of her husband. As he told us the story of how they met, dated and married, he said: "I don't regret a minute of it." This man gave everything to care for his wife for the last eight years of her life while she could give him very little. He was not "accomplishing" anything or successful in the eyes of our world. He was merely loving another the best way he knew how.

The family viewing for my uncle was held the evening of my aunt's funeral. We were simply blown away by the response. Over 1,000 people came to the viewing to remember his life and bless our family. Three hundred people attended the funeral service itself, and more left because there was no room to stand. Such numbers usually only turn out for someone famous or someone young. My uncle was neither. He never wrote a book, preached a sermon, or held a public office. His occupations included bread truck driver, owner of a construction company, and a school bus driver. He loved being with kids and enjoyed his last job the most. While my Uncle Wimpy—yes, that was his name—never did anything that might be worthy of historical significance, he lived a life that made an impact on everyone he met. He was a giver of life and was not worried about what he might accomplish or become on earth. He was just trying to be himself and love others while doing it.

Miller makes a startling proclamation about personal achievement and success. As a former comedian, he confesses,

> I was always focused first on the goals of my career—success in show business. All other matters, including relationships with family and friends, followed in priority. My view (unconscious, of course) was that family and other relationships were there for background support and enjoyment. It didn't occur to me until much later that it could or should be the other way around. The purpose of career ambition is to enable a life of emotionally close relationships. Whether it involves sustained connections to my own kin or a re-created network of new relationships, attachment to others is the end game in human living.[4]

My uncle understood this. However, many churches operate according to a system or way of doing things that does not.

The Operating System of American Life

The condition of individualism—along with that of pragmatism—forms the operating system that shapes life in America. Like a computer's operating system, our life's operating system dictates how all other programs work. Many churches adopt a small group program and attach it to the operating system of pragmatism and individualism. Instead of abandoning this root operating system for a better one, some churches have tried to develop small group programs that fit the American culture. Small groups and other ministry programs are adopted to help individuals "become all that they can be for Christ." The church finds itself ministering to individuals, helping them develop their private beliefs and live as individuals who are faithful before God. Small groups as a program promises individual fulfillment for those involved. It promotes personal development, if people so choose to participate. The church then finds itself trying to create the best possible small-group program so as to attract as many people as possible.

Such a program might produce more groups, but it has limited impact on how people live. Individuals meet as a group every week, but they still live in isolation, searching pragmatic answers to personal success. They don't become a part of a people who form an alternative society or contrasting city, one that lives differently than the culture. Instead, it only propagates the operating system of the culture because it uses the lifestyle of the culture as its measurement for success.

The church in America does not need more groups that function within the cultural operating system. It needs to adopt a relational operating system that helps people develop refrigerator rights. Churches don't need another growth program with small groups at the center. They need a way to help people connect with one another in meaningful ways so that they create a contrasting way of life to the environment in which society lives.

Miller also uses the analogy of the air we breathe to describe our condition of isolation,

> If something is nearly constant or routine, we tend not to notice it. Breathing is so automatic that you don't tend to consciously think about the mechanics of your body as you take a breath. In today's environment, our isolation from other people has become so routine that many of us don't even realize that this is our state of affairs.[5]

The church must help people realize that they are breathing polluted air and then provide an alternative way, a way based on the way of God.

The Operating System of God

The foundational part of God's operating system stands in sharp contrast to that of American life. God is love. Love defines the inner being of who God is. He cannot not love. At his core he is relational. First, we must see God as one whose life is one of self-giving, out-pouring love.

Many times, though, our individualistic, pragmatic operating system fails to see God for who he is. Our view of life often causes us to define God by his all-consuming power, omnipotence, and overarching authority rather than love. We begin with his transcendence or his "otherness." But in doing so, we define God by man's definition of power or our own picture of authority. We make God out to be the glorious one in heaven who dictates his will from a distance. One preacher put it this way: "It is popular to talk about God being relational. I don't know where people get this. The Bible is all about his glory and his power." This pastor's view has turned God into an authoritarian monarch. He has overlooked Christ as his definition of God.

Church leaders who take such a view of God often see themselves as sub-authoritarians, those with special connections with God who don't require relationships. They only need to figure out what God is saying and preach the truth. They become spiritual power brokers telling people how to live their lives. Pastoral leadership positions come with lots of authority, and people venerate pastors and set them on pedestals. "It is our duty to get off of them," as Chuck Swindoll has said.

We must follow the authority demonstrated by Christ. He displayed vulnerable power. When God pulled back the veil between man and himself, he came as a servant of servants, the weakest of all. The Word became flesh and dwelt among us. *"Christ Jesus, who being in very nature God, did not consider equality with God something to be grasped, but made himself nothing, taking the very nature of a servant, being made in human likeness"* (Philippians 2:6-7). God came shining forth "the love of all loves." He came relating.

Even more, he came relating to the cast-offs of society, those who did not "deserve" relationships with the righteous, much less God. He touched the leper, talked with divorced women, and embraced the children. He related to the least and little of society, not the great and powerful. He revealed his nature of love by demonstrating the power of relating to the nobodies.

He came but his own did not recognize him. Why? Because they were expecting a different kind of God. They were looking for a God of power and might, one who would establish Israel as a success story, one who would set things right and make things work properly. They wanted a God who would demand people to recognize his glory. However, Jesus did not enter the world with control and force. He did not seek success and fame. He did not look for platforms and political influence. He did not seek to establish himself so that he could influence as many people as possible. He came relating.

The fact is, he could not come any other way. Relational living is the only operating system that Jesus could adopt. It is just who he is. Jesus knows love because he lives in love with the Father and with the Holy Spirit. The statement, "God is love," reveals that God is a relational, triune God. God is relational within himself. The Father, Son and Spirit are one in love. Gregory of Nazianzen, one of the Cappadocian Fathers, wrote this about the Trinity in the fourth century:

> No sooner do I consider the One than I am enlightened by the radiance of the Three; no sooner do I distinguish them than I am carried back to the One. When I bring any One of the Three before my mind I think of him as a Whole, and my vision is filled, and the most of the Whole escapes me. I cannot grasp the greatness of that One in such a way as to attribute more greatness to the rest. When I contemplate the Three together, I see but one Torch, and cannot divide or measure out the undivided Light.[6]

God is not an isolated monarch who seeks to establish himself as an individual in power. Nor is God the omnipotent one who rules from a distance. God is the one who reveals power through the authoritative weakness of love. God is the one who strikes fear in others, not by force, but with confident servitude. He is the one who gets close in love and by this reveals true omnipotence, one that we cannot understand. God's greatness is one that does not fit what we think a God should be. We want to have a great God who walks regally, with all recognizing his power. However, God redefines greatness, by expressing his heart, by sitting with a friend, by healing a need, by revealing his love.

This reality of God is nothing but risky. Love has no guarantees. Love calls someone to commit to another regardless of the cost, potential danger, or possibility of hurt. God loves, knowing that he is taking the risk that his love will not always be returned. Love cannot be controlling or manipulating. Love is freeing, allowing the other party to choose how they will respond to love. This means that those who love run the risk of being hurt. The more one loves, the more hurt he will experience.

Relational love is the operating system that stands against the operating system of pragmatism and individualism. Love cannot be placed over our culture's way of living. It is either the basis of life, or we use the tactics that look like love to get stuff done or to meet "my" needs as an individual. Love by definition cannot be usurious or self-serving. Love cannot be orchestrated or designed. It can only be lived in experience with God and others.

What Does This Mean ... Practically?

Establishing the Way of Love

Relational love through small groups is a way of being the church. It is a way of doing ministry. It is a revolutionary manifestation of the kingdom in the midst of ways that stand against the love of God. In order to establish this love in the midst of the people of God, the church needs leaders who will choose to reflect the love of the Trinity by embracing God's operating system. Effective small-group structures start here, not with a vision for small groups or strategies for group oversight. God's relational kingdom way begins and ends with people not structures.

Paul writes a sentence in the first letter to the Corinthians, that if repeated today, would likely be greatly misunderstood. He wrote, *"Follow me as I follow Christ."* Wow! How would you respond if you heard your pastor say that to you? Some might say, "How arrogant!" Others might think, "I don't need anyone telling me how to live." Still others might reply with, "Just preach the Word; that is what I will follow." And most often, the pastor would hear, "We are supposed to follow Christ, not other people." But the reality is that everyone is following someone.

In a radio interview, G.K. Chesterton was once asked, "What do you see as the greatest problem in the world?" He responded, "I am." He understood that if he was going to change the world, he had to be willing to change. As a church leader, if I plan to lead the people under my span of care into this new way of love, I have to start by looking in the mirror. It matters not if those to whom I report or those who directly follow me change. I must personally break the pattern of this pragmatic, individualistic life. Someone must set the model and lead the way into God's operating system of relational living. People ultimately follow the leading of another; they don't change because a new program has been developed. They don't change because they read a book or sit in a training class. People change because they have been loved enough by God and others to see an alternative way of living and then move into it.

The problem though is the fact that we have inherited a system of doing church which undermines the relational way. As a result church leaders are required to operate according to anti-relational patterns to maintain this system. In many cases, the church has been established upon the culture of individualism and pragmatism. In order to establish the way of love, we must realize that leaders must stand for a different way of living and leading within the church.

This requires much more than the implementation of a small-group strategy. The way of love must flow through the entire church, from the way boards operate to the way corporate decisions are made. In other words, they way that church leadership operates must demonstrate the way of love represented in the Trinity or no small-group structure will every experience any form of community that puts God's life on display in this world.

Reflecting God

God sets a pattern of leading his people that stands in contrast to ways of the world. God is a shepherd. A shepherd is one who gives up his life for the sheep. Shepherds lead the sheep. They never drive them. In fact, sheep are almost impossible to drive because they are so easily scattered. This means that the only way to get sheep to go anywhere is to lead them in the direction you want them to go. Peter instructs church leaders,

> *Be shepherds of God's flock that is under your care, serving as overseers—not because you must, but because you are willing, as God wants you to be; not greedy for money, but eager to serve; not lording over those entrusted you, but being examples to the flock. And when the Chief Shepherd appears, you will receive a crown of glory that will never fade away* (1 Peter 5:2-4).

Church leaders are shepherds of God's flock, actually "under-shepherds" of Jesus, the Chief Shepherd. I grew up on a farm with sheep. Good shepherds invest in the sheep, gain their trust, and know each sheep personally. As such, there is no glory in shepherding. Sheep are by far the most frustrating animals I have encountered. They stink. They are noisy. They are easily frightened and vulnerable to the elements of the weather. They are also defenseless prey to predators. No wonder God referred to us as sheep in need of a shepherd.

I have to remind myself of this fact because I am so driven by vision that I can overlook the people I lead. I easily turn from leading to driving them to go in the direction I desire. When I do this, I no longer see the people I lead as persons; I objectify them and use them to accomplish my goals. In his book on church leadership entitled *They Smell Like Sheep*, Lynn Anderson tells a story that challenges me to avoid this pattern:

> Several years ago in Palestine, Carolyn and I rode a tour bus through Israel's countryside nearly mesmerized as the tour guide explained the scenery, the history, and the lifestyle. In his description, he included a heart-warming portrayal of the ancient shepherd/sheep relationship. He expounded on how the shepherd builds a relationship with his sheep-how he feeds them and gently cares for them. He pointed out that the shepherd doesn't drive the sheep but leads them, and that the shepherd does not need to be harsh with them, because they hear his voice and follow. And so on …
>
> He then explained how on a previous tour things had backfired for him as he was giving this same speech about sheep and shepherds. In the midst of spinning his pastoral tale, he suddenly realized he had lost his audience. They were all staring out of the bus window at a guy chasing a 'herd' of sheep. He was throwing rocks at them, whacking them with sticks, and sic-cing the sheep dog on them. The sheep-driving man in the field had torpedoed the guide's enchanting narrative.
>
> The guide told us that he had been so agitated that he jumped off the bus, ran into the field, and accosted the man, "Do you understand what you have just done to me?" he asked. "I was spinning a charming story about the gentle ways of shepherds, and here you are mistreating, hazing, and assaulting these sheep! What is going on?"
>
> For a moment, a bewildered look froze on the face of the poor sheep-chaser, then the light dawned and he blurted out, "Man. You've got me all wrong. I'm not a shepherd. I'm a butcher!"
>
> This poor, unwitting fellow had just provided the tour guide and all of us with a perfect example of what a 'good shepherd' is not.[8]

Good shepherds lead; they do not treat their sheep as objects to be used to accomplish a greater vision. They care for the sheep enough to gently guide them, serving them just as the Chief Shepherd modeled. They guide them by demonstrating a way of living with God and man, which includes elements like: taking Sabbath, maintaining a freedom from worry about success, staying put at one church for more than four years, trusting in God through prayer, and waiting on God rather than hopping from one ministry program to another. Such a way does not guarantee success, church growth, or wealth. If this were the measure of Jesus' success, he was the greatest failure of us all.

Being the Right Person

I will let a story Henri Nouwen tells demonstrate how easy it is for us to misunderstand the way of love because we have embraced a view of success that undermines the relational way. Nouwen was a Catholic priest who served as a professor at some of America's most renowned seminaries. After seeing great success in teaching and writing, he resigned his position as a professor and became the pastor of the L'Arch Daybreak Community in Toronto, a community for mentally handicapped people. During Nouwen's first fourteen months, he was asked to serve a young man named Adam. Adam could not speak or care for himself in any way, and seizures would throw his body into times of absolute exhaustion. To Nouwen, Adam was not a ministry or a project to take care of until he could move on to more important tasks. Adam became one of his best friends, teaching Nouwen how to live and enjoy life. Adam also taught Nouwen how to love God in a much deeper way.

One day, an old friend of Nouwen visited him. Nouwen writes about his response: "When my friend came into the New House and saw me with Adam, he looked at me and asked, 'Henri, is this where you are spending your time?' I saw that he was not only disturbed but even angry. 'Did you leave the university, where you were such an inspiration to so many people, to give your time and energy to Adam?'"[9] Nouwen's friend wanted him to produce and operate according to the system of pragmatism. Adam taught Nouwen how to relate. He taught him how to be real as a pastor. Adam changed Nouwen's operating system.

As I lead a system of over 100 small groups, I feel the pressure to grow more groups, produce more fruit, and have a greater impact on the St. Paul area. I pray that all of these goals occur. I am not against success. At the same time, I recognize that the one God most wants to change is me. This is not a selfish, inward looking, "fix me" focus. As I relate to my leaders, gather with my small group, and invest in my team of pastors and leaders, I see the greatest changes within myself. The primary way God is changing me is through the interaction with these people in relationships.

When I first assumed the role of overseeing these small groups, I failed to listen to the needs of one set of volunteer leaders. I made assumptions due to time pressures, and as a result I hurt them badly. I misunderstood them, and they misunderstood me. At first, I held my ground, but as I listened to their hearts (and to my wife's feedback) I realized that I was wrong. Soon after, I stood before them and asked their forgiveness.

Through this act of allowing them to rub up against me, I changed. I started listening to God and saw how he put this ministry on the heart of one of the pastors on my team. Through the actions of a group of volunteers and the leadership of this pastor, this ministry is taking on a new vision. This change has required lots of time and energy, relational energy on the part of this team of leaders, and this pastor. A program would have produced more immediate fruit, but relationships are the need of the day.

Is being the right person more important than producing results? I want the leaders with whom I work to falter on the side of being the right person and sacrificing the results. I believe that Nouwen charted a course that challenges our pragmatic sensibilities and will point us in the right direction for cultivating the kingdom of God in our world.

Battling an Anti-relational System

Few church leaders would disagree with my conclusion about being the right person, but as I stated above, we struggle against an anti-relational system that has infiltrated the church and in many cases controls it. As I work with churches, I consistently encounter the problem of church leaders not having enough time for relationships. I was sharing the small-group vision of relational ministry with the key pastors of a church of about 5,000. They had small groups and a relatively good structure, but they wanted to take things to the next level. The senior pastor specifically wanted to see his people enter into a radical new kind of life. When I challenged the pastoral team to set the model, the staff—and specifically the senior pastor—looked at me with concern. They performed some quick time calculations and soon realized that their schedules did not allow for refrigerator rights. Their lives were already overflowing with commitments and program-related relationships. To add deep intimate relationships overwhelmed them.

This problem is not unique to large churches. Often, pastors of small churches feel the pressure in even greater ways. They must lead the church out of being small and this requires all the effort they can muster to make things happen.

The pastoral system in America is a professional system. A professional is one who is trained to perform a certain set of tasks according to a proven program of operation. Doctors are an example of this. They receive training at a professional school to perform tasks which others with equal training and skill should be able to perform. The actual person serving as the doctor matters little; it is the duty that he performs that matters. For many patients, he is interchangeable.

The professional pastor is trained to perform a standard set of tasks that anyone trained as a pastor could perform (depending on the denomination). For instance, in certain traditions, the pastor serves as a professional teacher who informs the flock in the right way of living. He would perform marriages according to that tradition, bury according to that tradition, and baptize according to that tradition. But his presence personally as the pastor is not required for the flock to effectively live what he teaches or receive any of the sacraments from him. The pastor is relatively interchangeable.

Whether he expects the denominational headquarters to transfer him or he anticipates a move to another church, he knows that his time with the people of the church is short in comparison to their time in the church. The average tenure of a senior pastor in North America is less than five years, not long enough to develop refrigerator rights. Therefore, a professional distance is created between the pastor and his people, promoting the image of the spiritual individualist who does not need people to speak into his life. As a result, the pastor is often the most isolated person in the entire church. He does not look isolated nor does he feel so. He is busy beyond belief meeting with deacons or elders, counseling with the hurting, and praying with those in the hospital. His life is full of people, but he has no refrigerator rights. On top of this, the expectations placed on the pastor by the people are unrealistic, thereby creating an even greater pressure to perform. Since he has only four years to get all this done—and he must do his job with enough success to merit the recognition of another church with greater opportunities for pastoral consideration—he is left with pragmatic questions of getting programs going.

As a result, the lonely, focused, workaholic pastor sacrifices his family and personal relationships for the sake of the call to ministry. In his book,

Turnaround Churches, George Barna reports on his interviews of pastors who lead declining churches into success. He states, "None of these pastors was proud of being a workaholic, but most of them admitted that this was one trait that enabled them to lead the turnaround. ... A 60 to 80-hour work week was widely viewed as a job hazard for those called to this line of work."[10] The typical pastor is the super-human rugged individual, or what I call the "spiritual Marlboro man."

What kind of model is the professional pastor establishing for the people to follow? Here are some typical ways of living that pastors set for others to imitate:

"If you really want to follow Christ, you will become a workaholic for Christ like me."

"If you really want to follow Christ, you will be alone and isolated like me, with no one to share your deepest needs and hurts."

"If you really want to follow Christ, you won't ever put down any roots because you expect to move within the next five years."

"If you really want to follow Christ, you will establish a professional distance from the people you lead."

I pray that this does not describe you or your pastor. I pray that my life does not reflect these patterns either. However, the more I work with churches to help them establish groups, the more I discover that the model that people are following hinders actually doing groups well. My fear is that pastors are setting a model that operates according to the system of individualism and pragmatism, resembling the culture of the world. Miller states,

"The drift into individualism and isolation has not become so obvious that (at least to sociologists) American culture is unique. We are alone in the world putting such heavy emphasis on individual versus group identity. Ours is a culture of fierce, personal independence. We take pride in individual competition, mastery and achievement. We pay a steep price, however, as ours is also a culture of intense anxiety and psychic distress.[11]

While sociologists might see it, most pastors I talk with do not. I repeatedly hear the same thing that Barna found in his research, "None indicated that he or she was comfortable with the toll the job exacted on the family life. Yet, none of those who were workaholics in practice maintained that anything less than total effort and energy would have enabled the comeback."[12] I struggle with leaning this direction because I love my job and feel such a passion for what I do. But I also know that such a pattern will be counterproductive to the kind of life I want the people who follow me to lead. Henri Nouwen recognized this pattern 25 years ago. He wrote:

> The basic question is whether we ministers of Jesus Christ have not already been so deeply molded by the seductive powers of our dark world that we have become blind to our own and other people's fatal state and have lost the power and motivation to swim for our lives.
>
> Just look for a moment at our daily routine. In general we are very busy people. We have many meetings to attend, many visits to make, many services to lead. Our calendars are filled with appointments, our days and weeks filled with engagements, and our years filled with plans and projects. There is seldom a period in which we do not know what to do, and we move through life in such a distracted way that we do not even take the time and rest to wonder if any of the things we think, say, or do are worth thinking, saying or doing.[13]

The relational way will only flow from who we are, the character we possess and our willingness to cultivate the kingdom according to patterns that do not reflect the patterns of this world. We must develop a new system of being the church, one that cultivates relationships through the practicing of spiritual disciplines, honoring the Sabbath, communing with God and developing community in which church leaders develop healthy connections. As we do this, we establish patterns worth passing on to others who will lead others into the relational way.

Jesus' Relational Way

Brownson writes, "In the ancient world, the character of the king determined the character of the nation that served him. ... So Jesus is presented in the New Testament not merely as a 'role model' that one might, if one chose, try to imitate. Rather Jesus is the King, and the quality and character of his life define the lives of those who give allegiance to him."[14] In other words, the king sets the way of life for the nation.

Of course, we are to follow Jesus as his disciples. We are to be imitators of Christ, ones who lived like he lived. The best-selling book, *In his Steps*, where people live according to the question, "What would Jesus do?" illustrates the obvious call to follow Christ. Are pastors called to minister as Jesus ministered? When this question is raised the answer is not so obvious. We live in different times, in a different culture, with pressures and commitments that Jesus did not have. He never had to deal with committees, managing a building, organizing services, attending denominational meetings, or keeping the deacons or elders happy. Therefore, pastors often answer the question of, "What would Jesus do?" on a personal level and then do the best they can in the job they have inherited.

If Jesus were to become incarnate in twenty-first century North America, how would he minister? Of course, I can only speculate as others have done. For instance, one seminary professor who taught media classes stated that if Jesus were alive today he would use television. Would he? Would he use the written medium? What about the Internet? To tell you the truth, I don't know what media he would use to share his message with the masses. There is one thing that I think is quite transferable from the first century to our day: how he developed the movement. If Jesus were alive today he would establish his movement the same way he did 2,000 years ago. He would work with 12 people and develop them by imparting his life into them. He would demonstrate and equip them in the way of life in his kingdom and teach them how to minister the way he ministers. He would not do this with the masses. He would concentrate his energy on a small group of future leaders, investing his life into a few with whom he would share refrigerator rights.

Robert Coleman wrote, "Jesus was not trying to impress the crowd, but to usher in a kingdom. This meant that he needed people who could lead the multitudes. What good would it have been for his ultimate objective to arouse the masses to follow him if these people had no subsequent supervision or instruction in the Way?"[15] Few pastors will argue with Coleman's observation, but most find his way difficult, if not impossible to do today. One pastor used business terms to explain what he does: pastors lead people who are his employees (but unpaid); his stockholders (who can vote him out if they so choose); and his customers (who can take their business down the road to another church vendor). When pastors have all of the concerns and duties to oversee, how can they afford the time to invest in a small group of people?

Research on the Synoptic Gospels has provided estimates that Jesus spent about 50 percent of his time with 12 key leaders during his three years of ministry.[16] He did not ignore others outside of this group. In fact, there was a core group of about 70 who followed him. He also invested in these people, but with less of his time. And of course he ministered to the masses, as is illustrated in the feeding of the 5,000 and the 4,000, the Sermon on the Mount, and many healings. However, he prioritized his time, allowing him to give his best to the 12.

Levels	Jesus	Modern Pastor
Key Leaders	50%	10%
Core Group	35%	15%
Crowd	15%	75%

As I work with pastors in the church today, I ask them how they would break out the percentages among these three groups. Consistently, they share how 75 percent of their time is invested in ministering to the crowd through preaching, preparation for preaching, counseling, and organizing mass events. The other 25 percent is divided among key leaders and the core group of the church. The time spent with key leaders and core group members is typically spent in getting stuff done for the crowd.

The modern pattern of pastoral leadership often results in feelings of usury on the part of key leaders. Pastors only have a small amount of time to meet with leaders to accomplish a task so that they can better minister to the crowd. That crowd is comprised of individualists who often will leave as soon as something does not suit their personal desires or meet their felt-needs. The pastor then spends most of his time and energy investing in people who don't have the ability or the desire to pass on to others what he has given them. His ministry stops with what he offers. He invests most of his ministry preaching to, counseling with, and organizing events for the crowd who cannot reproduce life in others.

At the same time, Jesus did not ignore the crowds. He ministered to them through miraculous signs and wonders that revealed the kingdom. While ministering to the masses, he was demonstrating the way of the kingdom to his key leaders. His investment in the 12 was not that of individualized discipleship. He equipped the 12 and taught them the way through his ministry to the core followers and the masses. Jesus had his eyes on developing a movement of people following the way, and he demonstrated this way, for all to see.

The Pastor as a Mobilizer of the Relational Way

Paul followed a similar pattern, even though there is no evidence that he ever organized a leadership group of 12. Barnabas served as his mentor. Paul mentored Timothy, Titus and others. To Timothy, Paul wrote, *"You then, my son, be strong in the grace that is in Christ Jesus. And the things you have heard me say in the presence of many witnesses entrust to reliable men who will also be qualified to teach others"* (2 Tim. 2:2).

Throughout church history, the way of relational ministry is the pattern that mobilized leaders into impacting ministry. Concerning John Wesley's approach to ministry, Michael Henderson writes, "This sharing of the leadership role called for a totally different approach to spiritual and educational leadership. Rather than performing ministry themselves, the leaders' main task was the training or equipping of leaders at lower levels."[17]

Karen Hurston believes that the practices of small-group pastors have as much impact on small group success as any other factor. She observed this as she grew up in Cho's church in Korea. The staff pastors there are highly relational in their approach to group oversight. She writes, "Staff pastors in traditional churches spend most of their days resolving crisis situations, planning future events and programs, doing paperwork, counseling in the office, and taking uninvited phone calls. Staff pastors in a cell church are different. They focus more on raising up, equipping and encouraging leaders, and they are much more "hands on" in their approach."[18]

The traditional models of pastoral leadership—which results in spending up to 75% of ministry energy on the crowd—could be categorized under two basic models: the chaplain and the program leader. The chaplain is the traditional church pastor who cares for those who attend the church services. The program leader is the model promoted by innovative, growing churches; such a leader manages events and programs for people. Jim Egli contrasts the three models in this way:

Model	Chaplain	Program	Small Groups Pastor
Primary Role	Caregiver	Organizer	Mobilizer
Focus	Care of Members	Care of Programs	Care & Multiplication of Leaders
Qualifications: Character Plus...	Formal Education	Administrative Gifting	Proven Multiplication of Leaders
Orientation	Present Needs	Upcoming Events	Mission Goals
Approach	High Touch	High Tech	High Touch & High Tech

One could mistakenly assume that the relational model of pastoral investment endorsed in this chapter is very similar to that of a chaplain, as the approach of that model is "high touch." It is true that traditional pastors are high touch, but the difference lies in the people that are touched. The chaplain focuses on caring for individuals and families in need, whereas the small-group pastor serves as a mobilizer of others who can care for these individuals. As Paul instructed Timothy, the approach of the small-group pastor is to equip "reliable men who will also be qualified to teach others." The relationship approach of the small-group pastor is an investment approach, investing in people who in turn can invest in others.

My Last Word

Group structures only facilitate the experience of community when leaders embrace a way of living that manifests the practices of spiritual community. This sounds like an obvious statement. However, after 1,700 years of practicing church leadership in ways that rub against such relational community, this point cannot be emphasized enough. We must rethink how we structure our churches to facilitate the relational way, but I think it may be more important that we rethink how we lead our churches so that we facilitate the way of love. If we don't practice relational community in our leadership, then we should not expect community to result within our groups.

Gather Around the Presence

Small groups are not new to church life. At one point in my church experience, I attended seven different small groups almost every week. Of course, these groups possessed different intentions, and I assumed that I needed to attend all of them to serve God well. The different types of groups included a discipleship group, a Bible study group, a Sunday school class, a community building group, a leadership development group, an outreach group and a task group. These gatherings were valuable. They had model leaders who taught biblically. They sought to encourage people to obey the word and demonstrate the gospel to the world.

As I have reflected over my journey in small groups, I have asked the question, "What is the difference between the communities that have been a part of church life for generations and the kind of groups where God's relational way is experienced?" Many Christians seek practical answers to this question. They want to know how such groups are produced and unknowingly buy into the small group myth. They assume the key difference is found in such practical things as small group dynamics, the kind of curriculum used, or the quality of the training provided to leaders. As a result, church leaders purchase prepackaged small group curricula or training resources and hope that the small group magic will suddenly appear.

However, the difference is not found in practical methods. Jesus said, *"I tell you that if two of you on earth agree about anything you ask for, it will be done for you by my Father in heaven. For where two or three come together in my name, there I am with them"* (Matt. 18:20). The essential key is found in the presence of Christ. Only when a group experiences Christ's incarnate presence together will it be what God intends it to be. Only when it walks together—while allowing the head of the Church to be the head of the small group—will it truly create the kingdom community that changes the world.

Structural Myth #2:
Groups will succeed if they are built
around a specific practical strategy or method.

The Relational Truth:
Relational kingdom groups are based upon
the reality of Christ's presence within those groups.

Changing the Focus

When a pastor asks me for counsel in establishing small groups in his church, I seek to learn the kind of groups he envisions. Frequently, I have told pastors that I can help them organize group systems and even assimilate lots of people into those groups quickly. Then I explain that I am far more interested in helping churches reshape their culture around a vision for relational life. For many pastors, this requires a major shift in focus. Roxburgh and Romanuk put it this way:

> Organizational change occurs when leadership seeks to change the structures of the small group ministry of the church. This can be done by adding new insights about group dynamics, or another formula for putting groups together in terms of people mix, or a new kind of group process based on the latest studies and research. All of these are useful and helpful ways of restructuring and reshaping group life in a congregation. But what they miss is that research on small groups in congregations indicates that the focus of the vast majority of small groups is on the self or the needs of those in the group. Again, that is not a bad thing, but the focus of energy and attention of small group life in congregations is still on the care and resourcing of the self and others. What is not the center of focus and

energy of a small group is God. Cultural change looks at how to create a small-group environment in which the focus of group attention shifts from the self and one another to God.[1]

Organizational change in small groups focuses on strategic and structural issues of how to design groups. Cultural change seeks to discover the way that Jesus acts as the head of his body. If Jesus is the head of the church (Col. 1:18), then the church is only the church of Christ when it is living in vitality with the head. Unless the attention shifts from the self and one another to God, I think we can justifiably claim that the church fails to act as the church of the living God. Without the realized revelation of Christ in the midst of his people, the church ceases to be the church. The same is true for small groups. Without the presence of Christ in the midst of a small group, it ceases to function as the body of Christ because it is disconnected from the head.

Matthew records the first reference to the church in the New Testament. After Peter recognized the identity of Jesus when he confessed that Jesus is the Christ, the Son of the living God, Jesus said to Peter, *"Blessed are you, Simon son of Jonah, for this was not revealed to you by man, but by my Father in heaven. And I tell you that you are Peter, and on this rock I will build my church, and the gates of Hades will not overcome it"* (Matt. 16:17-18).

Much debate has transpired about the definition of the rock. Those of the Catholic tradition argue that Peter is the rock, while scholars from the Protestant world define the rock as the faith one has in Christ, not the person of Peter. What if there is another way to look at the nature of the rock? What if both views are correct in some way? Systematic theologian Trevor Hart explains revelation this way: "Something revealed is something disclosed or given to be known to someone which apart from the act of revealing would remain hidden, disguised or unknown."[2] Revelation involves the "something" that is hidden, along with the disclosure of that something. Revelation only occurs if this something is disclosed to *someone*. In other words, in order for revelation to be realized, someone must receive the truth into his being and embrace it. Without someone who receives the revelation, there is truth, but no revelation. The Father is the revealer of this revelation to Peter, turning static truth about Jesus into embodied reality within Peter. When embodied, this revelation changes Simon's character to that of "Petros," meaning rock. The revelation changed his identity.[3]

The church is built upon the rock of revelation of Christ that is embodied within people. The church is not built upon static theological dictums or ideology but on people who embody the reality of Christ's revelation through the encounter with his presence. This is not to discount the importance of creedal orthodoxy, but Jesus is more than a theological category of history that we discuss in our groups. Because Jesus is the Word made flesh who dwelt among us and rose from the dead, he is alive in his church, the center of his people. He does not intend for his people to analyze him and discuss him as if the cross were his last statement. He is to be encountered and loved as we receive the revelation that Jesus is the Christ, the Son of the living God.

As the head of the church, Jesus is directly connected to his church today. Therefore, the body need not strive to get good things done for Jesus. Such striving usually causes us to speed up the process and jump to the practical questions of finding the right strategy for group development without understanding how Christ is revealed in his small groups. As a result, we inadvertently put him in our box rather than letting him shape us into his life. Christ-centered small groups create a place where the presence of Jesus can be made real in the midst of his people, as the head of his people, allowing him to be the center that he is.

In order for the head to lead the church, the body must wait on the direction of the head. Dietrich Bonhoeffer begins his book *Christ the Center* with these words, "Teaching about Christ begins in silence. ... To speak of Christ means to keep silent; to keep silent about Christ means to speak. When the Church speaks rightly out of a proper silence, then Christ is proclaimed."[4] Too many groups talk so much about Christ or they try to do so much for Christ that they don't know how to be silent before him to allow him to speak about himself. When we talk and do, we miss the center of what it means to be the church. When he speaks, he reveals his presence, something that transcends talking about and working for him. He answers the question, "Who is Jesus?" In order for Christ to be the center of our groups, we must allow him to speak about and reveal who he is.

The Who Question

Upon the rock of the revelation of who Jesus is, he will build his church.

Upon the revealing of the answer to the Who question to his people, he will raise up the church. Jesus claims the ultimate responsibility to build the church. He does this through leaders, but often leaders fail to recognize Jesus' active role in the process. Leadership impatience causes us to press into the How questions too quickly, often skipping the Who question, which allows room for Jesus to reveal himself to the church.

When we ask the Who question, Jesus' presence becomes a reality in our midst. Usually, Jesus' presence comes as we wait on him in worship. Sadly, research on the state of North American Christians reveals that they do not expect to meet with Jesus in worship. Barna reports, "Eight out of every ten believers do not feel they have entered into the presence of God, or experienced a connection with him, during the worship service. Half of all believers say they do not feel they have entered into the presence of God or experienced a genuine connection with him during the past year."[5] Many Christians have become so used to not encountering Christ that they no longer ask the Who question. As a result, church leaders only have How questions at their disposal. Hence, the plethora of books by best-selling authors telling us how to have a better Christian walk, how to have a better church, and even how to have better small groups.

In the passage where Peter answered the Who question, proclaiming *"You are the Christ, the Son of the living God,"* Jesus said, *"whatever you bind on earth will be bound in heaven, and whatever you loose on earth will be loosed in heaven"* (Matt. 16:19). Jesus repeats this same sentence two chapters later (Matt. 18:18) in the context of Jesus' promise of his presence where two or three are gathered. Exact repetition like this is no accident. First century writers did not use computers and paper. Their method of recording words required that they use every word wisely. Therefore, we must ask why the repetition, especially when the two passages are so close together. Most likely, the two teachings are connected to one another in some way.

Within both paragraphs where Jesus states this sentence about binding and loosing, Matthew records the only two uses of the word *ecclesia*, "church," in the Gospels. In Matthew 16, Jesus proclaims that he will build the "church" upon the revelation of his identity, who he is. This statement is the foundation of the church. The foundation of the revelation of Christ gives authority to the church to bind and loose things on earth. The passage in Matthew 18 explains the on-going operation of the church. The church operates around the presence of Christ, which authorizes the church to bind the will of heaven to the things of earth.[6]

How the Church Operates

As quoted earlier, Matthew 18:18-20 records Jesus saying, *"I tell you the truth, whatever you bind on earth will be bound in heaven, and whatever you loose on earth will be loosed in heaven. Again, I tell you that if two of you on earth agree about anything you ask for, it will be done for you by my Father in heaven. For where two or three come together in my name, there am I with them."* I believe there are ingredients within this passage that should shape how the body of Christ should operate. To understand this operation, we must look at it on multiple levels.

On the first level, Jesus promised his presence to those who gather in his name. Pastors have quoted this verse often, but most seldom stop to ask what the phrase "in his name" means. We only use this phrase within the church context. Because I have heard the phrase "baptize in the name of the Father, Son, and the Holy Spirit" so often, I have assumed for most of my life that I understood what it meant.

Meeting in the name of Jesus means that people gather with a focus on Jesus and a commitment to seek what he has done and is doing. Another way to say this would be "under his rule."[7] To seek the rule and leading of Jesus requires his presence, and therefore he promises that he will so lead when two or three gather in this way.

There is a second level of meaning to these verses when read in the context of the verses previous to them, that of confronting a believer who sins. Jesus told his disciples:

> If your brother or sister sins, go and point out the fault, just between the two of you. If they listen to you, you have won them over. But if they will not listen, take one or two others along, so that 'every matter may be established by the testimony of two or three witnesses.' If he refuses to listen to them, tell it to the church; and if they refuse to listen even to the church, treat them as you would a pagan or a tax collector (Matt. 18:15-17, TNIV).

Jesus' presence is promised to those who are prayerfully going to a brother in sin with one or two other witnesses. Some have gone to the extreme of stating that the context of this passage demands an interpretation that concludes the presence of Christ is only promised to those who are confronting another. Such a limited interpretation fails to recognize the community nature of church. In the modern expression of church, where we gather as a dispersed set of individuals, this might make sense. In many churches, the only time people deal with intimate issues in someone's life is during a crisis that requires confrontation. However, in a church that lives in relational community, confrontation (in love) is a part of everyday life together. This was how truth was disseminated through the churches. Jesus promises his presence to those who love each other enough to say the hard things that they don't want to say.

A third level of meaning arises when one looks at the passage in the larger context of the entire chapter. Matthew 18 is comprised of five topics grouped together in the form of a discourse. All of these topics deal with how people relate to one another. These topics include:

- Relating to children
- Not doing anything to cause others to sin
- Going after those who go astray
- Confronting someone in sin
- Forgiving others

In the middle of these practical instructions, Jesus tells them, *"whatever you bind on earth will be bound in heaven, and whatever you loose on earth will be loosed in heaven. Again I tell you that if two of you on earth agree about anything you ask for, it will be done for you by my Father in heaven. For where two or three come together in my name, there am I with them."* The presence of Christ is the key to connecting the will of heaven to earth. His presence gives the church the authority to bind and loose according to the will of heaven. These five topics illustrate five ways that the church is to live with one another according to that will. But without the presence, the church lacks the key or the ability to walk in these five ways. Without the presence, all it has are "how" questions: How do we treat the children? How do we live in holiness? How do we reach the lost? How do we confront? How do we forgive? We can ask "how" questions forever and never find answers that will change our hearts. One encounter with the presence of Jesus can change everything, just as it changed Peter.

The Body of Christ

When Jesus spoke these words about how the church would operate, he was reshaping the Jewish picture of what it meant to participate as the people of God. They were looking for a conquering King; he was giving them his presence, which would change how they related to others. N. T. Wright explains, "Jesus ... apparently envisaged that, scattered about Palestine, there would be small groups of people loyal to himself, who would get together to encourage one another, and would act as members of a family, sharing some sort of common life and, in particular, exercising mutual forgiveness."[8] These scattered small groups would act as kingdom outposts that embodied his presence after his ascension.

Later in the development of the church, Paul clearly defines these outposts. I Corinthians 12 highlights how the body works. At the end of sixteen verses that reference the word "body" fifteen times, Paul writes, *"Now you are the body of Christ, and each one of you is a part of it"* (vs. 27). Much ink has been spilled on the nature of the body, how the gifts should work, and the mutual interdependence upon the parts of the body on one another. "Paul's basic concern was to restore the sense of unity in the Corinthian congregation by restoring the sense of interdependence among the believers. And this restoration required a true sense of their mutual relation to Christ."[9] To be the body of Christ is to act as a mutually interdependent group under the headship of Christ.

To be mutually related to Christ is to be mutually related to the anointed Messiah. The Greek word *christos* means Messiah in Hebrew. Many people miss this point as they mistakenly read Christ as a title representing Jesus' divinity, or even his surname. A first century reader of the Old Testament would have understood that *christos* means Messiah, the Jewish royal leader who would drive out God's enemies and restore God's presence on the earth.[10] Paul's audience included both Jews and Gentiles, and he was trying to help individuals in these ethnically diverse churches realize that they are mutually interconnected to one another through the life of the Jewish Messiah.

Immediately after Peter confessed that Jesus was the Christ, the son of the living God, Peter revealed his ignorance about what it meant to be the Jewish Messiah. Jesus told them he would suffer and die. Peter failed to remain silent and allow Jesus to reveal himself. Peter interjected his idea of the Messiah and Jesus rebuked him. Jesus, as "the image of the invisible God," does not manifest the kind of God one would expect. As *the radiance of God's glory*" (Hebrews 1:3), he surprised Peter with a different definition of what God looks like.

Jesus is our picture of God. It was scandalous to even think about God becoming a man, but it was immensely more scandalous for God to come as a suffering servant. Bonhoeffer writes, "The offense of Jesus Christ is not his incarnation—that indeed is revelation—but his humiliation."[11] Jesus demonstrated a kind of glory that does not look like glory to us. His power came not as a conquering king, but as a lowly king of love, a suffering servant, one who gave up his life so that others might have life.

While we are thankful for our salvation because of Christ's humiliation, we often miss the crucial fact that Jesus manifested the nature of God through his humiliation. He showed us the true way to love and to live through the passion of the cross. He taught us true power through vulnerability. He revealed how authority is not controlling, but gives freedom for the other person to respond or reject it. As the head of the church today, Jesus is still living the same way, his nature unchanged. He is not seeking to establish the church as a gloried authority on the earth. He was the suffering servant, and he still is through his presence in the church. As the head of his body, Christ is leading the church to operate in the same humiliating way that he operated.

To be the body of Christ is to function as the mutually interdependent body that expresses the same character that Christ demonstrated on the cross, "in service to God and for the benefit of others."[12] Immediately before facing death on the cross, Jesus instructed his disciples with this: *"My command is this: Love each other as I have loved you. Greater love has no one than this, that he lay down his life for his friends"* (John 15:12-13). As a church leader who looks around at other successful churches putting on big conferences, views other leaders on television, and reads endless books that explain how to be a successful church, I am constantly enticed to skip this verse. I am tempted to seek the glory of the resurrection without the death of the cross ... and I don't think I am alone. Most would prefer the experience of success without going through the trials of failure, the questions of misgivings, and frustration of disappointment. We want to hop from mountaintop to mountaintop without walking with God through the valley. We want great small groups, and we want them now. Moreover, we want them without the discovery of how much "I" am in the way of his presence. We don't want to be living sacrifices who wait in silence before the revealing Christ. The temptation entraps church leaders to act as *living contributors,* providing answers to the How question: How do I make my group—or groups in the case of a pastor—into life-giving experiences of biblical community?

What Does This Mean ... Practically?

Common Practical Answers
Because we live in a pragmatic how-to world, such statements as "meeting in his name," "encountering the presence of Christ," and "living together around the center of Christ" seem as amorphous as a bowl of Jell-O. These concepts are difficult to grasp. I get frustrated with such statements, finding myself searching for something practical I can use or do. So often the instruction to meet in the name of Christ is bypassed and groups meet in someone else's name. No church would overtly claim that their groups meet in these names. Yet I find that as I talk with church leaders, their interest lies much more in the four concerns below. These concerns act as a foundation to these names, as opposed to understanding how the presence of Christ lives through a group. I recognize them easily because I have sought after each of them myself.

The Name of Great Curriculum
Over the last few years, Christian publishers have saturated the market with many different kinds of small group study guides. Some church leaders have falsely assumed that if they use the right curriculum, great groups will develop. With the low cost of DVD production, we now have the option of inviting excellent Bible teachers into our living rooms to stimulate discussion.

Dependence upon publishing houses for curriculum is not new. Growing up in a denominational church, I saw the dependence on curriculum in Sunday school. Every quarter, our church would receive the Bible study curriculum sent to us by the denominational publisher. The church was dependent upon the professional writers at the headquarters to hear God and tell us what and how to study. Now that small groups are becoming the norm in church life, large churches have become the new experts in curriculum development. Some pre-packaged sets of material promise that their systems will launch groups and assimilate the majority of the people in a church within a few weeks. (Let me clearly state that well-crafted small group curriculum can be very helpful. My home church produces DVD's for our group leaders based on our weekly sermons.)

At the same time, I have questions: What did the church do before the invention of the printing press? How did the church of the first century grow so wildly without published study materials? While there is nothing wrong with using great curriculum and creative media for teaching that curriculum, it is dangerous to depend upon such resources as the source of success.

The Name of *the* Great Leader

One of the more common names around which groups gather is that of the "great leader." Many of us have seen such groups. There are those magnetic personalities in the church who have the people skills and the interactive skills that draw in others. People love to attend their groups. Because cloning is not an option, people use another approach to develop leaders like them. They make a list of all the things that these exemplary leaders do to grow their groups and then they train their leaders in these skills. The key to success in this system is in the training. Pastors look high and low for the best training on the market—and there is a lot of it out there—hoping to find the perfect training system to develop outstanding group leaders. They search for the best how-to books that will explain the practices or the habits of group leaders and believe if they can just get enough information into the heads of their group leaders, one day they will be great leaders!

While training is essential and how-to leadership books are practical, developing the perfect training system will not prove to be the magical gateway to producing "great leaders." In fact, I have seen churches develop such training systems under this premise, and they only end up sending people through training classes that fail to produce changed graduates. The participants only have more knowledge and a certificate of completion.

Character, passion for Christ, and living a life that is full of God are intangible elements that cannot be trained. Without them, no amount of knowledge will shape a great leader.

The Name of *the* Perfect Oversight System

Another popular name around which groups meet is the right oversight system. Pastors realize that they need to provide group leaders with care and oversight. Some of the most common questions pastors ask when they start developing groups relate to the care structure. "What oversight system should be adopted?" "Is the Groups of 12 model the best or does the 5x5 model or a variation of the Jethro structure fit better?" "I have heard about the G12.3 and the J12; which is superior?" Some ask such questions because they are looking to adopt the ideal oversight system so the small groups will be blessed by God.

This myth has been propagated most by those within the Groups of 12 camp. This model is based upon a strategy whereby a small group coach will develop 12 group leaders under his or her care and meet with them as a group every week. The number 12 is based upon the fact that Jesus developed 12 disciples. Over lunch, one G-12 advocate told me, "The 5x5 model that Yongii Cho developed is an Old Covenant structure because it is based upon Jethro's advice to Moses in Exodus. The G-12 model is a New Covenant structure because Jesus instituted it."

Such statements sadden me. The absence of sound theology and the poor exegesis frustrate me. But the manipulation of pastors angers me. Some who make such statements pastor large churches, and they routinely instruct pastors of small churches to follow their oversight model, promising magical growth.

The reality is that the Bible never prescribes an oversight model. We don't have any evidence for Peter developing a group of 12 or of Paul instructing Timothy to develop twelve leaders. There are great principles we can learn from the Groups of 12 model as well as the other oversight structures, but there is no perfect oversight model that will unlock the door to unlimited group multiplication.

The Name of *the* Perfect Group

A fourth name is that of "group format." If you were to make a list of all the different kinds of groups in which you have participated, I am sure that list would be quite long. From Sunday school classes to discipleship courses, mission groups, and Bible studies, the church has used a small group strategy for decades, if not centuries. In the traditional approach to small groups, we would identify goals of the Christian life like parenting, financial planning, or Bible study and base a group around that topic. Each group was formed around that specific goal and therefore created the name in which it met. A discipleship group meets in the name of growing as a disciple. A fellowship group meets in the name of forming friendships.

There are many examples of churches that organize their groups around group format. One church promotes a model of small groups that gathers around interests. They encourage people to connect with others with whom they share a common interest. Therefore, if someone has an interest in bike riding, she might start a group for bikers to ride together on Saturday mornings. Another might start a volleyball group. Still another might lead a book club group. And finally, a group might be a Bible study group, which would look more like a traditional small group. Such groups experience a sense of community, but these groups meet in the name of the unique interests that each member possesses.[13]

Another popular model is to create groups on four levels (i.e., 101, 201, 301, and 401). The lowest level is a low commitment group that might come in the form of a once-per-month social group. The next level might include a service or task group. Groups that might include a regular Bible study would comprise those found in the third level. And the fourth level is those groups that include a much higher commitment to one another, including accountability and weekly meetings.

The goal of models that encourage different types of groups is to connect people around their choices. However, meeting around volleyball, a task, or even deep accountability and Bible study, while a positive act, is quite different from a group meeting around Christ's presence.

Ministry on the Periphery

When we meet in any other name than in Jesus' name, we are doing ministry from the periphery. We have the goal of creating great groups that people will give up their favorite television program to attend, groups that cause people to connect to one another, build community, grow in Christ, and reach those who don't know Jesus. Our intentions are good, but we miss the center of what God wants to do. However, the programmatic air that we breathe drives us to "how-to" questions of the periphery. We want to know how to create groups that will grow, how to develop groups that will connect people, how to start groups to make our church more effective.

As I work with various churches, pastors often want to develop a strategy to start twenty or thirty groups as quickly as possible, launching a small group program. There are many ways to start lots of groups rapidly, but such groups will meet in many different names, not in the name of Christ. While impressive numbers might result, little change will occur in how people live their lives. The absence of refrigerator rights will go unchecked, and the creation of an alternative society—the manifestation of God's relational kingdom—will be ignored.

Following Peter to the Center

Peter sought to follow Christ from the periphery instead of the center. The keys of the kingdom Jesus spoke of in Matthew 18 symbolize the authority to connect the will of heaven to earth, thereby allowing Christ to be the center. But Peter misunderstood what Jesus meant. He thought that Jesus would enter Jerusalem as a power-type leader who would establish the kingdom with the keys of control. Peter wanted safety. He wanted to win. He wanted Jesus to force himself on people and establish himself with overwhelming power. To Peter, Jesus retorted, *"Get behind me, Satan! You are a stumbling block to me; you do not have in mind the things of God, but the things of man."* Peter wanted the keys of control rather than the keys of authority.

Small groups that meet in other names follow the path of Peter! Leaders of such groups have been trained. They have read the books and understand the job they are to do. They have also been set apart by the pastor to lead the group. They walk into the meeting with their chest out and chin up for the first few weeks. Then they realize that people are not responding the right way. In fact, the group is beginning to dwindle.

After learning the technical side of leading a small group, I too thought I understood the task ahead of me. I began with great expectations, dreams of seeing small members transformed, lost people reached, and new groups started. Nine months later, I had to step down as a leader because I had the wrong keys. My key chain was full of me and my desire to control people. I wanted people to grow in the Lord. But, I thought that my control and desires for them were the keys. While I had used the right keys in previous small group experiences, I exchanged them for leadership techniques that I thought would make for an effective group.

The need to control causes leaders to look for formulas that will make their groups better. They meet in the name of "being a good leader," "being a part of the perfect system," or "using the right curriculum." They have good intentions. They only want to make their groups more effective, but they do not realize that their approach is counterproductive. They seek to lead, imposing themselves upon their groups, feeling that they must carry the weight for group success. They assume the pressure in leading the group.

How to Make
The Group
Better

Leader

Even when the group improves, the pressure remains on the leader to keep it up. When the group struggles, the weight falls on the leader to make a change. The leader seeks to make things happen. She feels that she must assume the role of relating directly to the group. Such direct relationships can be very destructive. Leaders have nothing to give others in their groups unless Christ gives it to them. Dietrich Bonhoeffer writes, "Self-centered love seeks direct contact with the other person. It loves them, not as free persons, but as those whom it binds to itself. It wants to do everything it can to win and conquer; it puts pressure on the other person. It desires to be irresistible, to dominate."[14] Bonhoeffer continues by writing, "Spiritual love will thus speak to Christ about the other Christian more than to the other Christian about Christ. It knows that the most direct way to others is always through prayer to Christ."[15] When I first read these statements, I said "Amen," but I had no idea what he meant. I went right back to my direct ministry of trying to make my group better. I was clinging to the people in my group out of my need to remain in charge or in control of the group.

Henri Nouwen helps explain how this direct ministry often works: "Our loneliness makes us cling to one another, and this mutual clinging makes us suffer immensely because it does not take our loneliness away. But the harder we try, the more desperate we become. Many of these 'interlocking' relationships fall apart because they become suffocating and oppressing."[16] In my situation, I clung to the people in my group because I needed them to help me grow the group so that I could be a successful small group leader. In essence I was using them. But we cling to and use people to meet all kinds of needs. And when the group lacks the center of Christ, failing to gather in his name, this misuse will always happen.

Changing the Keys

Peter's keys of control kept him at the periphery, leading him to disillusionment and despair after he denied Christ three times. He gave up on Jesus and the promise of the keys of the authority of heaven. When the leadership of my group did not work out as expected, I had to re-think what it meant to be a leader. I joined another group, which was led by someone without all my how-to knowledge about leading groups. He had not read all of the books I had read, but I noticed something different about his leadership.

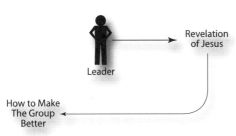

While I sat in the group, I watched with amazement how the group functioned. It was fun! People shared openly and the group grew. Our leader led us into the presence of Christ to set our lives up against what he says about us. My leader had the right keys, the keys of authority to lead us into the presence of Christ. These keys open a different door to a different path, one that leads directly to Jesus.

After this experience, I led groups differently. My stress level decreased immensely. I no longer felt I had to make my small group work. I realized that the shortest route to making a group great is actually the indirect one. The job of the group leader is to take people to Jesus and to take Jesus to people. Jesus is the authority and only his keys matter.

At the same time, Jesus provides practical ways to improve the group. He uses books and seminars to highlight activities and tools that work. However, these things are not the starting point. Jesus is. The books or seminars on group leadership describe the keys, but they do not provide them. A leader can only get these keys directly from Jesus. The keys are based upon the revelation that Jesus is the Christ, the Son of the Living God. Jesus is the one who brings life to a group. He is the one who causes people to share honestly. He is the one who touches lives and changes people. He is the one who moves through the group to reach out to the unchurched. He is the one who raises up leaders who begin new small groups. Jesus is the key, not the leader's hard work.

Ministering from the Center

There is an old saying, often used by barbeque establishments across the South: "If you've got good food, you don't need to advertise." Groups that offer good spiritual food do not have to twist arms for participation.

For a time, Bill Beckham was my pastor, and he constantly encouraged us to lead our groups with a focus on the presence of Christ. He repeatedly emphasized this truth. All I wanted to know was, "How?" The "How" question filled my mind so that I could not see who Christ was. Instead of asking "How," a better question is, "What does it look like?" I think it can be summarized with one word: revelation.

During the prayer time of a recent small group I was leading, I sensed that I should read a specific scripture after we finished praying. At the same time that thought came to my mind, another person picked up his Bible and read that very passage aloud. We then discussed that passage and talked about what God might be saying to us through it. In fact, those verses became a theme for us as a group.

This example is not spectacular, but I find that the most significant ways in which Jesus reveals himself is through the ordinary stuff. We need to ask for eyes to see what God is doing in our midst. Without those eyes, our Bible discussions, our ministry, and our love for one another will be less than revelation.

In small groups, revelation occurs when an individual shares a weakness and the group leads him to repentance and prays for him. It transpires when a "know-it-all" Christian remains quiet and listens, really listens, to someone else instead of telling everyone the "right" answers. It takes place when someone realizes that she had the wrong attitude toward another. Revelation manifests when a hardened man breaks down and allows others to love him. It emerges when a group member spontaneously prays for another without being asked and she is obviously being led by the Spirit. It becomes evident when an unbeliever confesses his need for Jesus when he sees the love between the members of the group. As a basic rule, revelation is the unexpected move of Christ in a group. In fact, when I lead a group meeting, I look for the unexpected. If the meeting went smoothly, with all the questions having been answered correctly without glitches or bumps in the road, I know we probably missed the revelation of Jesus. He is the head of the church and therefore he is the leader of the group and every group meeting. He has permission to do the unforeseen.

Remember Two or Three

Meeting in Christ's presence is connected to the numbers two or three. To be a church, it requires more than one person to meet in the name of Jesus. While I am not discounting the importance of private encounters in the presence of God, the Bible seems to place a much greater emphasis on the gathered people of God who meet in his presence. To cite one example, Paul writes, *"But if an unbeliever or someone who does not understand comes in while everybody is prophesying, he will be convinced by all that he is a sinner and will be judged by all, and the secrets of his heart will be laid bare. So he will fall down and worship God, exclaiming, 'God is really among you!'"* (1 Corinthians 14:24-25). Christ is revealed by the church, through the community of believers, not just through the words or actions of individuals.

When group leaders grasp the importance of Christ's presence, they often encounter a new struggle. Too many times, groups have more than one person present, but only one person meeting in the name of Jesus: the group leader. Everyone else is meeting in names such as, "frustration with my spouse," "fear my child will mess up his life," "exhaustion from a full day at work," or other preoccupations. While these feelings are valid and should never be ignored for the sake of a meeting, it often requires ninety minutes for the group leader to get one or two group members meeting in the name of Jesus; by that time everyone is ready to go home. It is not necessary for the entire group to meet in Jesus' name, but it is crucial that at least two or three volitionally meet in his name. Without this, most likely the group will miss the presence of Christ.

This is the reason that every group should be built around a core of two or three who are committed to meeting in the name of Jesus. Two or three can point to the center which is Jesus. An individual who leads a group by himself can only point to himself. Jesus sent out the disciples in pairs. Paul did not go on his missionary journeys alone. Even Jesus sought companions or partners in ministry.

Small groups work best when the leader first invites two or three people to join him or her in a vision. This team then establishes the vision of meeting in Jesus' name and invites others to participate in that vision.

There are many strategies to promote the principle of two or three. One strategy is that of having co-leaders, which protects the leaders from burn-out and from pride that might come from thinking it is "my" group. Another is to establish a core team. Still another is to ask specific members to serve as captains of specific ministries such as prayer captain, community captain, and outreach captain. The most long-standing strategy is that of raising up an intern or apprentice who works with the leader to care for the group.

Define the Role of Small Groups

When Paul wrote his letters to the churches in the first century, he was writing to groups of people that met in homes. Archeological excavations have revealed that typical homes in the first century were similar to homes today in that they would comfortably seat anywhere between nine and twenty people.[17] When Paul wrote the word "church" or *ecclesia* in Greek, he was envisioning small groups of people who gathered as a connected community in homes. His mental images of church and ours are vastly different after 2000 years of development.

Because the modern definition of church emphasizes the organization, the building, and large group worship, we impose these mental models onto Paul's use of the word *ecclesia*. In some ways his use of the word does include the gathering of large groups. For instance, in Corinth, he refers to the gathering of all the Christians in the city as *ecclesia* (1 Cor. 1:1).

Ecclesia was a word that the followers of Christ used to define themselves. It simply meant "an assembly" or "a gathering." It was used in the Septuagint to translate the Hebrew word *quhol* which means "assembly," often used to describe the "assemblies of the Lord." New Testament theologian James Dunn writes, "There can be little doubt that Paul intended to depict the little assemblies of Christian believers as equally manifestations of and in direct continuity with 'the assembly of Yahweh,' 'the assembly of Israel.'"[18] As a result, Paul could freely envision both small groups of believers meeting in homes and periodic gatherings of Christians of one city meeting in a larger venue as the *ecclesia*. One did not compete with the status of the other because both were gatherings or assemblies.

Due to our modern definition of "church," most of the time small groups are viewed as sub-units of the "real" church. Church leaders assume that the most important place of connection is the weekly large group service. As a result, small groups are labeled as something less than a gathering meeting around the presence of Jesus (*ecclesia*).

Some house church advocates swing the pendulum the other way and argue that the large group venue is not a valid form of *ecclesia*. I believe this goes too far. There is no need to denigrate such larger gatherings, as they are valid expressions of "church" when Jesus is lifted up. If the biblical definition of church is a gathering or assembly around the presence of Jesus, then both the small group and the large group are proper expressions of church.

While you may agree with the historical evidence about the Pauline church, it may be difficult for you to give your small groups this label due to your church tradition or to place this high of a value on small groups. If this is the case, then please be clear about your expectations. Don't expect people to see the value of the small group, because they will see it as less important than the Sunday worship service, and thereby they will most likely see it as optional.

However, if you do see a vision for groups that gather in the name of Jesus and experience his presence as being modern expressions of the church, then you must not only define them accordingly, but resource them accordingly. Paul, Barnabus, Timothy, Titus and many other leaders spent most of their life-long ministries investing in such small groups, and they still had many problems. While recognizing the biblical reality that small groups are "church," this alone will not necessarily change what happens within the groups. Teaching on the true nature of the biblical definition of "church" and being the body of Christ in the world must occur. Relational investment in the leaders of these groups must be a priority of the pastoral team. Pastors and church leaders must spend significant time in dialogue with small group leaders to help them process their understanding of church and small groups. Otherwise, people will misunderstand the label. Leaders may assume that the label "church" gives them permission to branch off from the big church and become independent.

My Last Word

Small groups as a Bible study or an optional fellowship gathering can be a good thing. However, when we understand the nature of church as it is practiced in the New Testament, the potential of what small groups can be transcends previous expectations. When small groups practice life together as *church*, Bible studies, fellowship groups, and task groups no longer possess the same value. Christ longs to be the center of our communities. When he is that center, the Spirit of God is released to accomplish the mission of God in this world.

Seeking God's
Relational Kingdom

As a teenager, I dedicated my life to serving in vocational Christian ministry. In my first years of college, I worked with youth, preached weekly at the homeless mission, and served as a summer missionary to Germany. I began my junior year as a depressed, sullen, but hard-working church leader. After two weeks of living in this sad state, I shared my struggles with the executive director of the campus ministry where I served as a leader. He responded, "It sounds like you have never trusted your life to Jesus." I was not shocked. I had questioned my relationship with God many times, but this encounter caused me to see how I had been self-dependent for my salvation. Upon realizing that I was self-dependent, I gave my life to Christ and invited him to be my Lord.

While my depression did not lift immediately, one thing did change in the blink of an eye: my heart was opened to the world of relationships. Before, I was plagued with loneliness even when surrounded by Christians. When I trusted Christ, I went from friendless to accepted. God had opened up my life to others so that I could connect with people in ways I never experienced before.

This heart change allowed me to participate and lead others into the world of God's relational kingdom, which was fun and different. While hanging out at someone's house, we would stop what we were doing to pray because it was fun. We were infectious and had something contagious to give to others. I tasted something that I never wanted to give up! I am very thankful for my Christian upbringing. However, this relational kingdom life was quite different from the kind of church relationships that I had known up to that point.

This new way of life sent me on a biblical quest to see how the church operated in the first century. I found a relational version of the church that caused frustration and even anger to well up within me when I thought about the churches I had attended my first two years in college. I asked questions: How could I serve in these churches without anyone noticing the lack of God's spontaneous life within me? How could I relate to key leaders on staff and they not discern what was going on in my life? How could churches offer me jobs when I obviously did not demonstrate a compassion for people? How could church leaders endorse me for ministry, when I had no one who knew my true heart? For some reason, I was able to slip through these church systems without ever revealing what was missing in my heart.

Amidst my search through Scripture, I read Dr. Yongii Cho's book on small groups in South Korea, and I became a small group fanatic. In my frustration with the traditional church, I concluded that groups are the missing link in the church today. I argued for the church to return to the New Testament structure. I expected churches to explode with growth if they would only fully adopt the small group structure and multiply groups. I idealized the small group vision as the single key to the future of the church.

During the 1990s, my work with TOUCH® Outreach Ministries reinforced this belief. As purveyors of small group training, our job was to provide pragmatic answers to the "important" question: How do we develop small groups? My myopic focus on the structure of small groups generated a narrow-minded legalism. Small groups (or what some call cell groups) became the all-encompassing goal of church life! I failed to see that the success of these small groups was based on a way of living in relationships with others, not on the fact that we met in small groups.

Structural Myth #3:
Meeting in small groups is *the* central source of biblical community.

The Relational Truth:
Relational kingdom life requires the church to address how people do life, not just how they do small groups.

What is the Point of Small Groups?

Over the years I have served as an editor of small group books, trainer and consultant, and I've heard lots of different motivations for adopting small groups. Some of the primary reasons provided for doing small groups include:

Church Growth. Small group ministry is a key ingredient to growing a church. All of the largest churches in the world have some form of small group structure.

Evangelism. Statistics have proven over and over again that most people are led to the Lord through relationships with either a friend or a family member. Small group evangelism is dependent upon friendship connections with the lost.

Church Health. Research on church health factors has revealed that small groups have the most impact on church quality. In fact, all of the healthiest churches around the world have developed effective small group systems.[1]

Interpersonal Connections. Small groups help connect disconnected people to one another, providing a venue for church relationships to extend beyond the examining of the backs of heads on Sunday mornings.

Personal Growth. People grow in their relationship with God when they have the opportunity to process what they are learning with other people. Small groups provide the environment for this kind of processing.

Biblical Model. Ardent advocates of small groups adopt this approach to ministry because they want to return to the way of doing church demonstrated in the New Testament.

I have used all of these reasons as a basis for doing small groups when talking with pastors because each one is valid. Most pastors like these reasons because they are very practical in nature. Each reason points to tangible results that small groups can offer. However, none of these reasons satisfied my sense of discomfort with the church. Each one pointed to the church itself; improving the church was the end game.

I was looking for a reason to do small groups that pointed to something bigger than the church. This examination required a different question: "Why do we do church?" To answer this question, we must first ask, "What is the mission of the church?"

My conclusion? To understand church, and therefore small groups, I had to look beyond the church itself and discover the bigger intention of God. The first words of Jesus recorded by Mark are, *"The time is fulfilled, and the kingdom of God is at hand; repent and believe in the gospel"* (Mark 1:14, NRSV). Jesus came preaching the kingdom of God, something much bigger than the structures of the church that would follow his ascension. He pointed to something that extended beyond the realm of the religious structures. He came preaching the kingdom of God, calling people to align their lives with the good news of the kingdom. The kingdom comes first in the order of God, not the church or small groups.

Jesus instructed us, *"Seek first the kingdom of God and all these things will be added to you"* (Matt. 6:33). I often find church leaders seeking first the development of their church through a small group structure. They seek church growth, evangelism, church health, interpersonal connections, personal growth, and a biblical model. All good things, but the good is often the enemy of the best. Many times, the good results that we seek stand in the way of the kingdom of God. Jesus says that if we seek the kingdom, he will take care of all our concerns. This means that he will take care of the concerns of church leaders: growth, evangelism, health, interpersonal connections, personal growth, and being a biblical church.

In a dialogue with a prominent church growth consultant about prioritizing the kingdom of God in my teaching on small groups and church leadership, he expressed that the goal of seeking the kingdom was too idealistic. He commented that pastors need more tangible or practical goals. After reflecting on his comments, I realized that he and I shared similar training in theology. We possessed a good understanding of the theological nature of the kingdom because we studied it in seminary, but this theology is disconnected from the ministerial practices used to do church. Little work has been done to connect the message of the kingdom with what it means to be the church in our current context. Therefore, when it comes to developing a small group strategy, Jesus' kingdom words seem to be quite impractical. However, this conclusion seems to be based on a misunderstanding of the kingdom of God.

Misunderstanding the Kingdom

Many Protestant church leaders don't connect the kingdom of God with practical church strategies. Modern interpretations of the kingdom simply lack practical meaning for us. Kingdom language is important for sermons to help people live as better individuals, but most pastors don't see the relevance of the kingdom for how we do church. Seeking first the kingdom of God is popularly interpreted as putting God first in "my" life, making him my individual king.[2] The kingdom of God is primarily related to individual salvation, individual commitment, individual sanctification, and individual glorification. The kingdom of God has become a private affair that has little to do with how I relate to my neighbor, much less those at church. With this individualistic understanding, the first concern is to focus on putting the kingdom first privately and then to allow God to move through me in the church as a second priority.

Such an understanding of the kingdom is not new. In fact, the roots can be traced back to the year 313, the year that the Roman Emperor Constantine converted to Christianity. His Edict of Milan marked the end of the persecution of Christians and the promotion of the church by the Emperor. Many writers on church organization have argued that Constantine's conversion marked a significant shift in the church structure, due to the fact that the Emperor built official buildings for church meetings, thereby eliminating the need for the small groups to meet in homes.

Many small group experts have called the church to return to the pre-Constantinian structure to experience the dynamic life of the New Testament. However, if the focus only lies on the structure, one only deals with the surface issues.

While the church underwent a structural shift with the actions of Constantine, we must acknowledge and explore the more subtle and hidden alteration that occurred.

When Christianity became the official state religion, the role of the church changed. Before Constantine, the responsibility of the church included both the private and the public. In other words, the church took on the responsibility to form both the private beliefs of Christians and the public practices that Christians lived in their everyday lives.

During and after Constantine's rule, public matters became the responsibility of the state. Because the state was assumed to be Christian, it set the boundaries for how Christians lived in their public lives and established the accepted norms for how people lived together in the everyday state of affairs. The state set the laws for public interaction with neighbors (the acceptable or unacceptable ways for treating one another). It took over the responsibility to take care of the public physical needs of people (welfare). The church was relegated to overseeing the private, internal development of religious truths. In essence, the church became the guardian for orthodox beliefs. It assumed the role of informing people how to think about God.

This pattern, inaugurated with Constantine and solidified by hundreds of years of church practices, created a division separating the realm of the public from the private. In such a society, Jurgen Moltmann concludes, "The church looks after people's souls and their salvation; the emperor claims their bodies and provides for the welfare of the empire."[3]

The Kingdom of God in America

While North American Christians don't live under the rule of a "Christian" emperor in a Christian state, the church remains under the influence of this privatized religion. The church holds the job of tending to people's private beliefs and morality, while the public way of living in the family, work, and school has been established by authorities outside of the church. Without an emperor, no central hierarchical system sets the parameters of public life. Instead, there is a general philosophy of public life that is outside the church's influence.

Randy Frazee has provided one way to illustrate how this philosophy of public life works in America.[4] In his book, *Making Room for Life*, he paints a picture of how life works, which seems quite neutral but in fact stands in the way of the kingdom of God. I have adapted his illustration to make this point.

Imagine Bob. His life is the epitome of success in North America. He is the VP of marketing at a large food distribution company. Because of his professional attitude and hard-work, he makes a handsome salary. Bob's level of income affords him a 6,000 square foot home and two cars, one of which he sits in each work day for a two-hour commute. He devotes a lot of energy to support his four kids—two live with his ex-wife—helping their moms cart them to baseball games, gymnastics, and piano lessons; therefore he has no time for relationships with his co-workers outside the office. Bob now knows what it takes to make marriage work, and he invests in his second wife, but this requires a lot of energy to relate to her large family who lives across town. He takes night courses to complete his MBA. He plays golf with a group of guys from his previous job. He tries to keep up with his parents and sisters who live in another state. He volunteers once per month at the local food pantry. And he really wants to please God, so he is involved in his church, giving his time to various committees and ministries.

Bob is a busy man, but with his time-management skills, he has found that he can juggle all of the balls. Frazee uses an illustration to help us imagine Bob's life. Each circle in this diagram represents a different activity and a different group of people.

What does "seeking first the kingdom" mean for Bob? Under the privatized interpretation of the kingdom, it means that God and church will take priority over every other activity in his life. So he draws the circle that relates to church larger so that everyone can see that God is his first priority. God is first, family second, church third, work fourth and then everything else follows after that. The key to seeking first the kingdom of God for Bob is priorities. If he puts God first, we assume that everything else will line up. Yet the reality is that Bob's way of living is under the control of another ruler. Another kingdom has shaped Bob's life. Ultimately, Bob's life is a form of an anti-relational kingdom.

First, Bob is at the center of his existence. This system of life requires him to manage all of these circles so that he can be and do what he feels is necessary for a productive life.

Second, most of the people in each circle have no relationship with the people in other circles. Bob has a set of linear, independent relationships that are only connected to him—he is the single common denominator. The relationships at the end of each spoke have little to no connection with other people at the end of the other spokes. This reinforces the need for Bob to manage his relationships.

Third, because Bob has so many different circles to manage, he feels that he has lots of friends, but in reality, he just has lots of acquaintances. He is so busy managing these unconnected acquaintances that he has no time for deep relationships with any one group. As a result, Bob often feels that no one knows him.

These three elements describe the anti-relational kingdom and create a dysfunctional lifestyle that Randy Frazee calls "crowded loneliness." Even still, this way of life forms the basis of existence for most people in North America. To attack this pattern of living is to attack the very core of how we live in America. Theologian Stanley Hauerwas states, "The very genius of our society is to forge a political and social existence that does not have to depend on trusting others in matters important for our survival."[5]

This anti-relational way of life has resulted in the most advanced society in the history of the world. It works, and has worked for me. I assumed that this pattern of living was the way to become successful, and I learned how to manage my circles accordingly. I never realized that I was managing my own little kingdom, at least until I read Frazee's book and wanted to toss it across the room!

To *manage* means to orchestrate or organize by controlling or manipulating a situation to attain a predetermined outcome. When Jesus instructed the people not to fret or worry about what they will eat and drink, he is telling them not to worry about how they will manage their lives. North Americans spend most of their lives managing how they will overcome the fears that control our society. They manage their work so that they will earn more money, allowing them to live more comfortably or keep their jobs. They manage their children so that they won't turn to drugs, or so that they can become successful in the future. (I heard of a family in Alabama who had their son in eight different baseball leagues at the same time. They live the Bob life so that their son can grow up to become a baseball star.) People manage their family relationships so that they will be perceived as good sons and daughters. They manage their church relationships so that they will receive their reward in heaven. Managing life puts the individual at the center of the equation.

What Happens When Bob Adds Small Groups?

Because Bob wants to be a good Christian, he will follow the leadership and direction of his pastor and join—maybe even lead—a small group. Every Tuesday night, he pulls into the driveway after sitting in an hour of traffic and eating fast food for his evening meal. He greets his wife, Roberta, when she drives up to the host home because she took their son to football practice, arriving in her own car. This couple is now about to enter the home of people they barely know. No one has time to connect outside of their weekly meeting. Because everyone else is as busy as Bob and Roberta, rarely does everyone attend the meetings consistently, causing more distance between the members.

Many churches in North America realize the power of small groups for church growth, evangelism, building community, church health, etcetera. They develop a small group structure, but they fail to address the root issues of how Bob—the typical church member—lives his life. They develop an "add-on" group system. They provide Bob with yet another circle to manage, asking overly busy members to add a small group to their already frenetic life.

Such an approach will result in the addition of group meetings that impact the private thoughts and beliefs of individuals; it might even give people some better friends. However, it will not address the problem of the anti-relational kingdom and the crowded loneliness that dominates our society. With the add-on approach, pastors feel compelled to cajole people into small groups, promoting the church's vision as the priority. This reality often frustrates some because they don't find small groups fulfilling while others experience guilt. The guilty are honest enough to admit that they cannot devote enough time to participate in one more program and reject small group participation.

God's Relational Kingdom

If the kingdom of God is relegated to private application, it is limited to the realm of personal salvation, personal discipleship, and personal commitment. Christianity becomes a private affair while social interaction is excluded from the influence of the church. However, this is not how Jesus used the word. The idea of the individual as we understand it today is a construct of the Enlightenment, which did not occur until 1,700 years after Jesus roamed the earth. Dallas Willard writes, "We are dominated by the essentially Enlightenment values that rule American culture: Pursuit of happiness, unrestricted freedom of choice, disdain of authority."[6] Independent, autonomous individuals who define themselves according to their individual thoughts and beliefs is a concept that first century Jews would not have understood. While the kingdom of God impacts each individual, it is impossible for Jesus' teaching to be primarily applied to our understanding of the individual.

If the kingdom of God is more than a private priority given to God and his church, then what did Jesus mean when he came saying, "the kingdom of God is near. Repent and believe the good news"? We must get into the skin of a first century Jew to understand the language of the kingdom.

First, Jesus' audience, the Israelites, knew that God had chosen them and set them apart for his purposes. Second, they knew that they were not experiencing the reality of what it meant to live as the chosen people. They looked back on the glory days of King David and saw a kingdom where God ruled in Zion. Third, while they had technically returned from Babylonian exile, theirs was still an occupied land. The Israelites still experienced a life of exile under the thumb of Roman occupation. Fourth, in order to be set free from this exile, their enemies had to be defeated. This is the basic social, as opposed to private, context in which Jesus came preaching the "good news" of the kingdom.

New Testament historian N. T. Wright states, "If, then, someone were to speak to Jesus' contemporaries of YHWH's becoming king, we may safely assume that they would have in mind, in some form or other, this two-sided story concerning the double reality of exile. Israel would 'really' return from exile; YHWH would finally return to Zion. But if these were to happen there would have to be a third element as well: evil, usually in the form of Israel's enemies, must be defeated."[7] To a first century Jew, this was "good news."

Of course, a typical first century Jew possessed a certain set of expectations or preconceived ideas about the kingdom of God. Their kingdom prototype was King David, and they envisioned a return to the days of David. James and John wanted to sit on the right and left of Jesus when he came into power. They expected Jesus, the Messiah, to enter Jerusalem with power and overthrow the enemy and bring back the glory of Israel. While we don't know Judas' motives, he may have betrayed Jesus because he was frustrated with his lack of action. Judas thought that he could force Jesus to do something if he turned him over to the enemy. Even after the resurrection, Peter asked Jesus when the kingdom would come. No first century Jew had an expectation that the kingdom would come in the form that Jesus brought. They expected power. In contrast, Jesus brought love, revealing a new kind of power, and thereby a new kind of kingdom. They expected war, but Jesus brought peace, showing people a new way to overcome an enemy. They expected glory. Instead, Jesus carried a cross to his death.

The kingdom of God is the reign of God, the rule of God where people operate according to the order of the King. Jesus came announcing the kingdom, inviting people to a way of life that would result in the return of God's people from exile, the return of God's presence to Zion, and the defeat of Israel's enemies. His call to the kingdom did not involve the annihilation of competing kingdoms. Instead, Jesus called people to a new way of living in the midst of a world that would not recognize their validity as a people. He called them to live as a chosen people, even though they had no land or officials in positions of power. He called them to a different life, a life that would establish a parallel kingdom in the midst of the kingdoms of this world. This is God's relational kingdom, one where the people of God relate to God and to one another in communion.

Such a kingdom is virtually impossible to explain. This may be the reason why Jesus told parables about the kingdom rather than providing a succinct definition of the kingdom. He realized that such a parallel kingdom could only be caught through experience. After all, his hearers were limited to their definitions of establishing a physical kingdom of power.

He did not call them to a private religion of personal beliefs. He called them to a corporate life as a chosen people. Jesus called them to establish an alternative pattern of life. To enter the reign of the King means to participate in the return of the glory of God to Zion, and to return from captivity, as God overthrows our enemies.

Therefore, when Jesus talked about the kingdom, his message had ramifications that extended far beyond individual belief in his message. It ultimately meant that Jesus was introducing a way of operating as a society that was radically different than how they lived under Roman occupation.

The Kingdom of This World

The story of Bob's life in American society is a parable of the kingdom that fights against God's relational kingdom. Recently, I learned of a large church that embarked upon a small group ministry with all its energy, arguing that groups are the only way to do ministry in the twenty-first century. After four years of mediocrity, the leaders declared their experiment a failure, stating the vision was too radical and will not work in our culture. Another pastor told me that he expects his church members to attend worship only twice per month. He said, "People are just too busy in the suburbs. That's why we created bimonthly small group meetings. We cannot expect more of our people."

Both of these churches have failed to see the root issue, the same issue I neglected to see as I originally promoted the vision. New structure (the skin and bones) without new breath makes the new structures unnecessary. By adding groups to a lifestyle that is shaped by the kingdoms of this world, a church might develop a growing small group system, but it will fail to call people into God's relational kingdom life.

John wrote, *"...I have written these things to you that you might not sin"* (I John 2:1). Jesus announced the good news of the kingdom so that we might not live a life controlled by sin. As I was flying into a large city a few months ago, I looked down upon the huge buildings, imagining the chaotic nature of life in large cities and the money that flows through them. As I looked at the high-rise buildings a thought became very clear. There are three types of sin: sins of commission, sins of omission, and sins of the principalities and powers of the air. Ethical teaching tends to focus on the first two. One is a good disciple of Christ if she does not commit great sins (such as adultery and stealing). She is an even greater disciple if she does not commit sins of omission (failing to pray or failing to care for the needy). However, sins of the principalities and powers are ignored by most.

The principalities and powers of the air create a pattern of living based upon a series of lies that establish a way of living that is contrary to God's relational kingdom. Therefore, if Bob remains preoccupied with this pattern—overwhelmed, busy, and stressed—he will miss God's kingdom, even if he goes to church every week or even leads a small group. Such "Christian" activities would only be added on top of a life that is controlled at the root by the kingdoms of this world.

The church can even find itself entrapped by the principalities and powers of the air. Imagine the most committed leaders in your church. Most likely these people have overcommitted themselves to a plethora of church activities. The more committed they are to God, the more circles they create: men's prayer breakfast, office Bible study, choir, youth volunteer, and others. They set themselves at the center of a spoked wheel and manage the activities at the end of each line, resulting in the condition of crowded loneliness within the confines of the church. I have lived under this pattern, thinking that if I was going to truly serve God I would volunteer for as many different ministries as possible. I was so busy serving God that I had no time to love or be shown love by others.

Paul writes in Colossians, *"See to it that no one takes you captive through hollow and deceptive philosophy, which depends on human tradition and the basic principles of this world rather than on Christ"* (2:8). The word "principles" could be translated "elements," "elementary spirits," or "ruling spirits of the universe."[8] Later in the same chapter, Paul states, *"Since you died with Christ to the basic principles of this world, why, as though you still belonged to it, do you submit to its rules?"* (2:20). While the principles "of this world" that the church of the first century was facing are different from those we face today, Paul recognized that behind these principles are basic philosophies of life. The philosophies are often assumed and go unchallenged. As such, they are the most dangerous. At the same time, the power of these philosophies has been disarmed by the cross, as Jesus made a public spectacle of them.

These principles are not just constructs of man. They are orchestrated by the powers and authorities of the air. Leslie Newbigin writes, "What is clear in these and in other passages is that the powers have been disarmed but not destroyed. They are put under the supreme dominion of Christ by what he has done on the cross, but they still exist. We have to wrestle with them. And the Church has to make manifest to them the wisdom of God as revealed in Jesus."[9] The enemy of our souls knows that if he can entrap us in the patterns of life according to the principles of this world, then he need not tempt us with obvious sins of commission or omission. By playing the game of life according to the anti-relational kingdom, all the church activity in the world will only bring a small slice of the reality of God's relational kingdom. The addition of small groups will only add one more activity to attend. With that, Satan is not too worried. However, he is greatly concerned when a people choose to participate with others in the church to set up an alternative way of living together in a parallel kingdom.

God's relational kingdom confronts the assumptions of the anti-relational kingdom. Small groups that understand this realize the reason for doing groups is much bigger than small group attendance. It is about doing life together in authentic biblical community and undermining the assumptions of this world that create the anti-relational kingdom. Such small groups don't accommodate the anti-relational kingdom. They confront it, challenge it, and offer a different way of living.

In particular, I believe that such kingdom small groups confront the assumption of success as defined by our North American culture. Why do we work the extra hours? Why do we want a bigger home? Why do we want new cars? Why do we run our children all over town to participate in every possible activity? The more we have, the more we want. This is the sickness under which the principalities have created for us to live.

Russian philosopher and novelist Alexander Solzhenitsyn sees the problem as an outsider who lived in North America. He writes "… every citizen has been granted the desired freedom and material goods in such quantity and of such quality as to guarantee in theory the achievement of happiness. In the process, however, one psychological detail has been overlooked: the constant desire to have still more things and a still better life and the struggle to obtain them imprints many Western faces with worry and even depression, though it is customary to conceal such feelings. Active and tense competition permeates all human thoughts without opening a way to free spiritual development."[10]

What Does this Mean … Practically?

Entering God's Relational Kingdom

The first time I shared the life of Bob with a group of leaders, I experienced something I did not expect. Most of the people in the room were successful, relatively healthy, and intelligent. With every circle I drew, the eyes in the room got bigger. The more I talked about how ridiculous Bob's life is, the lower their jaws dropped. It became obvious that the room was full of Bobs. These leaders quickly realized that leading a small group involved much more than organizing and facilitating a weekly meeting. They felt the need to change because they could not lead people into a different lifestyle unless they changed their own lives.

Herein lies the problem: people don't know how to change their lives. Presenting the problem of Bob's life is not enough. People have lived according to the principalities of this world for so long that they don't know how to live differently.

Therefore, the role of church leaders must change. Randy Frazee puts it this way, "Howard Hendricks, my beloved professor in seminary, suggested that pastors should not focus their ministry on teaching people how to do church but on how to do life."[11] Paul explains that the job of church leaders is to equip people for works of ministry when he wrote *"It was he who gave some to be apostles, prophets, some to be evangelists, and some to be pastors and teachers, to prepare God's people for works of service, so that the body of Christ may be built up until we all reach the unity of the faith and in the knowledge of the Son of God and become mature, attaining the whole measure of the fullness of Christ"* (Eph. 4:11-13). Equipping people for ministry is not merely about preparing people to serve in the church. It is also about providing practical patterns of living that serve as alternatives. This is kingdom equipping that impacts more than the scheduled activities of the church by invading the everyday lives of the people of God.

Calling People Out of Bob's Life

While Bob's life is typical in North America, the exact form of Bob's life will look different for every church. Randy Frazee presents the picture of suburban Bob in his book, which he wrote while leading a church in the Dallas/Fort Worth metroplex. He now serves as one of the leaders at Willow Creek Church, within a suburb of Chicago. Frazee seeks to teach busy Bobs—who commute for hours each day—how to reshape their lives around the kingdom. The life of suburban Bob is an ideal image of the American dream for all others who don't live like suburban Bob. However, "suburban Bob" is not the only way people live. My church sits between the suburban and urban worlds in Saint Paul, Minnesota. We attract people from many different socio-economic walks of life. In addition, this malaise is not limited to Bob. Roberta is affected by it just as much. The following are different ways that Bob's life can manifest in our culture.

Under-employed Bob. Many churches are trying to show under-employed Bobs how to live. Churches set in lower income neighborhoods and inner city settings have a different kind of Bob. When I first started researching how people live in America, I assumed that people in lower income brackets interacted with people more than those of a higher income. However, the actual research on this reveals just the opposite. People who make less money don't necessarily work less. And those who are not working don't necessarily have deeper relationships because they have more time on their hands. Robert Putnam, a Harvard sociologist, reports in his book *Bowling Alone*, that "Financial anxiety is associated with ... less time spent with friends, less card playing, less home entertaining, less frequent attendance at church, less volunteering, and less interest in politics. In fact, the only leisure activity that correlates positively with financial worry is TV viewing.[12]

Single-Mom Roberta. With two kids, two jobs and a bus schedule, Roberta's busyness has been dictated for her more than she has chosen it. She tries to make "ends meet" every month, but seems to fall short most of the time. The father of her children is absent and pays child support sporadically. Roberta has given her life to God, but she finds volunteering in a ministry beyond her capacity. She barely makes it to church on Sundays.

Rural Bob. Most people probably assume that country folk are more relational than city folk. The pace of life in farming communities is slower, but that does not mean that social interaction is greater. I grew up on a farm, and I realized that I needed to find a different profession because of the intense time demands farming requires. Twelve hour days are common. And for many farmers, it is twelve hours of isolation, sitting on a tractor or combine. At one conference where I was teaching, a woman told me that her husband could not attend because it was planting season. She confessed she had only seen him sporadically over the past few weeks.

Immigrant Bob. While training pastors in the life of Bob, I visited with three church leaders of Brazilian congregations in Florida. They told me that their greatest problem was the fact that most of their church members work twelve to fourteen-hour days. They also confessed that this pattern of work was new to these immigrants. They did not live this way in Brazil. The American dream often entraps immigrants. Some feel pressure to survive on American soil. Others must send money to their families back home. In addition to living in a foreign country where they struggle to understand the language, many are forced into transient living, boarding with friends or friends of friends until they can earn enough money to secure a home of their own.

Gen-X Roberta. The attitude of Generation Xers is characterized by a revolt against the life of workaholism displayed by their boomer parents. Gen-X Bobs want to experience life to its fullest, as opposed to wasting away their lives working for the machine of big business. They react to the absence of their parents, a typical characteristic of Suburban Bob or Roberta. Even still, they embrace a different form of Bob's life. Gen-Xers may have more relationships than their parents, but these connections are often very short-term in nature. They do not expect long-term commitment from their friends. Many times, the relationships are based on activities of interest such as rock climbing, video games, sports, online forums, blogs, chat rooms, or music. In addition, there has been an unusually high rate of depression, suicide and malaise within this generation, associated with very high rates of isolation.[13]

Church Bob. Most pastors with whom I consult confess that their church is full of Church Bobs and Robertas, people who are so busy with church activities that they don't have time for genuine relationships. One church leader told me that her parents, who live in the same town, never see her because of how busy she is at church. Such people have lots of circles, but almost all of them are within the church. Church Bobs (and Robertas) comprise the infamous 20 percent of the church who serve the church for the other 80 percent who are consumers. These people are the best candidates for leading small groups. However, they don't have time because they are so involved in various church activities—committees, ministries, and other church programs.

What kind of Bobs and Robertas does your church have? What kind of Bobs live in your community? This list is far from exhaustive, but it gives a broad understanding of the way Bob infiltrates almost every segment of American life.

Redrawing the Circles of Bob's Life

Churches must help Bobs of all types *"Seek first the kingdom of God and his righteousness"* by helping them redraw their circles around the kingdom. But what does that mean in today's society?

First, God being king today means that his people will return from exile. Too many Christians live in the church but under the rule of a foreign authority that has no place in the church: the principalities and powers of the air. It is time for the church to lead people out of this rule. We must reverse the trend of crowded loneliness and help people connect to others to become the family of God. Many churches in North America have taken a first step by embracing small groups as a structure of ministry. The church, whether through six-week small group adventures, small group Bible studies, task groups, holistic small groups, or cell groups, has recognized the need to provide points of connection for people. The previous sections in this chapter may have implied that adopting small group structures in this way is counter-productive. I may be guilty of overstatement for the purpose of making a point. Challenging people to experiment with small group connections seems logical. However, we cannot stop there.

Second, God being King means that his presence will be made manifest in Zion. God will become the center of life in his kingdom community, not a center where individuals are trying to manage their lives to attain success and happiness (more on this point in chapter three).

Third, God being king means that he will deliver us from our enemies. The problem is, the enemy in North American Christianity is not found in the form of an occupying force or in the form of an external government. We have internalized this pattern of life illustrated by Bob. We have found the enemy, and the enemy is within us! Therefore, not only do we need to connect with people in small groups, but we need to repent and turn away from the way of life that we have adopted and accepted as our own. As church leaders, we must help people redraw their circles.

Jesus modeled a way of living with others in the kingdom that starkly contrasts with the pattern of Bob. Jesus did not manage a series of relationships. Rather, he connected himself intimately with a small group of people. He surrounded himself with three intimate confidantes and nine other close friends. Jesus then related to a large group of up to 70 people who followed him in his ministry. Then he related to the crowds of people who did not know him personally.

Masses
120
30-40
8-12
2-3

Those around Jesus formed a web of connections where he demonstrated God's relational kingdom. Those closest to him saw it in a way that those who were further away did not.

Jesus lived the kingdom for us, and it was a relational kingdom. The kingdom is not something that we need to produce or achieve. It is something we enter as we learn to relate to one another, and thereby create an alternative lifestyle. At the same time, we must also be realistic. Jesus was single. Jesus did not have kids. He did not have a job, a commute, or a mortgage. He lived and ministered primarily in rural Galilee, not urban or suburban North America. So we must redraw the circles to fit the realities of our world, while at the same time resisting the trap of our world.

To begin, Bob and Roberta must recognize the value of connecting with a small group of nine to twelve people. They must choose to connect with a small group and seek out people who might become a spiritual family. Such a choice is risky and there are no guarantees. Relationships are built through trial and error. However, if they don't enter into a context where such connections are a possibility, Bob and Roberta will be left at the individualist center of life.

Participating in a small group is a step in the right direction, but it is even more effective if Bob and Roberta find two or three intimate confidantes that every person needs (see chapter one on refrigerator rights). This is represented by the inner circle. Jesus had Peter, James, and John. Such confidantes do not form a small group, but they may be fellow members of a small group. They could be a sub-group or a set of long-term best friends. The combination of the small group along with this group of two or three intimate friendships will then work with Bob to help him refocus his life. These two circles represent the place of primary kingdom connections.

In order for Bob to change within this group context, the vision for the groups must extend beyond the weekly meetings. The small group meeting is crucial to group life, but in my experience in participating and leading effective groups, the meeting contributes about forty percent to the life of a healthy group. The other sixty percent is a result of random life connections between group members. Good meetings are important, but Bob needs life connections with people who will love him, challenge him, pray for him and support him. This cannot be done in ninety minutes once a week or twice a month.

As Bob connects with the members of his small group and begins to live in community with them, he can take the next step, which is elimination.

Bob must discover the freedom to say "no" to requests made of him, and the group can help him with this. The inner circle confidantes will prove especially helpful with the elimination process. He must only do those things that the Holy Spirit leads him to do. This will mean the elimination of a lot of good activities. The biggest trap for Bob is not a list of bad things that he is doing, but rather overloading his life with too many good things. (Most of us need help in determining the best things in life because we struggle to say "no" to the good things.) As Bob eliminates extraneous activities, he can also learn to overlap circles in his life and include his small group in some of his other circles. Rather than Bob having to manage each circle independently, these circles can be connected and overlapped. For instance, most people have family relationships and church relationships. A couple of years ago at Christmas, I invited Jeremy and his wife Jessica, a couple from our small group to celebrate Christmas with my family in Dallas. Admittedly, this offer bucks tradition, but such an action of consolidation extends ministry beyond church activities and into the normal stuff of life. Imagine redrawing the circles described by the following diagram.

The ovals represent the overlapping of relational circles. Instead of seeing each oval as an independent and isolated group, Bob, with the help of his small group, can weave his relationships into an organic whole, rather than something that he must manage. For example, when my sister and her husband come into town, I have the option of spending all of my time with them, which only moves me deeper into an exclusive relationship with them. Or, I could overlap my relationships and invite some of our friends from our small group to join us for dinner and board games for part of our time together.

Kingdom-Centered Simplicity

Randy Frazee offers two specific suggestions for people who want to venture further down this path. He encourages the people he oversees to work only at work. When it is time to go home, he challenges them to "turn off" work and relate to others. Many of us allow work to control our minds during off-hours to the point where we have no time or energy for spouse, kids or friends. Frazee writes, "If work could be grabbed with our hands, we should seek to take only one fistful of work and in the other we should grab a handful of tranquility. This is a fifty-fifty proposition. Fifty percent of our day should be given to work and production—this is good. Fifty percent of our day should be given to relationships and sleep—this is also good and necessary. It is a matter of balance."[14]

The second suggestion Frazee makes is to eat together. With the advent of fast food, Americans have lost the practice of sitting down with others to eat and talk. Instead, we pick up fast food and eat "at the wheel." We must elevate the level of importance of eating together to the point where we can eliminate other activities that compete with it. Frazee proposes, "When we wake up each day to face the wonderful work that is before us ... we do so with a longing—a genuine passion to gather at the table at dusk to partake of a meal that sustains us and to listen to another page in the novel of the people God has graciously brought into our lives. When this event takes place, our souls send a signal to our minds that this is right."[15]

While families should carve out time to eat together each evening, the power of a meal can impact small group life in significant ways. Jesus understood this principle. Much of his ministry occurred while sitting around tables, eating with the disciples, sinners, and Pharisees.

These are just two ideas that could help Bob incorporate simplicity. Frazee has more in his book *Making Room for Life* while others like Richard Foster, Dallas Willard, and Larry Crabb are prophetic voices calling the church out of Bob's life into kingdom-centered simplicity.

Kingdom Organization

Practically speaking, there are some issues that churches face that would impede Bob's ability to change his life. One of the biggest barriers is how the groups are organized. In order for Bob to enter into community with his group and participate in life outside the group meeting, the participants should naturally overlap in some way with the other group members. If the only thing the group members commonly share is the same meeting night, they might have trouble entering into the relational way.

Therefore, the groups should be organized around some form of commonality to increase interaction and the potential for community life. Some churches do this around life-stage. Common interest is another option. Similar life experience can also form a good foundation. For instance, I know of a group that formed after returning from a missions trip to the Far East. Many churches organize their groups around gender, realizing that men will be more transparent with other men, and likewise for women.

The more I work with groups, the more I become convinced that the best way to connect people is around the commonality of proximity. This is especially true for churches set in larger metropolitan areas. Imagine if Bob must travel thirty minutes to attend a group each week and every other member of the group must travel at least fifteen minutes. How much interaction will those people have between the meetings? If they work very hard, Bob might connect with an individual once or twice per month, but the possibility of any spontaneous community life is out of the question.

On the other hand, if I live within five minute's drive or walking distance of the other members of my group, I can ask them for help on the spur of the moment. I can swing by their house and drop off a gift or invite a group member over for dinner at the last minute. And it is quite likely that we will run into one another while we are running errands. In other words, by organizing our group around proximity, we don't have to plan the sixty percent of the group life that is outside of the meeting. Much of it is spontaneous.

Imagining God's Relational Kingdom

To help people redraw their circles and develop a primary group of friends around the kingdom, they must imagine a new way of living together and move toward it. While selling their homes and moving to a commune is out of the question for all but a few, I do know of group members who have chosen to move into the same neighborhood. As groups of Bobs and Robertas choose to reorder their lives, they enter into the mission of the church. They are participating in an alternative society which establishes a way of life that defies crowded loneliness.

This mission of the church calls people to live as foreigners in the land of their legal citizenship. They serve as an enclave for resident aliens who belong to another country in which they have not fully entered. To imagine this mission, we often need exposure to a different context. The Epistle to

Diognetus, a Christian document from the second century, provides a picture of life in community that can stimulate our imaginations:

> The difference between Christians and the rest of mankind is not a matter of nationality, or language, or customs. Christians do not live apart in separate cities of their own, speak any special dialect, nor practice any eccentric way of life. The doctrine they prove is not the invention of busy human minds and brains, nor are they, like some, adherents of this or that school of human thought. They pass their lives in whatever township—Greek or foreign—each man's lot has determined; and conform to ordinary local usage in their clothing, diet, and other habits. Nevertheless, the organization of their community does exhibit some features that are remarkable, and even surprising. For instance, though they are residents at home in their own countries, their behavior there is more like that of transients, they take their full part as citizens, but they also submit to anything and everything as if they were aliens. For them, any foreign country is a motherland, and any motherland is a foreign country. Like other men, they marry and beget children, though they do not expose their infants. Any Christian is free to share his neighbor's table, but never his marriage-bed. Though destiny has placed them here in the flesh, they do not live after the flesh; their days are passed on the earth, but their citizenship is above in the heavens. They obey the prescribed laws, but in their own private lives they transcend the laws. They show love to all men—and all men persecute them. They are misunderstood, and condemned: yet by suffering death they are quickened into life. They are poor, yet making many rich; lacking all things, yet having all things in abundance. They are dishonored, yet make glorious in their very dishonor; slandered, yet vindicated. They repay calumny with blessings, and abuse with courtesy. For the good they do, they suffer strips as evildoers; and under the strokes they rejoice like men given new life. Jews assail them as heretics, and Greeks harass them with persecutions; and yet of all their ill-wishers there is not one who can produce good grounds for his hostility.[16]

Therefore, for groups to serve as seedbeds for God's relational kingdom, the call must be to radical conversion, not just group attendance. The kingdom calls all aspects of a disciple's life to repentance, not just the religious aspects, personal beliefs, or the obvious sins. The kingdom messes with everything. Jurgen Moltmann writes,

> If God is the reality that determines everything, then his kingdom is the new creation that heals everything and puts everything straight. This means that the conversion, to which the gospel about the nearness of God's kingdom calls, cannot be limited to either private or religious life. It is as all-embracing and holistic as the salvation of the new creation itself. Conversion takes hold of people and the conditions in which they live and suffer. That is to say, it takes in personal life, life in community, and the systems which provide an order for these ways of living. ... If it does not happen like this it does not happen at all. If it is half-hearted and only touches part-sectors of reality, it is not a conversion that corresponds to the kingdom of God.[17]

My Last Word

Groups are training platoons where Bobs, like me, learn to live the truth and leave behind the lie of the American dream. When we seek first small groups for the sake of making the church better or bigger, we fail to see the church from God's kingdom perspective, making life far more complex for people. If we seek first God's relational kingdom, then small groups will line up as an agent of the kingdom, and he will add the growth and all the other things that we long to see in the church.

CHAPTER 4

Write a New Story of Mission

After nearly three years of working with TOUCH® Outreach Ministries, I moved to Vancouver, British Columbia. While there, I served on the leadership team and then on the staff of a church that was developing small groups. As my introduction to the church leaders, I was invited to participate in a group leader training in which they were using one of the books that I had edited while with TOUCH®. Because of this, I thought that I understood the vision and direction of the church.

When I later took over the oversight of the small groups, it became clear to me that the vision of the senior pastor, Alan Roxburgh, went much deeper than small groups. In one of our meetings, he quipped how a small group structure does not address the key issues that actually transform a church. His off-handed statement sent me into "search mode" to understand what he meant.

Over the next few years, I wrestled with Alan's comment, searching for what could go deeper than the need for small groups and community. I reflected back on what had drawn me into the small group vision in the first place. The compelling message of Yonggi Cho was not about small groups or even church growth. Instead, he told stories about a people of mission who were mobilized to live in sharp contrast to the surrounding culture.

This caused me to recall the stories that Ralph Neighbour, the founder of TOUCH®, told me about his early experiments in creative church life. His motivation was not small groups or finding an efficient structure. He was motivated by the desire to mobilize the church for a mission. Small groups were designed to serve the mission. Because these small groups were not an end unto themselves, they were free to creatively write new stories about what it meant to be the church at that time.

The church needs to set small groups within a larger and more foundational understanding of God's mission. Church structures should facilitate the story of mission. Some have argued that the mission of the church is to become "a church *of* small groups" or "a pure cell church" or even "a community-based church." These terms describe structures designed to serve that mission, and structures don't make for a good story. Small groups and community flow out of the mission of the church; they are not the mission itself.

An innovative way to do small groups or even a singular focus on small groups will not deliver this "deeper goal." It will only cause people to live old stories of the church through new structures. Something more fundamental is needed, something of a grander scheme. Every church must rally around a grand mission, one that will call the church on a journey to write a new story of what it means to be the church in this day. This mission will reshape the imaginations of people to write a new script, to think outside of the current boundaries of what the people of God can be.

Structural Myth #4:
Building a new small group ministry structure on top of old stories of church will transform a church and build community.

The Relational Truth:
Relational kingdom life through small groups is founded upon a missional base which compels a church to write a new story of being the people of God.

The Story of Church
If you randomly asked ten people in your church, "What do you think the church should look like?" you would be asking them for their visions of

church. In their responses, most would imagine a picture of what kind of church they want to see, sharing a story to explain this picture. This story is their definition of church. Stories are what shape us.

The way we define church is a direct product of our story of church. Our experiences of church define our visions. Change experts have found that only about three percent of the population has the ability to envision something that they have not yet seen or experienced.[1] Therefore, 97 percent of your congregation will define church according to their history. Even if the pastor preaches on the meaning of church from a biblical point of view, most will define church around their previous church experiences. For example, some will call the church building the church because it has been called such their entire lives. Many will explain how church is what happens when a preacher preaches or when a priest offers communion. The stories that shape our definition of church are inherited from the church culture we have experienced.

The Old Story of Competing Visions

Let me illustrate how a common story of church impacts small group development. The story of competing visions is one that most Christian leaders know so well that they don't even know it is their story. It is just the way church is done. They assume that church will work if vision for each church activity is working correctly. After all, if the youth vision, the children's vision, the worship vision, the singles vision, the evangelism vision and the discipleship vision are all working well, then the entire church will be effective. Therefore, the goal must be to organize each of these visions into departments. Each department will then set annual goals, develop strategies to meet these goals, propose budgets, recruit volunteers and/or hire new pastors.

It is very hard to be critical of such a process, because most churches develop these departments around the biblical purposes of the church. No church intentionally develops strategies because they want the church to fail at God's mission. For example, a youth pastor will look at the purposes of the church and see that one of them is evangelism, based on the Great Commission. As a result, she will plan an evangelistic rally at a local high school because she wants her department to accomplish the purpose of evangelism. Problems arise when every department develops independent programs like the youth pastor has done, even though each program aligns with the overall purposes of the church. As more programs are started, increased levels of competition set in. Each department competes for the same people, financial resources, and publicity.

Overtly, pastors articulate the vision and the purposes of the church, usually basing them on the Great Commission and the Great Commandment. I wholeheartedly agree with such overt statements. However, the problem is not found at the level of what is seen or what is measured with vision statements and progress reports. It lies at a much deeper level, the level of the unseen stories. If we ever want to fully enter into the mission God has set for his church, we must understand the stories that pull at the church like a rip tide. We cannot see them, but they will pull us in a direction that we never intended to pursue. Unless church leaders actively seek to understand these factors, they remain unseen. New programs and even new small group strategies serve only as new clothes to dress up old, dry bones.

When churches base the development of such programs and ministries on the purpose of supplying spiritual goods and services for discriminating shoppers with spiritual needs, they continue to write an old story of church life.[2] The story of the church is that of a purveyor of the spiritual things that are required to support "real" life but don't have much impact upon how people do their "real" lives. In the book, *Stormfront*, the authors write, "When Christians accept a consumerist culture's definition at face value, they look to the church primarily to provide them with the means to improve their private lives, enhance their self-esteem, and give them a sense of purpose. Worship becomes a form of therapy whose sole aim is to improve the emotional state of individuals and to energize them for the week ahead."[3] Real life is done at the office, in schools, homes, or governmental halls. To a consumerist, the church is a spiritual sideshow providing a spiritual fix so that people can be successful in real life.

With a spiritual goods and services mentality, small groups become one good among many others. The small group program is designed to supply the spiritual good of relational connectedness to those who demand it. To accomplish the stated purposes, a senior pastor will hire a small groups pastor to champion the vision for small groups, while other pastors or volunteer lay leaders champion their visions, each having equal emphasis. Small group leaders are also committed to serve in many other capacities. They sing in the choir, chair a committee or lead a team, serve as a youth or children's volunteer, and perform many other activities. As a result, these leaders don't have time to invest in building relationships with the people in their small groups. Because of these other church responsibilities, the small group fails to experience life together in biblical community, settling for a weekly meeting which people feel compelled to attend. The leader feels pressured to lead the group because the pastor has a clear vision for small groups and speaks about it often.

As a result, the addition of small groups might add some benefit to the church for those who want to be connected. However, the reality is the church fails to enter into its mission. It remains in the land of competition, providing a spiritual good to meet the demands of the people.

The Story as a Pastor Reads It

One common trait found in all of the best small group churches around the world is the fact that the senior pastor carries the vision for groups. Yongii Cho writes, "The pastor must be the key person involved. ... The controlling factor in home small groups is the pastor."[4] Therefore, when the pastor catches a vision for small groups (usually by attending a conference or reading a book about another church), he shares it with a few leaders and secures their support for implementation. Because he has credibility with the people, they trust him to develop and implement a strategy. His strategy includes a clear vision statement, intermediate goals, and specific action steps for accomplishing those goals. He maps out a step-by-step strategic plan that will take his church into the land of the small group vision.

He sees some initial growth, both spiritually and numerically. Some groups work and others fail. Then the groups plateau and frustration sets in. The pastor, as the visionary leader of the small group system, searches for answers and tweaks the system. He looks to other small group models, changes how the lessons are written, modifies the leadership meetings, and even incorporates new strategies from other models. He presses on with this vision, no matter the cost because he believes in the value of small groups.

The story as this pastor reads it is a linear story. He has a vision of what the church can become, and he strategically seeks to move the church from point A to point B to point C. He preaches this vision, he even lives the vision, but he never sees the results he wants to see.

The Story As The Church Reads It

To lead the sheep into biblical community, a pastor must understand the story of church as the people read it. Again, these stories are not the overt declarations of faith that the people make in times of commitment. These stories are those unseen, unspoken ways of being the church that shape the ways people operate. They are the patterns or traditions of doing church that must be kept in equilibrium for it to operate according to the rules. Such stories establish a systemic structure. This structure is different than an organizational chart. It is the structure of life that includes attitudes and perceptions, the ways decisions are made, who leads what, and even who sits where.[5] If the people of a church live according to a story of church that competes with the missional story of the relational way, it does not matter how strongly the pastor holds the vision for small groups. The story will undermine his ability to lead people into his vision. The following illustrates three common stories that stymie the journey into the relational way.[6]

A Growing Church's Story

First Church was successful. It had grown to over 1,000 people. The pastor had faithfully led these people from a small congregation of 50 to its present prominence in the medium-size city. He realized that the church needed to develop a small group system to take the church to the next level. At that point, the pastor called me to work with his pastoral leadership team.

The senior pastor, the staff members, and the key leaders all believed in the need for small groups and were committed to participating in them. They were eager and invigorated to discover what God would do through this new vision.

As we talked, a major roadblock emerged. Each staff member had a different vision. The music minister had a vision for his area of responsibility. The youth pastor had a slightly different vision for the youth. The children's person possessed her own idea of what needed to be done. The discipleship pastor had spent years developing training classes and his vision was very clear, but he was the only one who had it. The outreach pastor articulated his dreams for his area of responsibility. And last but not least, the senior pastor had adopted a different vision for small groups through the many books he had read.

This church had been successful thus far by taking this approach to ministry. They had grown by identifying needs, developing programs to meet those needs, and managing those programs for continued growth. This is depicted by the left side of the diagram below.

The problem is that the same leaders were typically used for most of the ministries of the church. This created a leadership shortage and stress on the system (depicted by the right side of the diagram above). Eventually, this growing church will plateau because the leadership is hopping between the various programs and ministries to lead them. In the not too-distant future, this church will need to create a ministry for burned-out ministers!

I worked with one church that had over 40 different programs and ministries, all which were good when evaluated independently. When the staff and leaders got honest, they confessed that they were worn out from all of the recruiting and planning required to make these programs work. When I demonstrated to them the absurdity of adding small groups on top of their already overworked leaders, we entered into a process of seeking God about his mission and evaluating how their current programs fit within that mission.

The Leaderless Story

In this story, the members of a church assume that God's way of revealing his will is through democratic polity. It is through congregational voting that the people determine God's direction by attaining a majority vote. After this vote has been secured, it is the job of the pastor to implement the decision of the congregation.

While the intentions are good, the majority will rarely make hard decisions to take the church into missional places. Typically, the majority does not have the time, energy or insight to think in such creative ways. Therefore, the pastor who senses God speaking about the mission becomes frustrated. She[7] will try to secure the support of the right leaders for what she senses God is saying, resulting in a power struggle. Because her role is not that of leading people, she looks for greener pastures at another church, failing to recognize that she is only going to experience more of the same at the next place.

The short tenure of a pastor increases the level of distrust the people have of pastors in general. Moreover, it increases the perception that the church should operate under a leaderless system. This process might be depicted like the diagram below.

Research has shown that pastors don't enter into effective ministry until they served in a church for five or six years.[8] The average tenure of a pastor is five years. George Barna writes, "Our work has found that the typical pastor has his or her greatest ministry impact at a church in years five through fourteen of their pastorate. Unfortunately, we also know that the average pastor lasts only five years at a church, forfeiting the fruit of their investment in the church they've pastored. In our fast turnaround society where we demand overnight results and consider everyone expendable and everything disposable, we may be shortchanging pastors—and the congregations they oversee—by prematurely terminating their tenure."[9] Entering into mission requires a synergistic relationship where pastoral leaders are willing to invest their lives in a congregation, and congregations who are willing to stick with pastors over the long-term to see results. When this occurs, it is far more likely that the church will break the pattern and create new doorways for creativity, allowing the Spirit to lead a church into a new story. We won't see a high percentage of churches experience this, but it will only take a few to start the process and begin a movement that will catch fire.

The Autocratic Story

A third story is one that is a reaction to the Leaderless Story. A pastor tries to undermine the democratic church by forcing his desires as the leader upon the church. He makes decisions and then tells people that his decisions are God's will for the church. He encourages and blesses those who agree with him. Those who want to talk with him about alternative points of view are accused of being rebellious. As a result, those who follow him become his worker bees jumping at his every whim, illustrated by the left half of the illustration below. Those with the most leadership potential exit for another church, illustrated in the right half. Whether people agree or disagree with the decisions of the pastor, the result of this system is a focus on the pastor being in charge, making all the decisions.

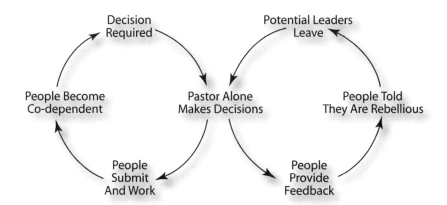

Many pastors think they are doing the church a service because they are exhibiting strong leadership. They feel that they have heard a clear direction from God—many of them have—and they don't want backslidden voters to hinder God's call. Other pastors find themselves in churches where the position of pastor is elevated to such a high level that no one would dare challenge the "man of God." While both situations are based on noble desires, the Autocratic Story perverts a good thing. While the pastor has the ability to make decisions, no single individual has all of the spiritual gifts or the ability to carry out his ideas. Therefore, he starts lots of ministry projects, but none of them produce the fruit he promises or expects.

Leadership by mandate is not the same thing as missional leadership. When caught in the Autocratic Story, a pastor who wants to embark on mission must develop new patterns to facilitate discovery of God's mission within other leaders. It might not generate as much activity as the old story, but it will write a new story.

The Story of Mission

Traditionally, missions is considered to be something missionaries do in unchurched countries. Or, it is something people do on a mission trip to Mexico or on a week-long project across town with another church. With this understanding of missions, the church's role is to support missions with money, prayer, and by sending people to work in these lands. It does this through church services back in the Christian country. Here is what the authors of *The Missional Church* have to say about this situation:

> "Church" is conceived in this view as the place where a Christianized civilization gathers for worship, and the place where the Christian character of the society is cultivated. Increasingly, this view of the church as a "place where certain things happen" located the church's self-identity in its organizational forms and its professional class, the clergy who perform the church's authoritative activities. Popular grammar captures it well: you "go to church" much the same way you might go to a store. You "attend" a church, the way you attend a school or theater. You "belong to a church" as you would a service club with its programs and activities.[10]

The New Testament reveals a story that was set aside when Constantine officially recognized the Christian church and married it with the state. At that time, a different church story was written called Christendom. Even in democratic nations, the patterns developed under this story have remained. The noble desire of many church leaders to return to a biblical structure often obscures the fact that the people in these structures are carriers of Christendom stories. When small groups are practiced within a Christendom mindset, people "go to group," "attend a group meeting," and "belong to a group" following the pattern of the story they know.

By contrast, we cannot assume that the church in western society is set in the midst of a Christian culture; whether or not this was ever true is debatable. We cannot assume that God's mission is limited to countries that are labeled non-Christian. Many segments of North America and Europe are the home to some of the most unchurched groups in the world. Mission is not something the church does; rather, it is something that lies at the heart of the church's essence. The church is the sent people of God, the body of Christ in the world, sent to embody the character of God to a world that spurns him.

The mission is much greater than a church's effort for growth and evangelism. To be the sent people of God on mission is to be a missionary people, not just a group of people who gather for worship and attend small groups. To be the sent people of God is to manifest the character and compassion of God's heart in tangible ways in a particular time and a specific location. One theologian writes, "This story of sending at a particular time and place in history has its roots in an eternal sending of God."[11] The story of God should shape the story of the church that we write today. The Father sent the Son who was empowered by the Holy Spirit to minister to a specific people in Galilee and Jerusalem. The Holy Spirit was sent to the church to bring God's life to those outside of the land of Galilee and Jerusalem. Each individual church is sent by God via the life of the Holy Spirit to be the body of Christ in a specific time and place.

This truth is larger than having a vision for church growth. It transcends any strategy for being "a church of small groups." It means the church actually allows the triune life of God to flow through it. God has always been on a mission to redeem the world. He called Abraham to be the Father of the multitudes. He set apart Israel to be a light to the world. The Father sent the Son to be what Israel could not be for the world. Then the Father sent the Holy Spirit to empower the church to be his body.

With this understanding of the church on mission, the vocation of the church changes from simply attracting and feeding spiritual consumers. Its goal is not to get as many of these consumers into small groups as possible. Instead, the mission of the church is to allow the Spirit of God to redeem spiritual consumers and transform them into a kingdom people who live as an alternative society. The church is the local manifestation of God's kingdom. The people of God comprise the church, exhibiting a life together that serves as a contrast society or a representative city in the midst of this world.

As well, this will require much more than a creative way to do small groups. It will require a new way of thinking, a new imagination for the writing of a new church story. It will require the freeing creativity of the Spirit of God rising up within his people to generate fresh perspectives and risky adventures. The missional adventure is one where we embark on a journey with an unclear destination. The missional call invites the church to go where it has not been, to be what it has not been, and to do what it has not done. The end is the manifestation of the kingdom, and this is something that we cannot control or know from our limited perspective. This requires leadership that invites the Spirit to impart a new imagination. Turning back to the book, *The Missional Leader*, Roxburgh and Romanuk write of this kind of leadership:

> Missional leadership is about cultivating an environment in which this relationality of the kingdom might be experienced. The gift of the Spirit means the church is the place where we are invited to risk, in relationship to the open-ended adventure of the Spirit's presence. Leaders cultivate an environment in which the boundary breaking Spirit constantly calls forth new ways of being God's community. Missiologist David J. Bosch describes Acts as the story of how the Spirit breaks the boundaries of planning and expectation of the young church. Things just don't turn out the way the early leaders plan. They are drawn into a journey that didn't fit into their categories and plans.[12]

To enter into the missional call of the church, we need leaders who hear a different call and lead people to embark on the adventure with God into new Spirit-led ways of being the church.

What Does This Mean ... Practically?

Before Hong Kong reverted back to Chinese rule, I had the privilege of taking a train into the interior of China to visit a house church. I was honored to sit in the same room with people who risked their lives to meet illegally, pray together, worship God, and have their lives shaped by the

Word of God. One of the men with whom I traveled, a native of Hong Kong, had been imprisoned the previous month. The police strung him up with ropes like a pig being skinned and beat and tortured him. He was released when they realized that they had mistakenly arrested a British citizen.

If God were to call you to be a church planter in China or another culture not directly influenced by Christendom, your call would be very clear. You would have no question about whether the church fit with the traditions of the culture. Your only alternative would be to find appropriate ways to live out the kingdom as an alternative society.

Today, many pastors in North America are seeing themselves as missionaries in this sense. They see their role as inviting people into an alternative lifestyle that is contradictory to that of the Western culture. The kind of leadership required to lead the church into this missional life is different than the leadership patterns practiced in the church when the future of the church was more predictable. When church plays the role of attracting people from the culture to receive "spiritual goods and services," then the leaders clearly understand the goal and strategy for providing those goods and services. But now society has shifted. The place of church has changed. Therefore, leadership of the church must also change. How God is reshaping the church is not yet clear. We do not know what church will look like in the future.

For those schooled in the traditional ways of doing church, leading people into relational kingdom life is like a seasoned farmer trying to sail a ship across the Atlantic without any training. He knows how to work a farm, but he doesn't know how to navigate the open seas. As pastors, we are skilled in providing religious services, how to visit the sick, marry, bury, and provide counsel. However, we are novices in the art of aligning people around a mission that will call people into a life of biblical community.

Pastoring on Land

I grew up working the land with my father. Tractors, harvesting grain, hauling hay and lots of sweat were a way of life. Such a life is relatively predictable. Farmers know what to expect, even with the variations in weather. They do the same things year after year, plowing, planting, and harvesting during the same time of year. A successful farmer's life is marked by a rhythm that changes little from one year to the next.

For many pastors, their job looks similar to that of a farmer. They know what to expect. They preach every week. They visit hospitals when needed. They hold deacon meetings once per month. They have their weekly counseling sessions. Life is relatively predictable. They know what they have to do in order to keep the people of the church happy.

Pastoring on land is the image of leading the church within the confines of Christendom. According to Ephesians 4:11-12, Christ has established apostles, prophets, evangelists, pastors and teachers in the church to equip people for works of service. Leading an attractional church focuses primarily on performing the jobs of the pastor and the teacher. This usually means that the pastor finds himself as the caretaker of sheep, actually "doing" the work of the ministry, rather than "equipping" others. In other words, the predictable job of the pastor is based on the rhythm of ministering to those who come to the church services and programs.

Usually this is manifested in three roles. First, he is the professional teacher, providing the best Bible teaching possible. He is also the professional counselor, ministering to all who come to him with their spiritual and psychological ills. Finally, he is the professional manager, spinning all of the plates, keeping the church programs humming so that people will have something religious to do.

Because pastoring on land is fairly predictable, strategic planning is a foundational leadership tool. The job requires pastoral leaders to lead from a linear process where the end goal is very clear and the steps toward that goal are logically mapped out. This is the linear process explained earlier in this chapter. Strategic planning requires a stable system whereby the leader can articulate a clear end goal, but it does not describe the reality in which the church finds itself today.[13]

Pastoring on the Open Seas

Sailing is unpredictable. Imagine if you were to sail from Miami to Jamaica this week and then make the same trip next week. Even if you use the same boat, each voyage will be unique. The winds, the currents, the weather will all change over the period of a week and therefore change your journey.

Leading people into the relational kingdom is like sailing a ship. Pastors want to find a refined model for doing church that they can copy. Finding a model to copy might work when things are predictable within Christendom, but on the other side of Christendom, it is impossible to know exactly how to set a course for a destination. First of all, it is not clear what the church will look like ten to twenty years from now. We must trust the leading of the Spirit of God. Secondly, the climate, barriers, and currents are impossible to predict. One ship cannot sail exactly like another ship previously sailed, even if the destination is the same. The exact pattern that works in one church won't work tomorrow in the same way for the same church or a different church. I depend upon Roxburgh and Romanuk for help in communicating this:

> Most congregations are facing discontinuous, challenging, and unpredictable change. It's not a matter of small adjustments in a stable system. We are in a period that makes it impossible to have much clarity about the future and how it is going to be shaped. Therefore those leaders who believe they can address the kind of change we are facing by simply defining a future that people want, and then setting plans to achieve it, are not innovating a missional congregation. They are only finding new ways of preventing a congregation from facing the discontinuous change it confronts.[14]

This discontinuous change is illustrated by the fact that the church no longer exists in a place of privilege within society. A pastor's influence within the community is on the decline. People turn to talk-show hosts and popular self-help gurus more than they turn to the church when life gets rough. Secular "prophets" like Oprah and Dr. Phil are rapidly replacing people like Billy Graham and Oral Roberts. Phyllis Tickle states in her book, *God-Talk in America*, "more theology is conveyed in, and probably retained from, one hour of popular television than from all the sermons that are also delivered on any given weekend in America's synagogues, churches, and mosques."[15] In this world, the church cannot sit back and wait for people to come for spiritual goods and services.

Sailing is far from a linear process. While living in Vancouver, I had a friend with a sailboat. I learned two things about sailing. First, it is better to have a friend with a boat than own one yourself, because he was always working on it. Secondly, sailing from one point to another is unpredictable. The search for the right currents and winds meant that we cut a path that zigzagged toward our destination.

Today, many church leaders are getting in the boat and learning how to sail, experimenting with new leadership patterns that they did not learn in their pastoral training nor have seen in their pastoral heroes. They are following the patterns of New Testament apostles, setting new models, and laying new foundations for the church. They are novices at "ship sailing" leadership, but they know that they can no longer lead people to do church on the land. They have to give up strategic planning because they realize that they cannot set a clear future. Instead, they "cultivate a way of life among a people through which God's future is elicited among the people."[16] They are learning to listen to God and listen to what the Spirit is saying through his people. They are writing a new story.

Writing a New Story of Church

The story of a church will shape the imagination of the people. The story of a church will either limit it or free it. These stories require certain things to happen so that the story line works according to expectations. Stories like the examples described previously are often so deeply entrenched that attempting to change them comes within a hair of heresy. Change interferes with people's expectations. To them, their programs are the church. To others, the church is defined by the revolving door of pastors. Doing church on land is deeply entrenched in the church in North America. We don't know how to do church on the open seas. Getting people in the boat and heading toward biblical community is not a quick or easy process. There are no "seven steps to adopting relational kingdom life" or an "add water and stir" method to being the church that God wants us to be.[17] The church must re-imagine what it means to be church. This will require re-engaging biblical texts and re-discovering what it means to be the people of God.[18] Church leaders find themselves at an interesting crossroad. They can continue doing church—and thereby continue doing small groups—according to the old stories. Or, they can close that chapter of the old story and pick up a pen and begin writing a new story of church.

Missional Leadership

Missional leadership describes the role of the lead story writer. To understand this role, let me contrast it to a few models of leadership that are clearly understood.

Missional leadership is not democratic. Those being led will not understand why a new story is required, at least not in the beginning. I have yet to find a biblical story that demonstrates that God is a democratic God. Every time the people of God took a vote, it seems that they missed God's will. God initiates his mission. He spoke to Moses to go to Egypt and called the people out. When they left, the masses wanted to return to slavery and the populace wanted to worship idols. Ten of the twelve spies voted against going into the Promised Land. Voting on God's will is contrary to the pattern of God's order.

At the same time, missional leadership is not autocratic. Just because God speaks to the pastor in the church, it does not give him permission to stand up and proclaim where the church is going and the strategic plan for getting there. That is a dictator, not a leader. Dictators believe that they have the perfect plan and the perfect system for the people, if only they would listen to their ideas and follow their plans. Moses did not become the mind of the people. He was not the only one who had a say in how the people followed God. He worked with a team of people, including his brother Aaron, his sister Miriam, Joshua, and the 70 elders.

Missional leadership is also different than leading from a clear sense of vision. Many pastors lead from the perspective that God gave them a vision. They cultivate the discipline of listening to God's plan and hearing God's ways. Such leaders are often good at vision casting and inviting people to join that vision. Over the last few years, many pastors have taken this approach to the vision for small groups. The vision was so heavily laid upon their hearts they felt *forced* to do small groups. Some pastors so strongly believed in the vision of small groups that they made the mistake of denigrating the old way of doing church by telling their people how unbiblical it was in retrospect.

Devaluing the church of yesterday does not make for a good story; it only breaks hearts. It only causes people to lose confidence in the church and in the leadership of the church. The only way to proceed into what God has for the church tomorrow is to start where the church is today. If leaders castigate the church models of today, people won't know where to start as they look to move into something new.

Missional leadership requires leaders to extend beyond the predetermined boundaries of the leadership models we have inherited. To move into the zone of a missional leader, one must dispense with the search for leadership methods. We cannot identify superhero pastors, make a list of all their traits and work to measure up to this model. The challenges that the church faces need far more than exceptional leaders with unique skills. Instead, missional leadership is founded upon the character and identity of the leader, not his or her methods. "Before anything else, leadership is about our identity as people who are participating in God's life and given work to be done in the world. ... Therefore leadership is fundamentally about forming character and living a life shaped by virtue."[19]

Robert Quinn is an organizational consultant who writes of personal deep change as the catalyst for collective change. In his book *Building a Bridge as You Walk on It*, he writes, "When we make deep change, the people around us respond to us differently. When we change ourselves, we change how people see us and how they respond to us. When we change ourselves, we change the world."[20] The future of the church will flow from the inside out, from the center of one's identity, character and honesty.

When I studied the art of writing, I read how difficult and frustrating the creative process could be. After many hours of editing and writing, I see what the experts mean. When I sit down in front of a blank screen, I can go a thousand different directions. After the work is complete, I could refine my work endlessly. Regardless of what I write, the content flows out of the beliefs that reside within me. I cannot write what I do not currently possess.

In the same way, missional leadership is a creative art. It calls for leaders to create from within themselves, allowing the Spirit of God to make room in their lives to facilitate the writing of a new story. The leader is not the author of this new story. This is God's story that is realized as the people of God enter into his relational ways. Leaders make room for the creation of this story. Here are some shifts we must make as leaders to facilitate the writing of a new story of mission.

From Normal to Fundamental Leadership

To facilitate the writing of this new story, we must move from what Quinn calls "The Normal State" of leadership to "The Fundamental State" of leadership. He labels the normal state—the kind of leadership in which most people operate—as self-focused, internally closed, externally directed, and comfort-centered. Each person possesses a default response that tends to put self-interests ahead of the collective, remains within the confines of personal comfort zones, defines one's self on external responses, and remains in a reactive state that seeks to hold on to comfort. Such defaults are normal. They are practices that we adopt to survive. But at the same time, they resist the creation of a learning environment whereby individuals embody change. Leaders who operate within the normal state might convince people that they need to change their story of church. They may strategically use their leadership weight to force a move into small groups or move people to admit their own need for community within a church. However, this kind of leadership will ultimately not write the story of a relational culture within a local body of Christ.

Quinn writes, "To remain in the normal state, refusing to change while the universe changes around us, is ultimately to choose slow death. To enter the fundamental state of leadership is to reverse the process by making deep change."[21] In the state of fundamental leadership, a leader becomes purpose-centered, internally driven, other-focused, and externally open. Living within this state is to put the common good ahead of personal welfare, seek feedback from others and adapt it, deal honestly with personal hypocrisy and personal values, and clarify the results.

One of the most impacting observations made by Quinn is the need for leaders to reveal their personal struggles and examine discontinuities between the leader's personal ideals and actual behavior. He writes, "Here is a surprising point: recognizing our hypocrisy is a source of power. When we become willing to monitor our hypocrisy, we discover that intense personal shame drives us to close our integrity gaps. Accepting this truth about our hypocrisy helps us to transform ourselves and others."[22]

Without such honesty about the gap between our ideals and our lived-out values, real change will not occur. I have found this to be the case with my personal struggles around entering into the life I describe in the third chapter. By default, I know how to live Bob's life. I have only begun to enter the alternative that I propose here. For me, to stand before those I lead and act as if I know exactly how to live this way would be a lie, and they would see right through it. However, when I am willing to share my personal struggles while living in a frenetic culture, they are much more willing to engage me and deal with their own struggles. I don't have to have all of the answers or be some kind of super-hero leader. Instead, it is much more effective when I share my story and ask them to enter into the struggle with me.

From Pastoral Chaplain to Apostolic Forerunner

In the traditional model of the church, there are official "ministers" who play the role of a chaplain, pastoring the Christians under his care. He marries, buries, and counsels, helping people be the best Christians they can be. He performs his religious duties, leads religious services, baptizes, and administers the sacraments. He basically does the best he can with the hand he has been dealt, which is serving those who come to him.

The metaphor of an apostle, "one who is sent," stands in contrast to the chaplain. Such a leader is one who is sent forth by a group of people to go out and act as a forerunner for them. He is the one who is a few steps ahead of the group, establishing new ways of being the church. The apostolic role is not one of a title: it is one of action. The apostle shows the people how to live in the body of Christ, a people of mission. The church is the sent people of God, an apostolic body that requires someone who will venture out of its "unsent" or static state and into the mission in which God has called the church. Quinn drives this point home with, "A leader ventures to say: 'I will go; come with me!' A leader initiates, provides the ideas and the structure, and takes the risk of failure along with the chance of success. A leader says: 'I will go; follow me!' while knowing that the path is uncertain, even dangerous."[23]

While I lived in Vancouver, I frequently drove across Lion's Gate Bridge which spans the Burrard Inlet connecting West Vancouver with downtown Vancouver. At times, the clouds were so low the bridge "ended" in the clouds. An apostolic forerunner crosses a bridge that leads into an unseen future. He goes over to the other side and discovers what the relational kingdom looks like. He comes back and invites people to continue discovering new aspects of this relational kingdom. He continues going back and forth to pick up people so more and more discovery might occur.

From Solo Pastor to Facilitating of Five-Fold Equipping

Christ has established apostles, prophets, evangelists, pastors and teachers for equipping of the saints for the work of ministry (Eph. 4:11-12). This list of gifts is different than those found in Romans 12 and 1 Corinthians 12. These are the equipping gifts, the roles that leaders fill in the church so that the saints of the church can receive the equipping they need to fulfill their calling within the body of Christ.

Within the traditional model, the focus lay on the solo pastor, the one who primarily fulfilled the role of the pastor/teacher. He shepherded the flock and taught them the Word. In successful contemporary churches, the pastor is often a super-star personality who has the unique ability to perform four or even all five of these roles. As a result, the membership is not equipped for ministry as much as it sits in awe of their wonderful pastor.

The early churches never operated around solo pastors. No single individual can truly operate in all five of these roles in a way that equips the saints for the work of ministry. These five roles work together to build up the body of Christ. The senior pastor then is called to be a *facilitator of equippers* who can operate in these roles. Every church needs people who operate as apostles, establishing God's new patterns of life as the church; as prophets, speaking forth his timely word that cuts to the issue; as evangelists, equipping the body to share the good news of Christ; as pastors, mentoring other pastors in the ways of shepherding; and as teachers, demonstrating how to teach others in the patterns of the Word.

The role of those in the five-fold ministry is "to equip the saints for works of service." While those in these roles will do the actions of that role better than most, their jobs are much wider in scope. They have the responsibility of equipping people in the church to be mature, equipping them to do the work of evangelism, to care for others as pastors, and to mobilize and train teachers. It is not enough to do these things. They are also equippers of others who can do these ministries in the body.

By contrast, the modern understanding of the evangelist, for example, is one who is an itinerant speaker and convener of mass rallies. It seems to me that this misses what Paul is talking about in this passage. This role is about equipping the body, not about actually doing the work of the ministry. The Ephesians 4 evangelist is an equipper, not the doer, of evangelism. He is the evangelism coach who helps the players—the church—do the work of service effectively. The role of the prophet calls for leaders who can equip others in how to hear God and speak forth his truths.

In the recent resurgence of five-fold ministry, many churches have appointed five different people to head up different departments under these five headings. This structure is motivated by good intentions, but provides less than acceptable results. It only creates competing ministries. Those in the prophetic prayer ministry elevate themselves because they hear God as his intercessors. Those in the evangelism ministry focus on calling people outside the walls of the church because they believe they are doing the "real" ministry. Small groups usually get lumped under the pastoral role, communicating that what they are doing has nothing to do with the other four roles.

Instead of seeing specific individuals filling the five roles, it is better to imagine various people performing the duties of these roles as the Holy Spirit sees fit. If this is the case, these five-fold anointings are not positions, but conduits that flow through the various groups. Like the warp and the weft of a cloth, the five-fold anointings are the vertical threads and the small group organization is the horizontal thread.

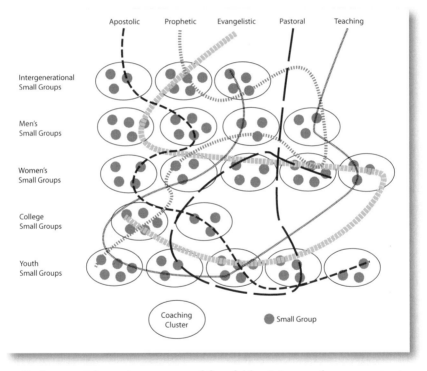

Such a model requires a team of five-fold ministers who are equipping the saints for the work of ministry and to build up the body. When this occurs, the focus is removed from the solo pastor who must become the superhero minister and the focus returns to Christ, who is the one who sets these five-fold ministers in the church.[24]

From Strategic Planning to Facilitating Dialogue

When discussing leadership and strategies for accomplishing goals, there is something within our blood (at least there is in mine) to get down to the practical how to's so that we can get busy doing the work of ministry. I enjoy the strategic planning process. Put me in a room with a marker and large sheets of paper and I will lead a team to develop an extensive strategic plan. The problem is that the church is about people, not about strategic plans. People don't conform to our plans nearly as much as we would like them to. They have families, jobs, and problems that get in the way of our plans for them. They take vacations. They move to another city for work. Sometimes they don't hear God like we think they should. The trip from Egypt to the Promised Land was about a three-week journey. The Israelites were afraid to receive what God promised so they wandered in the desert for 40 years. I am sure that this was not in Moses' strategic plan!

Since this is an unpredictable time and strategic planning does not work, what tools do we have at our disposal? I believe the greatest tool is that of dialogue. Dialogue is a discipline that is as old as thinking itself. It is the art of reflecting and reasoning together. William Isaacs, an expert on fostering communication through dialogue, writes, "[Dialogue] is not something you do to another person. It is something you do with people. Indeed, a large part of learning this has to do with learning to shift your attitudes about relationships with others, so that we gradually give up the effort to make them understand us, and come to a greater understanding of ourselves and each other."[25] Through dialogue, the missional leader listens to what the Spirit is saying through the people of God. He asks guiding questions to stir the imagination. Through the use of the biblical stories, he calls people to dialogue around how the text might inform the reshaping of God's people.

Strategic planning involves a leader who determines a set destination for a church. He might work by himself or with a few key leaders to establish benchmark goals and strategies to arrive at that destination. Dialogue takes a much more humble approach. It requires a team of people to think together and listen to God together about the destination. This destination will not be defined by the model church down the road, but by listening to the dreams and visions that God has laid out in the Bible for the church. To understand this destination, the senior pastor must lead key leaders to discover the vision God has for that church. He cannot force people into that vision. He must trust the Spirit of God to raise up the vision through the people. After all, if God does not speak through a few people about the vision, moving the masses to leave the land and board a ship will prove impossible.

Practicing dialogue also requires that teams of people will listen and think together about the steps of the journey toward the vision of being the church. To keep moving where God wants us to go, church leaders must learn the art of finding the "next step." Any long-range plans that are established must be continually adjusted to fit the new contingencies that arise on the journey.

For such a team to enter into dialogue, every member of the team must be fully committed to that team, entering into a covenant relationship with team members. This means that no one has an excuse to leave when times get tough. It also means that the team members are committed to honesty. If the team feels like one or two persons are not committed to the others, members will not risk being honest because they don't want to risk the loss of a friend.

The discipline of suspending one's attachment to his contributions can be addressed when commitment and honesty have been achieved. If a team member honestly shares his idea or assessment of the situation, he must let it go and allow the team to listen to his contribution to discover what is best. Most of the time, team members know the art of discussion (how to defend an idea or assessment, often resulting in a scenario that pits "my" opinions against "your" opinions). In a discussion, someone must win and someone must lose. Dialogue allows the team to discover a "third" option, one often prompted by the Holy Spirit.

From Silo Ministries to Integration

Church improvement strategies take the path of improving the departments that operate as independent silos. The children's ministry works to set goals and improve their strategies. The youth department develops ways to grow the ministry to the youth. The music ministry dreams about the future potential for their ministry and organizes the budget around those dreams. Missions, outreach, facilities, college ministry, singles ministry, women's ministry, men's ministry and senior's ministry all do the same thing. They act as individual silos sitting next to one another, isolated in their busyness from the other aspects of a church's ministry.

Then the silo of small group ministry is introduced. All of the isolated ministries might operate according to a small group pattern, but often they don't work together.

Imagine youth small groups that meet weekly in a church set in a large city. The youth that meet in these groups live throughout the city, which requires the parents to devote one night per week to drive their teenager to a home or a church building in another part of town and wait for two hours to pick them up. On top of this, the parents attend another small group for adults. One can only fathom the stress these parents experience. Both the youth department and the adult ministry are organized around a small group philosophy, but they operate in isolation from one another.

Integration is hard work. It requires lots of communication and time. Trust and willingness to risk, along with a commitment to listen hard to one another, must be a part of the culture. Most of all, those involved in each silo must be willing to engage those within other silos and discover how they can work together. Each ministry area must be rooted in the grand missional call of the church. Nothing can compete or distract from that, and each must have an absolute commitment to simplicity. No program or ministry should be allowed to become so cumbersome that it requires more and more to do less and less.

There are no easy answers for breaking out of the isolation paradigm of building the church. The way forward is found in the journey, the cultivation of a way of life among a people, whereby answers are discovered as the Spirit speaks through the people. Integration of ministries may be the tangible goal, but God uses that goal to call leaders into personal integration as a team of leaders who exhibit what it means to be the church, instead of just managing the church.

God's Dreams

Jeremiah 29 records a letter the prophet wrote to the Judahites who had been taken into Babylonian captivity. In this letter, he told them that they would live in captivity for 70 years and that they should *"build houses and settle down; plant gardens and eat what they produce. Marry and have sons and daughters; find wives for your sons and give your daughters in marriage ... Also, seek the peace and prosperity of the city to which I have carried you into exile. Pray to the Lord for it, because if it prospers, you too will prosper"* (Jer. 29:6-7).

In other words, "Don't fret about getting back to Judah. Instead, find God in the midst of exile." In addition they were told, *"Do not let the prophets and diviners among you deceive you. Do not listen to the dreams you encourage them to have. They are prophesying lies to you in my name. I have not sent them"* (Jer. 29:8-9). These lies were promises of quick return and quick blessing.

The church in the West finds itself in a similar situation to that of the exiles, displaced and without a home. No longer is the church at the center of society. No longer does the church hold a place of privilege and respect. The church has been exiled by society and now it is searching for its new role. There are prophets today proclaiming that the church only needs a few tweaks, a new idea, or even a small group program. Then it will return from its exile to enter revival and take Christ to this culture like never before. Small groups laid on top of the model of Christendom will not live up to God's dreams for the church. Such an approach reinforces an institutional model of the church that is becoming more and more distant from our culture.

Through Jeremiah's letter, God told the exiles, *"For I know the plans I have for you, plans to prosper you and not to harm you, plans to give you hope and a future."* These plans of blessing would only come through the hard lessons learned in exile. They could not return to the glory of "yesterday." They had to get back to the foundational issues to discover what it meant to be a people. They had to find new dreams, a new imagination, regarding what it meant to be a people of God while surrounded by pagan authorities.

My Last Word

In the life of the church today, such an imagination can only be cultivated as those within the church re-learn what it means to live in vital relationships with one another. As we relate to God and each other through the power and inspiration of the Holy Spirit, an organic mission will arise that will foster a new future for the church. Mission and the relational way cannot work without one another. Mission without relationships results in an army. Relational Christianity without mission will only produce a country club. When mission and relationality join forces, God's plans for the church generate hope, just as Jeremiah foretold.

Create Contagious Relationships

When I read Yongii Cho's book on small groups, one of his stories sold me on the vision for a relational way of being the church. It was the story of a couple that came to Cho and told him, "It is impossible to escape this church." They explained to him how a small group leader (who was also their neighbor) heard about the troubles of their son. She came and prayed for him, and his life turned around. Afterward, the small group included the couple in the life of the group. Because they did not want to become Christians and they did not want to disappoint the group, they decided to sell their house and move. When they did so, the small group leader went to the town hall and found their new address, giving it to the church staff who in turn gave it to the group leader in that area. Over the course of the next month, the new group reached out to them. After such expressions of love, they finally realized they belonged to the church and they received Christ.[1]

Up to that point in my church experience, small groups were designed for the Christian. Evangelism was something that I was encouraged to do as an individual. Cho's groups loved and included unchurched people. I was challenged by the view of evangelism where members were empowered to take the gospel to people rather than trying to attract them to a building. The groups lived the gospel with nonbelievers so that they could see Christ in addition to hearing about God. I remember thinking: "I can do that kind of evangelism."

Small group community life actually works with small group outreach. Contrary to the experiences of most small groups, we don't need to have groups that are focused on believers and other strategies for outreach. The small group is an outreach unit. Cho taught his groups to include outsiders in the life of the groups. They sought to create contagious relationships within the groups, relationships that would stimulate organic evangelism and growth that is based upon the groups incarnating the presence of God within their midst. Such an approach to community confronts the myth that a preferable design for community is found in closed fellowships of Christians.

Structural Myth #5:
Small group community is best fostered in a context whereby the group members focus solely on ministering to the needs of one another.

The Relational Truth:
Relational kingdom groups follow Jesus' mission to the world and develop deep, contagious fellowship.

The Mission of Jesus

Jesus said, *"My Father is always at his work to this very day, and I, too, am working. ... I tell you the truth, the Son can do nothing by himself; he can do only what he sees his Father doing, because whatever the Father does the Son does also"* (John 5:17, 19). With this statement Jesus put himself in the proverbial "dog house" with religious leaders. He was saying that he lived and ministered in absolute unity with God, thereby making himself equal to God. Jesus went on to say, *"For the Father loves the Son and shows him all he does."* Jesus did not just think he was doing God's will; he proclaimed that the Father showed him *exactly* what he was doing in the world.

While Jesus no longer walks on the earth as flesh and blood, the church is his body and he is the head of the church. We are the manifestation of Christ to the world. This means that if we are going to truly manifest what God is like, we must ask the same question that Jesus asked, "What is God up to in the world?" Would the answer to this question change some of what we do in our churches? I wonder if we would be as busy, engulfed in ministerial activity that steals our time for relationships with others and with Christ.

At the beginning of his ministry, Jesus proclaimed his mission, or what God is up to in this world: *"The Spirit of the Lord is on me, because he has anointed me to preach good news to the poor. He has sent me to proclaim freedom for the prisoners and recovery of sight for the blind, to release the oppressed, to proclaim the year of the Lord's favor"* (Luke 4:18-19). Jesus took on the messianic mission of becoming nothing so that "nothings" might become whole in him. On that prophetic day, Jesus announced to the poor, the prisoners, the blind, and the oppressed that they would find favor in his presence. Since Jesus is the head of his body, it makes sense that his mission through the church is the same today. If this is his mission in the church at large, could we also conclude that his missional activity is the same for small groups that experience his presence?

The presence of Christ creates groups that live in contagious community that are on mission with him. This concept means that the mission of groups is not limited to the experience of community by believers. Bruno Bettelheim makes the point by stating, "I am convinced communal life can flourish only if it exists for an aim outside itself. Community is viable if it is the outgrowth of a deep involvement in a purpose which is other than, or above, that of being a community."[2] Groups must have a mission that looks outside of the group in order to propagate life in Christ.

On Mission with Christ

Small group pastor and consultant, Jim Egli, summarizes the mission of groups with four words: Upward, Inward, Outward, and Forward. He uses the image of a three-legged stool to illustrate the necessity of each part. Upward forms the seat, while Inward, Outward and Forward serve as the legs. The interesting thing about a three-legged stool is how all the parts work together. All four parts must work properly for the stool to be of use. If any one leg is missing, the other two are deemed useless. The seat integrates or connects the three legs.[3]

Groups enter the Upward movement as Jesus leads people into worship, prayer and intercession. Groups have a calling to follow Christ into relationship with the God of the universe, to enter into the mystery of the Trinity and relate to the Father, Son and Spirit. This experience is more than one of teaching people how to pray as individuals. The Upward movement leads the group to follow Christ together into communion with the Triune God. The way people pray with others in a group will shape how they pray alone. As the group enters this Upward life, individuals will discover the joy of being with God in the presence of brothers and sisters.

The Inward movement is the call to love others in the group, to create an atmosphere of true love, acceptance, and forgiveness, to sacrifice for one another, to risk telling the truth to one another, to embrace one another in weakness, and to receive the gifts others have to offer. The Inward movement is often called building community.

Jesus is moving Outward on his mission. He is going out into the streets to invite people to his banquet, his wedding feast. He is reaching out to those who have rejected his love with more love, embracing them even if they reject his life. He came not for the healthy but for the sick. If groups are going to experience the presence of Christ, they must go with him and open their doors to those who do not know his presence.

The fourth movement is Forward. The largest complaint of pastors that I have talked with is not that of finding members for groups, but that of finding leaders. Jesus' mission contains a leadership development strategy. Jesus is leading his people Forward into new places. He does not want his children to remain immature group members who attend the same group year after year. He wants them to grow up, to take on spiritual responsibility and to pass on what they have been given. The Forward mission contains two specific elements. First, there is the process for growing up young Christians into mature believers. Second, the Forward movement results in the development of new leaders and the birthing of new groups.

Following Jesus into these four missional movements creates small groups that experience contagious relationships, connectedness that infects outsiders with the life of Jesus. Christ's life leads each group to discover its unique way of manifesting God's love to the world. Such groups are so good that they don't need to be advertised. They create word of mouth and a lifestyle that outsiders see and desire.

Satan's Small Group Half-Truth

Satan has played a trick on the small group world. He has told the church a half-truth, which might sound like this: "You can choose between a group that focuses on community and one that is open to adding others. You can experience unity with other Christians without sharing that with others." The basic lie is that a group can follow the presence of Christ in the Upward and Inward movements without following him in the Outward and Forward movements.

This lie has resulted in two types of groups, both of which appear to provide biblical community at first glance. The first is the closed group, one with an exclusive membership list that cannot be expanded without agreement of everyone in the group. The second is the officially open group that is in reality closed. The vision of the church is that groups will grow, but the fact is the groups don't. People could be added, but the group members focus on themselves so much that they are in essence closed. Bill Donahue and Russ Robinson state that this is one of the seven deadly sins of small group ministry: "A closed group mindset is a death sentence to true community. The dying is slow and initially imperceptible, like a degenerative illness whose outward effects are not yet fully manifest."[4]

These groups only provide a partial experience of community. Group members often feel connected to one another, and some will even argue that their closed group status generates the safety needed for this community. While this conclusion is true for some groups, sadly research on small group experiences has revealed otherwise. Robert Wuthnow, a Princeton sociologist, performed an extensive research project on the religious small group movement in America. He found a lot of positive results of these groups. But he also writes about another side:

> Some small groups merely provide occasions for individuals to focus on themselves in the presence of others. The social contract binding members together asserts only the weakest obligations. Come if you have time. Talk if you feel like it. Respect everyone's opinion. Never criticize. Leave quietly if you become dissatisfied. … We can imagine that [these small groups] really substitute for families, neighborhoods, and broader community attachments that may demand lifelong commitments, when, in fact, they do not.[5]

When groups choose to focus only on Upward and Inward, they fail to tap into the power that Outward and Forward possess to increase community.

The four don't compete; these missional movements enhance one another. Each group has something unique that Christ is doing in the midst. As a group gives it away to others, it will receive more, not less.

I am always blown away by what happens when an honest seeker attends a group. The belief that he "messes up" the level of connectedness is truly a myth. I have found that he actually adds to it. The stranger causes us to open our hearts in a different way. He requires us to look for new ways that God is moving. And many times, he shakes us out of our comfort zones. For many weeks, Kevin was coming to our group with his girlfriend. She had just returned to the Lord, and he was seeking. For weeks he sat silently in our meetings. I would ask him to give input, and he would say something polite. Then one night we discussed forgiveness. He piped up and said, "The hardest person for me to forgive is myself. This is the reason I cannot receive God. I have done some pretty horrible stuff." This excuse is commonly given by those trying to avoid God. In Kevin's case, he really felt this way. While he was taking steps toward God with his honesty, the comment had a much bigger effect on the group. Here was a non-Christian who was willing to be real, while the room was full of shocked Christians of experience who must have been thinking, "I have never been that real before." As we included Kevin, allowing him to take steps toward Christ at his own pace, he challenged us to be transparent with him and one another.

The Problem of the Outward Mission

The root issues that limit the Outward mission in small groups go much deeper than whether or not a group is open or closed. Most churches embrace and even preach the Great Commission. However, if church leaders were truly honest, they would confess they have a sizeable problem with relational evangelism. George Barna reports that only 57 percent of evangelical Christians believe that God has called them to personally share their faith. And most of these will never talk to their friends or family members about Christ.[6] Leonard Sweet tells of an executive from the Southern Baptist North American Mission Board who stated that 92 percent of Southern Baptists will die having never shared their faith in Jesus with another person.[7] I grew up in this denomination, and if there is any one thing that Southern Baptist leaders emphasize, it is personal evangelism. I attended more training sessions on this topic than I can count!

When I teach on evangelism, I often start by asking the seminar participants to share the words or pictures that come to mind when they think about that word. They usually share things like knocking on a stranger's door, passing out tracts, crusades, Billy Graham, or Christian programming on television. Next, I ask them to share words that describe how they feel about participating in evangelism. Words like "pressured," "uncomfortable," "awkward," or "manipulative" are given. Evangelism, which means "good news" in the Greek, is no longer "good news" to those in the pew, even though they are all glad they were evangelized. Rebecca Pippert poignantly states, "Christians and non-Christians have one thing in common: They both hate evangelism."[8]

As an undergraduate, I recall a sermon preached by a senior student leader at the campus ministry in which I participated. I will never forget a haunting statement he made: "If you don't share your faith with a non-Christian at least once per week, I question your salvation." I walked away feeling guilty, pressured, and definitely distant from any sense of the good news.

Why does evangelism leave such a stigma? Why does it feel like we are trying to sell someone a bill of goods instead of proclaiming good news, the year of the Lord's favor? Some might argue the flesh is the problem and believers simply need more boldness. Others will state that not everyone has the gift of evangelism. Argue all you like, but none of these is the root answer.

This demand for evangelism has often resulted in a focus on individual achievement. Most of the stories I have heard at evangelism conferences have been told by a "Michael Jordan" of evangelism. These super stars have that winsome outgoing personality that gives them the ability to talk to anyone. I met a man in Nashville who started a conversation about God in a very natural way with the people in the car next to ours while waiting at a red light. I was impressed because he applied no pressure and the people in the other car were quite comfortable. However, most people don't have this ability. When people share their stories of an evangelist's success and boldness, they are speaking from how God uses their natural abilities. What about the majority of people who don't have such a personality?

There have been many studies performed on how people were led to the Lord. All of them reveal that over 80 percent of the people who are in church today where influenced to come to Christ by a friend, relative, neighbor, or co-worker.[9] Matthew 28:19 reads, *"Therefore, go and make disciples of all nations, ... "* in most translations. Because the word "go" is a participle, this verse can also be translated, "As you go, make disciples of all nations, ..." instructions for people to make disciples as they go about their lives. Eugene Peterson paraphrases, "Go out and train everyone you meet, far and near, in this way of life ..."

Evangelism, then, is not something we do; it should be something that flows out of our lives as we move through life with others. Steve Sjogren, pastor and author of many books on evangelism, writes, "Evangelism is something I just continually do—with everyone in my life, all the time. I evangelize my next-door New Age neighbor at the same time I am evangelizing my wife, who is the most godly, 'saved' person I know."[10] To participate in evangelism is to share the good news with those in our lives. Evangelism is living in such a way that that we demonstrate the Christ life to others and invite them to taste it through us and our life together.

Incarnational Mission vs. Attractional Evangelism

The four missional movements of Upward, Inward, Outward and Forward are not novel. They are rooted in the Great Commandment and the Great Commission. At the end of the Great Commission, Jesus said, *"... and surely I am with you always."* The power of Christ's mission is based upon his presence and life within a group. In other words, these groups are incarnational, revealing the presence of Christ as they act as the body of Christ. They are not mere sub-groups with a limited vision based around Bible study or mutual care. While these two outcomes occur, the mission of the body of Christ extends beyond taking care of those currently within the fold.

Groups that incarnate the presence of Christ embrace his mission. They look outside themselves and beyond the confines of the current group to take Jesus to those who do not know him intimately. All too often, small groups try to do evangelism with the "come and see" approach. This approach is attractional, which seeks to get people to attend small group meetings. Attractional evangelism assumes that if we do small groups right, then the lost will come. The goal of attractional evangelism is to invite people to "something Christian," hoping that they will come and be like the people within that group. This approach only works with those who are seekers, not with people who don't know they need Jesus.

Groups that embrace incarnational evangelism take Christ to those in need. It sends the group outside of the meetings to meet people on their turf. Instead of asking people to "come and see," such groups "go and show." Because it is incarnational, the way that Christ manifests his life will vary from group to group depending upon the gifts and callings within each group. There is no one-size-fits-all approach. Each group must listen to Christ and follow him. One group might sense a call to work with under-privileged children, while two or three from another group might serve meals at a homeless mission on a regular basis.

Because proximity and repetition is crucial to effective evangelism (I will share more on this in the next section), many groups target a neighborhood or a geographic area of town and begin to pray for people they know in that area. They begin to prayer walk neighborhoods as a part of their meetings—breaking into small groups of three or four. Then, they host a cookout or work with neighbors to organize a block party.

Many churches are shutting down their Sunday evening services due to a lack of attendance, and some are using this to their advantage. Before they shut down the meeting, they cast the vision for people to use that time for incarnational evangelism. They encourage them to take walks in their neighborhoods, hang out at a local coffee shop, or attend a book reading club. These activities mobilize them to connect with people in natural ways.

The Key to Incarnational Evangelism

In John 17, Jesus prays for the church that would rise up after the disciples by saying,

> My prayer is not for them [the disciples] alone. I pray also for those who will believe in me through their message, that all of them may be one, Father, just as you are in me and I am in you. May they also be in us so that the world may believe that you have sent me. I have given them the glory that you gave me, that they may be one as we are one: I in them and you in me. May they be brought to complete unity to let the world know that you sent me and have loved them even as you have loved me (John 17:20-23).

Unity of the church is incredibly important to Jesus—and therefore cru-cial to living in his presence—as he prays twice that his people will be one with each other just as he and the Father are one. Some have applied this pas-sage to unity between churches. While ecumenical work is important, how can church institutions live in intra-unity when they cannot live in inter-unity? Jesus possesses much more than organizational or theological unity with the Father, like that of many ecumenical movements. He has personal, ontological unity with the Father. They know the heartbeat of one another. They are dancing partners who have been dancing together for an eternity. Jesus knows the Father's next step so well because he has the same heart as the Father.

This unity is radical and mysterious. The wild reality is that Jesus prays for the church to experience this same kind of oneness. He wants us to learn to dance together in such unity that we know each other's steps before we take them. He wants us to embrace others deeply and experience the radical love of the Father for the Son through the love of other Christians.

Then Jesus takes his prayer one step further. He says that our unity in the church has a purpose: *"to let the world know that you* (the Father) *sent me* (Jesus)." The unity in which I live with others is God's evangelism strategy. The oneness of my group is God's apologetic to the world. God does use books, crusades, tracts, door-to-door evangelism, and Christian television to reveal Christ. But the value of these methods is hindered unless the people demonstrate a different way of life. Francis Schaeffer states, "Our relation-ship with each other is the criterion the world uses to judge whether our message is truthful—Christian community is the final apologetic."[11] What greater message is there than the visual manifestation of a group of people who live in unity with one another as they have been drawn up into the same love and oneness that the Father and the Son share? As D. A. Carson writes in his commentary on this passage, "It is hard to imagine a more compelling evangelistic appeal."[12] Evangelism, then, is a by-product of our life together in community.

True oneness in a small group will lead to evangelism. The good news of God's love becomes so apparent within a group that those outside cannot help but notice. Stanley Grenz writes, "Only as we live in fellowship can we show forth what God is like. And as we reflect God's character—love—we also live in accordance with our own true nature and find our true identity."[13]

A group's unity actually shows God to others. This concept makes sense, being that the church is the body of Christ, and the small groups are a part of the body. How better for God to speak to the world his message than through the body language of love?

An Epidemic of Love

The spread of disease is studied by experts called epidemiologists. In *Redefining Revival*, Bill Beckham writes of a chance meeting with an epidemiologist who applied his profession to the sharing of the gospel. Bill explains how these professionals seek to understand patterns of disease growth and how the spreading is best controlled. The key to understanding how a disease will migrate through a population is to understand those who are infected, not those who are susceptible to the disease. They have found that five basic questions determine how the infection will spread. These same questions relate to the spread of the good news. The key to understanding the rate that the unchurched will become followers of Jesus is found within the church, not outside of it. The questions related to disease infection also help us understand how the gospel will spread through a church:[14]

1. How serious is the disease? Is it a simple common cold or a life threatening disease such as AIDS? How critical or life impacting is the message of Jesus Christ?
2. How contagious is the disease? How easy is it to catch? Is the good news of Jesus easy to share with others?
3. How long will the person be infected? Will the infection period endure a long time and thus increase the number of people infected? How long will Christians seek God passionately and allow him to rule their lives?
4. How infected is the person with the disease? Does the individual have a mild case or a virulent dose of the disease? How deeply has the message of the gospel impacted individuals?
5. How many people come into contact with the disease? How many people are in danger of being exposed to the disease? Is the impact of the disease widespread through the church or is it something only a few have caught?

Questions four and five are especially crucial. The need in today's small groups is for a serious infection, one that changes the way a person must live because of it. And it must be caught by many people who will choose to share this state of infection within biblical community.

People need more than a call to a private belief system. They need an invitation to a way of life that leads to radical freedom and a transforming relationship. Robert Putnam reports: "TV watching comes at the expense of nearly every social activity outside the home, especially social gatherings and informal conversations. The major casualties of increased TV viewing, according to time diaries, are religious participation, social visiting, shopping, parties, sports, and organizational participation."[15] When the world sees something inside the church worthy of sacrificing their TV addiction and other numbing pleasures, we might well see the revival that we so often talk and read about.

How Infected Is the Community?

The fourth question above seeks to measure the level of infection with an individual. However, if we take Jesus' prayer for his church in John 17 to heart, his evangelism strategy seeks to measure the level of infection of the community, not the individuals. The way Christians relate to one another determines the level of infection that can be spread to those outside the community.

There is something innate to our flesh that resists the kind of relational life that demonstrates Christ's incarnated presence. Love costs. It costs my security, my time, and my emotional energy. It means that I must embrace those I don't like in my group, those who are weak and needy, and those who have open wounds.

Every one of us has at least one type of person that we would rather not bond with. I know my type: the nice Christian who hides behind religious rhetoric, quoting scriptures and trying to build himself or herself up as someone special. I'll call him Religious Rob. When he talks in my group, I lean forward, lower my head, and let out a loud "Huff!" I can think of numerous times this has happened. In my heart, I want to get up, grab him by the shirt collar and lead him out the door. Give me a young struggling believer or even an honest searching non-Christian any day of the week, but not another Religious Rob!

Religious Rob becomes my enemy. He impedes the accomplishment of my group goals, which sound so right. I get frustrated because he quotes scriptures to belittle people and doles out rhetorical advice. Jean Vanier writes in his excellent book *Community and Growth*, "But in community we are called to discover that the 'enemy' is a person in pain and that through the 'enemy' we are being asked to become aware of our own weakness, lack of maturity, and inner poverty."[16]

Why does Religious Rob bother me so much? Because God uses him to hold up a mirror in front of my face. His presence week after week in my group reveals my own struggles with being religious or how I perform for God to attain accolades from him and others. I don't like this mirror image. It causes me to shut out Religious Rob and exclude him from bonding with me. Thereby, I refuse to allow a contagious bonding relationship to develop.

Other people in my group are often given as mirrors, especially those whom I feel are my enemies. Reality hurts. In transparency I begin to see myself in truth. No one has to point out my faults. The Spirit just starts shaving off stuff as I rub up against others and confess my own sin. But there is something in my flesh that runs away from this. I stifle it, and thereby stop the creation of any way of life that is contagious.

Jean Vanier also writes about what God has taught him about community while living with and caring for mentally handicapped people: "Community is a place where people can live truly as human beings, where they can be healed and strengthened in their deepest emotions, and where they can walk towards unity and inner freedom."[17] Every human being cries for such relationships. When the church embraces God's creation for such community, it begins the movement Outward.

Contact with the Community

According to question number five regarding the spread of disease, coming into contact with the disease is essential to its spreading. When people are first infected with spontaneous community and connectedness, they are often surprised by how good it is. Most people have never experienced true acceptance and loving encouragement. The taste of trusting friendships is addictive.

In some groups, the fear of losing this intimacy causes group members to hoard that which God has given. They seek to protect the group from any threat that might weaken or test the new bonds of friendship. The flesh calls people to turn inward and raise walls around our relationships as a fortress: it wants to create a separate unit or a single group that has something special.

This turn inward to the sole focus of maintaining community results in setting boundaries. The group members create entrance requirements, all of which they have fulfilled. They tell "would-be members" that if they want to belong to their group then they must first change. Outsiders hear the message, "You will be accepted if you think like us, embrace our theology, conform to our standard of behavior, and adopt our pattern of dress." Of course, groups don't say such things overtly, but their unspoken behaviors communicate quite well. For instance, a group might use "church-speak" that isolates, throwing around terms like "justification," or "sanctification," and phrases like "washed in the blood of the lamb." The discussions become heady and theological, often with many cross-references that leave a Bible novice in the dust. They laugh at inside jokes without explanation. This group is typically critical of alternative views and passes judgment on those who fail to act as they do.

The longer a church has been established the more difficulty it will have in moving into the Outward mission. New churches tend to be much more effective at reaching outsiders because they have not yet established these boundaries. Therefore, established churches that start small groups should recognize that their groups will bond well, but bridging relationships with outsiders may be quite difficult.

Bonding That Leads to Bridging

The best way to promote the continuation of community is to follow Christ in the intentional Outward movement of bridging. A group will resist this at first, believing that outsiders will mess up the bonds, that the group cannot afford to risk being honest with newcomers, that new people will not understand how the group works. While all of these concerns present realistic challenges, it is exactly these challenges that God uses to deepen the bonding relationships. It seems inverted and backward, but God's ways are not our ways. He gives more of community when we share it.

When a small group has a permeable boundary, it demonstrates the nature of God to those without God. This value is exactly what God did in his act of demonstrating love in the incarnation. God did not establish a hard boundary of heaven around the Father, Son and Holy Spirit so that they could enjoy their fellowship with one another to the fullest. Rather, the Trinity is a permeable fellowship, with God inviting us to enter into the dance with him. The problem is that no matter how hard we might try, it is impossible for us to enter into that dance. Jesus had to leave the safety and comfort of the heavenly community that he shared with the Father and the Spirit to take on human flesh.

Some of the early church fathers used the word *ek-stasis* to describe this act of Jesus, meaning "out from one's being." He opened himself up totally and moved out from his boundaries of being toward communion with man. He journeyed to the far country of our humanity to transform creation from the inside.[18] In Christ's descending, he then draws us back up into the life of the Trinity and intimacy with God. As our "Great High Priest," he has offered up the ultimate sacrifice, and thus lifting us up into fellowship with him.

If we are to have the same mind of Christ who did not consider *"equality with God as something to be grasped, but made himself nothing, taking the very nature of a servant, being made into human likeness … humbled himself and became obedient to death"* (Phil 2:6-8), it only makes sense that our fellowship with one another would embody a life that chooses to move out from its boundaries towards communion with those who are not a part of the kingdom humanity. Groups that journey to the far country of those outside the group reflect the life of God. (This journey need not be physical, as one only needs to go to work or visit with a neighbor to understand how far people are from God's country.) As groups do this, they are drawing people into fellowship with the Father and fellowship with the group.

What Does This Mean … Practically?

Creating Contagious Relationships

In the Korean culture, Yonggi Cho has taught his leaders and group members to use strategic methods for reaching unbelievers. For instance, leaders will listen to conversations that people are having in the crowded city of Seoul. As they hear a neighbor sharing a struggle, they will pray for God to show them how they might minister to that person. After they talk with them and find out where they live, they will often purchase flowers and arrive at their door offering to pray for the needs of the family. This strategy works in Seoul, South Korea. Sharing flowers with a neighbor and asking to pray for someone is not an intrusive strategy in that context. North Americans might find such an act odd or even invasive. Flowers do not deliver the same message in our culture as they do in South Korea.

Most groups have the potential to enter the Outward mission; they only need some initial ideas to help them get started. Christians who have been a part of an established church have learned to live church in the boundary mindset, requiring outsiders to change what they believe and how they act before they can participate. This truth does not mean that they don't want to see people come to Christ or that they don't have a passion for the lost. It only means that they need help to get started from a different approach.

Paul instructed the church at Philippi, *"Consider others more important than yourselves"* (Phil. 2:3). I have long tried to apply this verse to my treatment of fellow small group members, but the instruction extends beyond the fellowship of believers. Paul did not say, "Consider other Christians more important …" he said "others." This verse includes those outside the church, those who do not belong yet to the church of God. This truth means loving people right where they are without any expectation that they will change; accepting people in their current beliefs without the condition that they must accept Jesus to continue accepting them; and including people when they don't think like me, act like me, or dress like me. In his excellent book *Evangelism Outside the Box*, Rick Richardson writes,

> Evangelism is about helping people belong so that they come to believe. Most people today do not "decide" to believe. In community, they "discover" that they believe, and then they decide to affirm that publicly and to follow Christ intentionally. People are looking for a safe, accepting place to develop their identity and sense of self in community.[19]

The rest of this chapter provides ideas that will help jump-start the Outward movement. It is important not to think "evangelism program" or "outreach ministry" as you read. The Outward mission is a way of sharing life as people carry the infection of the Gospel to others.

Empowering Carriers

If we are going to see incarnational evangelism where people carry the gospel in a "go and show" manner, the church must clearly cast a new vision for such an approach. Most people who populate churches and small groups assume that evangelism is "come and see." They expect the church to do something to attract the people. They only need to do the inviting. Within the "come and see" paradigm the focus lies on designing the evangelism program, not upon empowering people to become carriers of the Christ life to share with others. Missiologist Charles Ringma writes about the "come and see" assumptions:

> No thought is given to establish what church members are already doing in their neighborhood and places of work. No attempt is made, for example, to identify the medical practitioner who has changed the approach to patients by providing counseling and practical support rather than just curative care. No attempt is made to identify the local [public official] in the congregation who is tackling certain important quality of life and social issues in the community. … No attempt is made to support prayerfully the teacher who has just started work in an inner-city school with many pupils from broken families.[20]

The church needs to re-think its vision for equipping people to be "fishers of men." The reality is that every Christian has the call to be a local missionary within their given context. They need not go to Africa. Most of them are surrounded by unbelievers everyday, people they have the potential to reach. Because each Christian is set in unique situations and has unique gifts to offer, there is no single way for individuals to serve on their mission fields. Each individual must discover the unique ways they can serve the lost with the powerful spiritual gifts God has given.

One way to empower carriers is to ask the question, "What is your calling?" With this question, you are seeking to discover what God is doing within individuals and to help them put practical feet to the passions that the Spirit of God has placed within their hearts. This question is great for small group leaders to ask of individual members on a regular basis, not just once or during special meetings. Most individuals do not have the ability to put words to their inner stirrings when they first hear this question. They need time to process their passions, and they need space to openly share what they sense. One might express a desire to work with kids in lower income neighborhoods. Another might discover a desire to minister to men who have been released from the prison system. Still another might find an unexpected passion to consistently minister to people living in a homeless mission.

These three examples are rather radical in nature. However, deep inner callings are not required. An individual might possess a desire to invite a neighboring family to dinner once a month. Another might feel led to start a Bible study at work. Or someone might feel impressed to fast and pray for their co-workers once a week. The calling cannot be predetermined.

As individuals listen to God's call, many conclude that they need to start the ministry as a separate entity from their small group life, separating mission from community. I know of one leader who felt called to minister to people in her neighborhood on a consistent weekly basis but did not consider it a group initiative. She did not see how the small group should have a mission, and how the inner callings of each individual member of the group would shape the unique calling of her small group. The small group should serve as a resource for mission and be on mission.

For years, I have trained small groups in this principle using Jim Egli's workshop book, *Upward, Inward, Outward, Forward*. In this workshop, I lead small groups through a series of activities to help them discover their mission. One of the activities is to write a mission statement that defines the unique gifts the group has to offer and the unique situations that comprise their mission fields. Many times, groups do not reach anyone because they don't realize the specific nature of God's mission for each specific group. As the individual group members listen to one another, they will discover how God is moving them into mission. As a result, fellowship within the group will increase as they serve together.

Sharing Hospitality

Peter instructed the church to *"offer hospitality to one another without grumbling"* (1 Peter 4:9). The Greek work for hospitality is *philoxenia*, which means love of strangers. The word *xenia* in the Greek has a dual meaning, as it was used to identify both the stranger and the host, signifying that a stranger is only a stranger in relation to another stranger. A host is just as much a stranger to the stranger as the stranger is to the host.

A stranger is one with whom we share little in common. What greater stranger is there to a Christian than one who does not share the common bond of Christ? Of course, Peter's admonition to be hospitable involves opening our homes to Christians, but even more so it pertains to opening ourselves to receiving those who have the least in common with the believing community.

The love of the stranger is not a love which seeks to convert or change. Instead, it is one which receives people where they are. Non-Christians are not an object to be won. They are people loved by God. The art of hospitality allows others to enter our hearts without expectation. Henri Nouwen states, "Honest receptivity means inviting the stranger into our world on his or her terms, not on ours." When we say, 'You can be my guest if you believe what I believe, think the way I think and behave as I do,' we offer love under a condition or for a price. This leads easily to exploitation, making hospitality into a business."[21]

To embrace a stranger, the one who must take the first step is the host. The host is the one who must change, who must go out and draw in the stranger. Therefore, the only way hospitality works as an approach to creating contagious bridging relationships is if the group members change, opening their hearts to receive strangers as they are.

Receptivity is only one side of the coin of hospitality. Receiving the stranger does not mean a group should abdicate what it believes, becoming neutral because of the fear of offending. In true hospitality, the host enters into dialogue with the stranger. Again, Nouwen steers us correctly: "When we want to be really hospitable we not only have to receive the strangers but also to confront them by an unambiguous presence, not hiding ourselves behind neutrality but showing our ideas, opinions and life style clearly and distinctly."[22]

To begin embracing the stranger is quite simple. Groups only need to make a list of people whom members know locally—people who do not know Jesus—so they can pray for them on a weekly basis. The list need not be long; two people per member is sufficient. From there, the group can host a party. (Mark Mittelberg of Willow Creek Community Church calls these Matthew Parties, in honor of Matthew the tax collector.) Jesus related to sinners and tax collectors at parties, people who were the rejects of first century Jewish society. Such parties are easy to include unchurched friends, family members, neighbors or co-workers. For example, every small group member has a birthday that can be celebrated. The group can throw a party for each member and invite unchurched friends to celebrate with them.

On a simplified and less organized level, group members can use the power of a shared meal or meeting for coffee to embrace the stranger. The entire small group need not be involved, possibly only a couple or a member from the group.

Recognizing Other's Level of Openness

Christ manifested love by coming to earth. He met us where we were. To meet the unchurched where they are with Christ's love, we must understand where they are. James Engel developed the *Engel Scale of Conversion Stages*. Conversion to Christ does not occur through one decision. It is a process that transpires over time. It is a journey that people take from being unaware to the point of receiving Christ. The following illustrates the steps of this journey:

-8 Awareness of Supreme Being but no Effective Knowledge of the Gospel

-7 Initial Awareness of Gospel

-6 Awareness of Fundamentals of Gospel

-5 Grasp of Implications of Gospel

-4 Positive Attitude toward the Gospel

-3 Personal Problem Recognition

-2 Decision to Act

-1 Repentance and Faith in Christ

 0 The Person Becomes a New Creation in Christ

+1 Post-Decision Evaluation

+2 Incorporation into the Local Church Body

+3 Conceptual and Behavioral Growth

Most evangelism programs assume that everyone is in the same place. They explain how to share Christ with someone who is ready to make a decision to receive Christ (i.e. −1 on the Engel Scale). Our evangelism must go to where people are and help them take steps toward Christ, rather than assuming that people are just unrepentant or hard-hearted because they have not received Christ or don't regularly attend church meetings.

The small group is a great place for those whom the Spirit has awakened, often called "seekers" (-4 to −1 on the Engel Scale) to experience the good news. In other words, those who have a strong resistance to Jesus might not find a small group meeting a positive experience. Groups are not the preferred medium to awaken people to the reality of God or to the message of the gospel. Taking Christ's love to people requires creativity, friendship, prayer and time, all of which can be done outside of meetings.

There are two points in the life of a group when seekers are easily added. The group is always open, but experience shows us the door to a group is most open at two points. The first door opens wide when a group first starts. It is natural to add those who do not know Christ to a group where everyone is getting to know one another. Therefore, one of the easiest ways to add new people to groups is to start more groups. (More on this in the next section).

The second door opens after a group has passed through the conflict stage of group development. When a group first starts, it enters the *forming* stage. In this stage, most members will see the group meeting and other members through rose colored glasses. After a few weeks, the "honeymoon" feelings diminish and reality sets in. Group members learn more about one another and some of what they learn is not what they expected. This point is called the *storming* or conflict stage. During this time of truth, group members have a choice. They can either work through the things that cause conflict, stuff their feelings and hide, or judge each other and cause hurt. If they choose to be transparent and forgive each other, the group will move past the storm of conflict and on to the next stage of *norming* or community. At this point, the door opens wide because the life of the community becomes attractive to outsiders.

A few years ago, one of my small group leaders invited me to his house to talk about his small group. He shared how his co-leader and another member almost got in a fistfight at the altar of the church after the Sunday service after weeks of getting on each other's nerves. He was at a loss as to what to do. My response was, "What good news!" Then I explained why flaring tempers are a sign of growth and how needed it was for them to become friends. Over the next few weeks, these guys worked through their issues. The group dynamics changed dramatically, and the group started growing. Eventually, it multiplied into three groups. Without some conflict—a small disagreement or a large blow up—it's nearly impossible for a small group to mature to the point of unconditional love for one another.

Sharing with New Groups

Because people connect more easily when new groups are started, churches that have a birthing mentality are much more likely to see people receive Christ than churches that don't emphasize starting new groups. The vision for groups to give birth to new groups should be stated clearly, early, and often. Such a vision calls group members to move the focus off of themselves to an outward look at those who are disconnected from Christ and from community.

Some find birthing new groups a traumatic experience. They invest in the development of the group, take risks and build trust with one another, and feel that they have established close friendships. Therefore, church leaders must be very sensitive to the fragile emotions of a group when they are preparing to birth. Much like a woman who is nine months pregnant, at the time of birthing a group, those involved should be treated with great care.

For this reason, it is very important to consider two things. First, the way the vision is communicated is crucial. Many small group leaders and members have become exasperated with the birthing process because their pastors have told them they must multiply because their group is too big: "When your group has 12-15 people, it is time to multiply the group into two." Communicating the vision this way is often counterproductive. People feel that they have invested their time and energy into growing the group and now it is being taken away from them. Now they have to start all over and invest in another group which will also be taken away from them. No pastor would birth a new church just because his current church is too big. That doesn't make sense. New churches are birthed because God has raised up a leader to start a new church. Likewise, new groups are birthed because God has raised up a new leader to start a new group. Therefore, the birthing vision must always be communicated to reflect the reality of why a new group is started. Therefore, the vision might be communicated "God is raising up new leaders within this group. As you are trained and prepared, you will be empowered and released to birth a new group."

Secondly, it is important to prayerfully consider the method used to birth a new group. Many churches have frustrated the birthing of new groups because they have only used one way to multiply groups. The reality is that there are many different ways to start new groups:

Option #1—Traditional Multiplication: In this strategy, a group of 14 will multiply into two groups of seven with the apprentice (A) taking one of the groups, and the existing leader (L) taking the other. This method has come under a lot of criticism because group members (M) feel that the group is dividing. In reality, the group is not dividing, it is coming to an end, and two new groups are starting out of two new visions. In addition, this method has been used the longest in churches all over the world with much success.

Option #2—Leader Birth: The leader (L) of the group would invite two or three members (M) of the group to join his or her vision to start a new group, leaving the old group in the hands of the apprentice (A).

Option #3—Intern Birth: The apprentice (A) would share his or her vision with the group and invite a few of them to join a new birth, leaving the old group in the hands of the group leader (L).

Option #4—Member Plant: This method, developed by Groups of 12 churches, sees every member of the group as a potential leader. The small group leader (L) encourages all members to prepare themselves to gather people and start a group, even with only three or four people. This method works best in churches that have lots of experience with multiplying groups and in cultures that are very open to the gospel.

Option #5—Joint Venture: Two groups send out people to form a third group. The new leader (A in the group at lower left) shares his vision with people from both groups and invites them to join him in getting this vision off the ground (typically requiring the help of a coach or pastor).

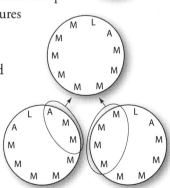

Option #6—Group Strengthening: Sometimes a group filled with very strong people will send out a few of its members to help a weaker group that has too few.

Option #7—Sub-Group: Create an additional sub-group, led by committed members (M) specifically designed to reach the lost (LP). When people come to know Christ, they can be added to the sending small group or the sub-group can be transformed into a "regular" small group. (See "Interest Groups" below.)

When people are empowered to develop a vision for starting new groups, the options are almost unlimited. The key is to develop a process of discipling and training new group leaders (see chapter 9) so that new groups can be started. Without new leaders, there will be no new groups, thereby limiting the ability to enfold new people from the community and the congregation.

Sharing through Redundancy

To follow Jesus into bridging relationships with others, we must consider redundancy of contact. We cannot express the love of Christ to the unchurched without repeated contact with them. Robert Putnam reports from his extensive research on social capital, "Again and again, we find that one key to creating social capital is to build in redundancy of contact. A single pitch is not enough, whether you are pitching unionization or Christian salvation. Common spaces for commonplace encounters are prerequisites for common conversations and common debate. Furthermore, networks that intersect and circles that overlap reinforce a sense of reciprocal obligation and extend the boundaries of empathy."[23] Evangelism expert George Hunter believes that non-Christians need between twelve and twenty "gospel touches" to move along the Engel scale to the point of receiving Christ. They need gentle nudges through redundant contact with Christians.

Practically speaking, this requires exposure to more than one Christian. When group members contribute two names to the prayer list and then get to know the unbelieving friends of other group members, the potential for contact redundancy increases. In addition, if those being prayed for live close to other members within the group, the potential is increased again. It is good to pray for the aunt of a group member who lives three hours away, but it is unlikely that anyone in the group will run into her while doing errands.

Sharing through Assimilation

The church must have a process by which people who have been sitting in a pew for years are challenged to embrace community and connect with others. Many churches have developed a small group preparation class to help them make the shift. Also, newcomers to the church must also be connected in groups.

At the same time, assimilation can become a growth crutch for groups. It provides new group members without much sacrifice on the part of the group and creates a false sense of confidence that the group is effectively reaching out. The stark reality of this usually hits when 75 percent of the church attendees have been assimilated into the groups. If the groups have not learned how to reach out to non-Christians by this point, the growth rate will level off and the groups often turn inward. Therefore, while assimilation is important, it is not enough and it can have a negative impact on group health.

Churches that attract large crowds deal with a different assimilation struggle. In some of these churches, the group growth rate cannot keep up with the new attendees. In such situations, groups can fill up very quickly with people interested in joining a group. A new group can start with twelve to fifteen people, leaving no room for others to be assimilated. Practical necessity demands that these kinds of groups should be closed to assimilation growth. Therefore, it might be officially closed in public forums like the church web site and brochures by way of omission, but privately it remains open to lost friends, neighbors, and family members who are invited by members of the group.

Sharing through Interest Groups

Those who are not ready to attend a small group might be willing to participate in a short-term (no more than 13 weeks) interest group. Such interest groups would be used to awaken people to the reality of God and to the gospel through relationships. They might be formed around any common interest from mountain biking to reading novels, from a discussion on evolution to a weekly game of volleyball.

With this information at hand, it is worth mentioning that such groups are not the same as holistic small groups. Their primary goal is to gather people around an interest, not the presence of Christ. Therefore, the holistic small group is a Christian community in which the interest group leader would be a member. The interest group would be an *extension* of that community.

Sharing through Servanthood

One of the problems found in our culture is that many believers have been Christians for so long that they don't have any non-Christian friends. Therefore, to gather people in a small group and then tell them to reach out is an exercise in futility. They need a way to touch people outside the church and initiate new relationships.

The concept of servant evangelism has been promoted by the work of Steve Sjogren and the church he pastored in Cincinnati. This evangelism method is a low-risk way of sharing Christ with people that any believer can do. It is also a high-grace way of sharing Christ that most anyone will gladly receive because it meets people at their point of need through active kindness. Sjogren defines active kindness as "demonstrating God's love by offering to do humble acts of service, in Christ's name, with no strings attached."[24] This evangelism format is a means by which a group can show people God's love without forcing people to listen to a Gospel message. Sjogren writes, "People don't necessarily remember what they are told of God's love, but they never forget what they have experienced of God's love."[25]

Such acts of kindness might include a free car wash (no donations accepted), giving away cold drinks on a hot day at a park, washing car windows at an intersection, blessing needy families with bags of groceries, raking leaves for neighbors, or cleaning restrooms at local businesses. (For more ideas, see Sjogren's book *101 Ways to Reach Your Community*). These and other acts of kindness are designed to make contact with the unchurched by showing them the love of God without any expectations. When people are asked why they would do such a thing, the response is something like, "We are doing this to show you God's love in a practical way."

My Last Word

Community without mission results in in-grown selfishness. Community with mission expresses the God-life and displays the kingdom of God in this world. The presence of Christ draws people into community and then creates an infectious wonder that draws people to God's life. Jesus always moves and leads beyond the boundaries of the small groups. Whether through reaching out to friends, service projects, hosting a neighborhood cook-out or just praying for specific people who need Jesus, ordinary people can participate in God's mission as they follow Christ and his life as it is manifest in the midst of groups.

Embrace the Relational Dance

When I was simultaneously involved in seven different small groups, all but two would be best defined as some form of a Bible study group. Since that time, I have practiced the value of connecting more deeply with one group of people at a time. Through each of these groups, I have seen how Bible study was merely the starting point for group life. In fact, it would not be accurate to label them as Bible studies, even though the Bible has played a crucial role. Instead, I have found that these groups have come to dance together with God. Through prayer, the Holy Spirit was released to apply what we were studying. The presence of Christ, which I highlighted in chapter two, was revealed in a personal way through the Holy Spirit.

Over the years, I have found that the experience of the Holy Spirit brings the groups I lead to life. My wife and I were leading a youth small group one night. During the discussion, one of the youth felt led to read a specific verse. This young guy was not especially devoted to his faith. He was a typical fifteen year old who attended church with his parents. After he read this verse, it was clear that God was speaking to Shawna and me. It spoke directly to the struggle we were going through at the time. That night, our group knew that the Spirit was present, and we had entered into the dance.

The Word tells us that God is Spirit. When Jesus was preparing the disciples for his ascension, he told them that he would send the Paraclete, the Counselor, the Holy Spirit. Luke concludes his Gospel with Jesus' words,

"... stay in the city until you have been clothed with power from on high." Then he opens Acts with the story of how the first church was empowered through the descending of the Holy Spirit.

Without the life of the Holy Spirit, a small group can do some good things. The members can study the Bible, serve the community, encourage one another and even look like an effective group. However, if one looks beneath the activities, one would discover that such positive activities are easily accomplished in the "flesh." The enemy of God's best is not the overtly evil temptations. Satan knows that if he can get us to work hard for God and ignore the Spirit, he can limit the impact that a small group might have on its members and the world.

Structural Myth #6:
Small groups can develop biblical community
without an overt dependence upon the Holy Spirit.

The Relational Truth:
Relational kingdom groups are a product of the
dynamic life of the Holy Spirit.

Spiritual Diversity

Opinion regarding the Holy Spirit is polemical if anything. On one side are the hyper-cessationists who claim that all of the supernatural activity of the Holy Spirit ceased with the closing of the biblical canon. They argue that the signs and wonders in the New Testament were necessary to substantiate the revelation of Christ through the work and words of the apostles. Now that the Bible is closed, no supernatural revelation is needed. On the other side are the hyper-charismatics, those who promote God's supernatural work in the church above all else. They typically elevate acts like prophetic words, speaking in tongues, and praying for miracles over the preached Word of God. Most churches exist somewhere between these two extremes.

The key to successfully writing a book on the Holy Spirit is to target it toward a specific audience, and it is best if this audience already agrees with the basic point of view of the author. This issue has presented me with a unique challenge while writing this book. Those interested in the topic of a relational way possess a diverse cross-section of beliefs about the life and work of the Holy Spirit today. Some readers come from the tradition that embraces the gifts and often look down at others who are not "Spirit-filled." Other readers don't embrace the supernatural gifts, finding excesses and abuses in those who claim to be "Spirit-filled." A moderate view includes those who are open to the Spirit and pursuing the gifts, but they do not center their churches around the spiritual gifts. And last, there is another approach taken by churches that state they are open, but not actively pursuing the gifts.

While this book does not allow me the space to wrestle with the various camps along the spectrum,[1] it is hard to ignore the fact that the Holy Spirit has a direct and overt place in the most effective small groups. However, I have observed too many North American churches trying to do small groups with a very limited view of the third person of the Trinity to ignore this issue.

Such a trend is not surprising considering the history of discussion surrounding the Holy Spirit. Not only is the Holy Spirit a point of major controversy in the church, many theologians have added to the problem as they have determined the Spirit to be the mysterious person of the Godhead and therefore must be left unknown. Alister McGrath points out this problem when he wrote, "The Holy Spirit has long been the Cinderella of the Trinity. The other two sisters may have gone to the theological ball; the Holy Spirit got left behind every time."[2] People believe in the Holy Spirit as a part of good orthodoxy, but they don't know what to do with him. Gordon Fee quotes a former student who confessed, "God the Father makes perfectly good sense to me; and God the Son I can understand; but the Holy Spirit is a gray, oblong blur."[3] Our confusion about the Holy Spirit often leads us to seeing him not as a person who is a full member of the Trinity, but as an impersonal power, an "It" or something that is less than fully God. While we confess our orthodox creeds, how we talk about the Holy Spirit and how we relate to him often reveals that we are functional "binitarians."

Part of the problem is related to our language about the Holy Spirit. The word "spirit" in Western literature connotes what is disembodied, impersonal and immaterial. This idea has led us to believe that the spiritual is not physical. The Holy "Spirit" is hard to understand because our use of language tells us that his work is really not of this world.

This idea is not the case in the Old Testament's use of the word for Spirit, *ruach*. "If we talk in Hebrew about Yahweh's *ruach*, we are saying: God is a tempest, a storm, a force in body and soul, humanity and nature."[4] The *ruach* of God is the breath of life, the wind of God. He is no impersonal "It," but life itself. Without *ruach*, there is no life because the Holy Spirit is God's personal presence to us on earth. "The Spirit is more than just one of God's gifts among others; the Holy Spirit is the unrestricted presence of God in which our life wakes up, becomes wholly and entirely living, and is endowed with the energies of life."[5]

Fellowship of the Holy Spirit

Paul concludes the second letter to the Corinthians with one of the most power-packed verses in the Bible: *"May the grace of the Lord Jesus Christ, the love of God, and the fellowship of the Holy Spirit be with you all."* This verse reveals the triune theology of God held in the early church. But it is much more than a theological statement. Paul does not share his theology for the sake of theology. He uses theology to stimulate the church to be the church.

The grace of the Lord Jesus Christ forms the bedrock of life in the church. We are children of God and members of his body by grace and not by works. We have done nothing to deserve the right to enter into the throne room of God, much less to enter boldly. The church is constituted by the grace of the cross, which opened the door to fellowship with God.

The love of God—when Paul uses this formula he means "God, the Father"—goes beneath the bedrock of grace, as love defines the very essence of the Father's nature. Self-giving, self-sacrificing, life-extending love lies at the heart of who he is. God was never content to watch people from afar while they maimed themselves in sin. His love is an active love that caused him to make a way for people to receive his love. The point of God's activity in this world is to draw people with his love so that he might relate with them.

The grace of the Lord Jesus Christ and the love of the Father are elementary truths of the church. But the "fellowship of the Holy Spirit" is a little more mysterious. At least part of the mystery is based in how the term "fellowship" has been used in the church. Growing up in a small country church, I thought fellowship was something that happened in the "Fellowship Hall" after church on Sunday nights. While I looked forward to the apple pie, banana pudding, and good conversation, I don't think this is the kind of fellowship that Paul is talking about here. The Greek word for fellowship, *koinonia*, carries the meaning here of "participation in."[6] To participate in something means much more than just relating to it. It means joining God's life through participation in life together, and the sharing of that life with others who don't have it. It means that we are to enter into the life of the Holy Spirit, thereby joining the life of God.

Early church theologians often described the Trinity by using the image of *perichoresis*, or a holy dance. *Perichoresis* is a metaphor that "suggests moving around, making room, relating to one another without losing identity."[7] In this dance, the one God—who is tri-personal—is a life of self-giving love, as the Father, Son and Holy Spirit dance together in perfect love and unity. Our participation in the Holy Spirit is the invitation to dance with God in his life of love and unity. True fellowship occurs when beings who are different share something in common, when they dance the dance of life together. It requires those involved to give themselves fully and openly to one another. The Holy Spirit comes to the church to sweep us up into the life of God. This truth is the mark of the church, the seal which has been placed upon the people of God. It is not merely a theological seal. It is experiential. Paul is not praying for the church to understand the doctrinal fact that they participate in God's love and grace. He is praying that they will experience his love and grace. In reference to the last verse in Paul's second letter to the Corinthians, Gordon Fee writes,

> The participation in the Holy Spirit continually makes that love and grace real in the life of the believer and the believing community. The *koinonia* of the Holy Spirit is how the living God not only brings people into an intimate and abiding relationship with himself, as the God of all grace, but also causes them to participate in all the benefits of that grace and salvation—that is, by indwelling them in their present with his own presence and guaranteeing their final eschatological glory.[8]

The illustrations that follow describe the meaning of "participation in the Holy Spirit" in the form of helpful diagrams. The overall size of the triangle indicates the level or amount of participation as a whole (larger is better). The circle within denotes the level of participation by a church (the

Power

Koinonia
of the
Holy Spirit

Order   Sharing

largest circle possible within the triangle is best). Each of the corners of the triangle represents three aspects of participation in the Holy Spirit (power, order, and sharing). All three of these must be embraced in order for a church to fully enter into the dance with God.

To the left is a diagram of a church that is participating in the Holy Spirit to the fullest extent of what I am describing.

Dance Step One: Power

Acts 1:8 sets the tone for the rest of Luke's account of the early church: *"But you will receive power when the Holy Spirit comes on you; and you will be my witnesses in Jerusalem, and in all Judea and Samaria, and to the ends of the earth."* Before Jesus ascended, he told them to wait on the Spirit. For ten days the 120 met in the Upper Room. While we don't have a detailed account of what they did, we are told that they were *"all joined together constantly in prayer."* The second chapter of Acts then records how they were *"filled with the Holy Spirit"* resulting in power for evangelism, power for miracles, and power to operate in unique giftings.

In Ephesians 5:18, Paul tells the church, *"Do not get drunk on wine, which leads to debauchery. Instead, be filled with the Spirit."* We receive an initial filling of the Holy Spirit, or baptism by the Spirit, upon receiving salvation by grace. Without the Holy Spirit, no one is saved. But the initial salvation experience is not enough.

We are to be filled in an ongoing fashion as well. Billy Graham states, "The filling of the Holy Spirit should not be a once-for-all event, but a continuous reality every day of our lives."[9] Even Jesus depended upon the filling of the Spirit for his ministry. When he was baptized in the Jordan River, the Holy Spirit descended upon him as a dove. After this, the Spirit led him into the wilderness to fast for 40 days. Jesus began his ministry with the declaration that, *"The Spirit of the Lord is on me ...."* The power of the Holy Spirit filled Jesus and rested upon him. Jesus was God incarnate, but he was also fully man. Therefore, he had to rely completely upon the Spirit to empower him to minister according to the plan established by the Father.

This Spirit's empowerment results in the grace to dance with God in the things that only he can do: Miracles, healings, and prophetic words that speak directly to the heart of individuals and entire groups. There is much debate about the textual reliability of the last few verses of the Gospel of Mark—the earliest and best manuscripts do not contain these verses—which emphasize the workings of signs and wonders in the church. In reference to these verses, Martin Luther once said, "We must allow these words to remain and not gloss them away, as some have done who said that these signs were manifestations of the Spirit in the beginning of the Christian era and that now they have ceased. That is not right; for the same power is in the church still. And though it is not exercised, that does not matter; we still have the power to do such signs."[10]

We possess the same power to do such signs, even in small groups. However, too many lack such power. Leaders study the lessons. They get everyone in a circle. They work to make people feel welcome. Then they perform their duties according to the instructions of the small group experts.

When an individual reveals issues of need or hurt—whether through personal confession or by simple observation of his or her actions—the community often responds in one of two ways. The first is the response of judgment. A group that does not possess the power to pray and see God move and touch a hurting person will often become that person's judge. Judgment never changes anyone. It only sets one person above another. In one group I led, Brian was petrified to share his life history. One night he found the courage to share how he had come out of a life of homosexuality. We embraced him and committed to work with him through his struggles. He shared how this was the first experience where he was able to reveal his issues without the judgment of other Christians.

The other typical response to the absence of the power of the Holy Spirit is absolute acceptance (which is in stark contrast to the story I just shared about Brian). Such groups call "all things good" because they fear being labeled as judgmental. Many small groups—in the name of wanting people to feel accepted—allow people to share their sins, their struggles, and offer them no hope for change. They only share their pain, commiserating together in their failures. Everyone in the group knows what is right and what is wrong, and they feel sorry for the poor guy who is struggling in his soul, feeling the weight of guilt and shame. They believe that sharing alone will bring healing, but James 5:16 states that it is the prayer of a righteous man that comes after the confession of sin that brings healing. Such prayers require the power of the Holy Spirit.

Those from more charismatic backgrounds are inclined to focus on power so much that it becomes the sole emphasis, neglecting the other two points of the triangle that will be explained below. In some cases, these churches embrace emotionalism that looks like a move of the Spirit because people respond to it, but the order of the Spirit is absent. Such a singular focus limits or diminish as the *koinonia* of the Holy Spirit, and pulls the church away from order and sharing as illustrated to the left.

Power

Koinonia
of the
Holy Spirit

Order   Sharing

I was a member of a small group that had such a form of power. A man visited our group who often operated prophetically. After we answered a brief icebreaker and worshipped, we opened up the Bible and began discussing a specific passage. As the leader asked questions, it became obvious that this self-appointed prophet in our midst felt a great deal of freedom to talk. As more time passed in our meeting, the less we talked and the more he talked. He had a personal word for almost every person in the group, including me. Most of his words were innocuous because they lacked any substance. A few were misleading because he was flattering people's egos. According to I Corinthians 14, such words should have been limited to two or three and then tested by others in the group, measuring them up against the Word of God. That night, our leader failed to bring order to the meeting and it continued for almost four hours. We left emotionally stimulated, but after the let down, it became obvious that the time was wasted on words with little substance.

Such accounts could be recorded endlessly. Many have become enamored with the specific words of prophecy or unique revelation while ignoring the general revelation of the Word. They have found prophetic words more stimulating than the preached Word. They have found experiences that stimulate them emotionally of more value than theology or doctrine.

Dance Step Two: Order

Chapters in I Corinthians are favorites of churches that emphasize the power of the Holy Spirit. Chapter 12 lists the charismatic or miraculous gifts that Paul recognized in operation in the church at Corinth. Chapter 14 provides instructions about the use of the gifts of tongues and prophecy. While Paul exhorts the readers to use spiritual gifts saying, *"eagerly desire spiritual gifts, especially the gift of prophecy"* (I Cor. 14:1), Paul's letter is not an argument for the power of the Holy Spirit in the church. Instead, he was correcting misuses, abuses, and improprieties of that power. Paul was trying to establish spiritual order because the Corinthian church placed an inordinate amount of emphasis on spiritual power.

The primary component to spiritual order is the Word of God. The Bible is called the sword of the Spirit, meaning that God's Word is used by the Holy Spirit. It is not man's sword which he can use and apply as he sees fit, resulting in legalism and manipulation. It is the Spirit's sword which God uses as he sees fit, according to the law of love, which leads people to repentance and restoration. The Holy Spirit is the Spirit of truth who has the task of guiding the church into all truth (John 16:13).

Small groups must possess a healthy understanding of the Word of God if they are going to operate in biblical order. Historically, the church is known to be a people of the Book. The church does this because the Bible was inspired by the Holy Spirit himself, as he worked through the various authors. The Bible is God's book of divine order for the Spirit's ongoing life in the churches. Martin Lloyd-Jones used to say, "The Bible was not given to replace direct revelation; it was given to correct abuses."[11]

Many churches have reacted to this "power" focus and have opted to set aside the miraculous spiritual gifts like words of prophecy or messages in tongues. Instead of praying for a miraculous healing, they have determined it much safer to pray for "the will of God." Therefore, they limit or diminish the *koinonia* of the Holy Spirit in another way. The diagram to the left illustrates the over-emphasis on order and how it pulls a church away from power and sharing.

Power

Koinonia of the Holy Spirit

Order   Sharing

While abuses of spiritual gifts and manifestations of power have been documented extensively, is the best approach, then, to exclude the power of the Holy Spirit from the small group life? There must be other options apart from walking away from the power of the Spirit. The church must heed Paul's instruction, *"Do not put out the Spirit's fire; do not treat prophecies with contempt"* (1 Thessalonians 5:19-20).

This begs the question: Can power and order work together? Former minister of Westminster Chapel, R. T. Kendall, writes:

> I believe there has been a silent divorce in the church between the Word and the Spirit. Because there are those on the "Word" side saying: the need of the hour is for preaching of the Bible generally and expository preaching particularly... There are those on the "Spirit" side saying: the need today is for signs and wonders; the world will not be shaken until we recover apostolic power; we need to see healings and prophetic words that will show the world the Church is alive. What is wrong with either emphasis? Nothing. Both are right. There is a need for the remarriage of the Word and Spirit.[12]

The story of David's attempt to return the Ark of the Covenant to Jerusalem illustrates the need for a union of Word and Spirit. Being zealous for God and his presence, David developed a plan to bring back the Ark of the Covenant—which was the symbol of the presence of God's Spirit—to Jerusalem. David did not skimp on his plan to honor the Lord. *"David and the whole house of Israel were celebrating with all their might before the Lord, with songs and with harps, lyres, tambourines, sistrums and cymbals"* (2 Samuel 6:50). David recognized the significance of the Ark, involving the "whole house of Israel," leading them in worship and praise. He understood the need to practice the presence of God's Spirit. But during the singing and the celebrating, the ark became unsteadied due to the stumbling of an ox. Uzzah reached up to steady the ark and God struck him dead due to this irreverent act. What David failed to do was to seek the Word about his biblical order regarding the Ark.

On the surface, such an act of God seems quite unfair. In fact, David became angry because Uzzah had good motivations. He just wanted to keep the ark from falling off the cart! But herein lies the root of the issue. The Ark was not to be transported on a cart pulled by an ox. The Torah specifically instructed that priests were to carry the Ark by using two long poles that slid through rings on each side of the Ark. The Ark was the sign of God's presence. God had established an order for God's presence to be carried. To ignore that order is to ignore God.

Dance Step 3: Sharing

It is possible to enter the dance at the point of the Spirit's power by one's self. I can be filled with the Holy Spirit alone. I can feel his presence alone. I can sense God's love and acceptance alone. I can attend church on Sunday morning, worship him, hear his direction, and do all of this alone.

It is also possible to enter the dance of order by oneself through the study of the Word of God. I can understand God's ways as I study the Bible. I can attain direction and purpose through memorizing verses. I can receive encouragement through meditating on his truths. I can hear a sermon and feel it is directly preached to me, which will cause me to change my ways.

By doing these two things within the world of individualism and a focus on individualistic spirituality, I can create a participation triangle that might look something like the diagram at the right.

The Bible adds a third dimension to the Spirit and the Word that expands the participation in the Holy Spirit. Most of the books of the Bible are not written to individuals. These are written to groups of people, the people of Judah or Israel in the case of the Old Testament, and to specific churches in the case of the New Testament. This fact is often missed as we read English translations. Take Ephesians 2:1 for example, *"As for you, you were dead in your transgressions and sins, ... "* In English, the second person personal pronoun "you" can be either singular or plural. In Greek, there is one word for the singular "you" and another for plural "you." In this passage, all three uses of the personal pronoun are plural in the Greek. This is the case for almost all uses of the word "you" in the New Testament. The Bible was not written for individuals to experience the participation in the Holy Spirit by themselves. Paul wrote his letters to be read publicly in the churches. He was writing to a people who were relationally intertwined.

The *koinonia* of the Holy Spirit cannot be fully experienced alone because *koinonia* implies sharing. It is something that we do together in the church. The Spirit does not come to the individual first. His primary activity is for and in the community. We participate as individuals in this community, not as independent persons, but as members of the body of Christ. Jesus is the head of the church. He sets the pattern for life. The Holy Spirit is the nervous system of the church who connects us to the head and to one another, making us a body. Through the *koinonia* of the Holy Spirit, we are drawn into a life together that is more than the sum of the individual parts. We are dancing together in the life of God through the Holy Spirit.

I graduated from Texas A & M University, an alma mater rich in tradition. When attending an Aggie football game for the first time, you will learn an important lesson: the corporate identity of the student body is far larger than the sum of the individual fans. Let me explain.

A football team always has 11 men on the field. At A & M, the student body is called "the 12th Man" because of the impact the home fans have on the football team and the outcome of the game. Because of our role as the 12th man—notice this is not 12th men, as we are one group—we stand the entire game, signifying we are ready to enter the game and play ourselves if needed. This long-standing tradition is based upon the original 12th man, a student who suited up to play during a game due to numerous player injuries.

Many other universities have as much enthusiasm about their teams as mine, but another unique tradition sets us apart. A & M doesn't have typical cheerleaders. We have what we call "yell leaders." These are students who roam the sidelines and coordinate 70,000 fans in an organized chant. When a yell leader gives a signal, those in the lower section repeat that signal for the fans behind them and the signal is passed all the way up. As a result, everyone knows what we are doing and we are able to do it together. This reinforces the strong corporate spirit of being a Texas Aggie.

In the West, the church has a long heritage of emphasizing the individual experience over the corporate. One theologian believes that Augustine provided this pattern for subsequent generations. "The mystical traditions which followed Augustine provided one of the essential foundations of

Western individualism, for which the dignity of every individual soul is higher than the dignity of the body, the rights of individual persons are more important that the rights of the community, and human dignity itself is higher than the dignity of other earthly creatures."[13] Western philosophy advanced this further as it set the boundaries for the definition of a person. Descartes saw a person as a "thinking individual, and in his view social relationship does not enter the picture. The human is defined as an individual substance of rational nature, not as a person related to other persons essentially."[14]

While I can hear the Word of God or experience the power of God alone, I can only dance with God in the *koinonia* of the Holy Spirit in a limited way. Maybe this is one of the reasons for the polemic battles over the manifestations of the Holy Spirit in the church today. If we see our relationship with God as primarily private, then we are open to all kinds of problems, abuses, and misapplications. However, if we are dancing together as a church with the Holy Spirit, there are more than enough opportunities to learn together how the dance works, giving us room for making mistakes because what someone does can be tested, corrected, and affirmed.

Peter tells us that we are *"participants in the divine nature"* (2 Peter 1:4). His nature is love. Paul's primary writings on the Holy Spirit are found in First Corinthians 12 and 14. Set in between them is the love chapter. Without love, all the giftings in the world have nothing to offer. They don't change anyone's life. All the biblical exposition through preaching offers nothing without love. The fruit of the Spirit that Paul lists first in Galatians 5 is love. God's love has been poured out into our hearts by the Spirit (Romans 5:5). This fruit of love is not something that can be experienced alone. In fact, all but the last of the nine fruits of the Spirit focus on how people relate to one another. The fruit of the Spirit manifests as we relate to one another.

As we participate in the Holy Spirit with others, we are participants in his love. The Spirit is the person of the Trinity who carries the love of God and the grace of Jesus out to include others. The Spirit is oriented to others, the created world, reaching down to the church to draw into the perichoretic dance of the Trinity.[15] The Spirit is the agent sent by the Father through the Son to draw his people into communion with the Trinity.

What Does This Mean ... Practically?

Dancing in Small Groups

Small group members can attend groups every week while remaining isolated individual Christians. They can live Godly lives, experience the presence and power of the Spirit, and even know the Word, but their participation in the Holy Spirit may be quite limited. In such groups, the members attend group meetings, but have little to no commitment to one another. They fail to experience any spontaneous life which occurs when people love one another. God uses his body to reveal his love to individuals. Every human being needs more than a relationship with God to understand and know God. Humans need God with skin or other human beings to speak the Word of God to us. We need others to pray for us and have faith for us when we are lacking. We also need other humans to show us how to live. Even Jesus needed this. During his greatest time of trial, immediately before the cross, he invited Peter, James and John to pray with him. He desired support in his time of trial. While they failed to do this, Jesus still longed for them to understand and support him.

Jesus understood a basic truth about life. He knew that he could not be a healthy person by himself. Humans are created in the image of God, and are therefore relational in nature. This view of the person is vastly different than how we often define the person in Western society. If you ask the average person how they define themselves, they will tell you what they do for a living, what they enjoy doing in life, or the goals they have created for themselves. They define themselves as autonomous individuals.

Under this definition of a person, if you want to get to know me, you will have to get to know my thoughts. And to be a truly Godly person, all I need to do is to think rightly and act rightly. However, if we are relational in nature and you want to get to know me, then the only way you can truly know me is if you also see me as I relate to others. My wife and sons, my parents, my pastoral team, our closest friends, and our small group shape who I am. I am a part of them and they are a part of me by the Spirit.

Dance Lessons

The place to begin is with the realization that the Spirit already resides in every Christian. Every Christian, every church body, and every small group has a degree of the *koinonia* of the Holy Spirit. No one is powerless to enter into all three steps of the dance. There are no excuses. The Holy Spirit resides in us all. Now the three elements of power, order and sharing might be minimal or disproportionate, but the Holy Spirit is at work in every church, small group and believer, drawing them up into the dance.

Paul uses the phrase *koinonia* of the Holy Spirit in one other place in the New Testament. In the second chapter of Philippians, Paul writes:

> If you have any encouragement from being united with Christ, if any comfort from his love, if any fellowship [*koinonia*] with the Spirit, if any tenderness and compassion, then make my joy complete by being like-minded, having the same love, being one in spirit and purpose. Do nothing out of selfish ambition or vain conceit, but in humility consider others better than yourselves. Each of you should look not only to your own interests, but also to the interests of others.

These verses hold a key to learning his dance steps. This dance is one of self-giving love, self-emptying sacrifice, and costly servanthood. This dance will not bring any glory or power, and as soon as we think it will, our ability to dance diminishes. We are to have the same attitude of Christ who made himself nothing and became a servant and died on a cross. This is the kind of dance into which the Spirit is leading his church. This is the dance that makes small groups fun and life-giving. Following are a few dance lessons that can help us experience this *koinonia* of the Holy Spirit.

Dance Lesson #1: Edification

"Knowledge puffs up, but love builds up" (1 Corinthians 8:1). The Greek word for "build up" is *oikodomeo*, which means to edify, to encourage, or to cause to grow. In chapter fourteen of the same letter, Paul uses the word *oikodomeo* six times, emphasizing the fact that the purpose of spiritual gifts, the movement of the Holy Spirit in the church, is to edify the body. In Greek, *oikodomeo* is related to the word *oikos*, which means house or household. In English, edification is connected to the word edifice. One who edifies is actually building an edifice around another person. When someone has been edified, he has a spiritual house built around him to protect him from the lies of the enemy. When he has not been edified by others, he lacks that wall of protection from

the enemy and is much more likely to fall prey to the enemy's traps.

The practice of edification is connected to the Old Testament pattern of blessing and cursing. God promised his blessings to Abraham. He proclaimed that the nations of the earth would be blessed through Abraham. Jacob sought the blessing of his father Isaac, and he wrestled with God and would not let him go until he blessed him.

God's love for the nation of Israel caused him to turn curses into blessings for them (Deut. 23:5). In Ezekiel 34:25-26, we find these words of blessing, *"I will make a covenant of peace with them and rid the land of wild beasts so that they may live in the desert and sleep in the forests in safety. I will bless them and the places surrounding my hill. I will send down showers in season; there will be showers of blessings."*

God's blessings are often blocked by curses, curses that have been spoken over our lives since childhood. Think about three of your best friends. Do they realize that they are blessed and that God's blessing is for them? Are they stuck behind a curse of rejection from a childhood authority figure? Are they living under the lies of self-deprecation due to comparing themselves to other people? How about fighting condemnation due to past failure?

Jesus said that he would build (*oikodomeo*) his church. This statement does not mean that he is in the business of building church buildings or of even establishing the church as an organization or an institution. He is building up the people that are the living stones of his church. To do this the Sprit often uses the gift of prophecy. This gift has come under much fire due to abuses and the lack of testing what has been prophesied. Prophecy is to be weighed against the revealed, unchanging Word of God. Paul writes, *"Two or three prophets should speak and the others should weigh carefully what has been said"* (I Cor. 14:27).

The problem is not with the gift of prophecy; it is with our misuse of the gift. We have not been sharing prophecy in the full dance of the *koinonia* of the Holy Spirit. Some churches prophesy in the power camp, and the more ecstatic the prophecy the more it feels like God. Other churches prophesy in the order camp, claiming that prophecy is only done today through the preaching of the Word.

"But everyone who prophesies speaks to men for their strengthening (edification), *encouragement and comfort"* (1 Cor. 14:3). Paul instructs the church, *"Follow the way of love and eagerly desire spiritual gifts, especially the*

gift of prophecy" (1 Cor. 14:1). God speaks through the members of his body to other body parts for the purpose of *oikodomeo*.

In Paul's context, it can mean both supernatural words and preaching the Word. In addition, it is the simple sharing of truth to others with whom we share a relationship. In our formal church context—where small groups have been seen as a sub-group to the church—we read Paul's letter as if his churches were having similar church experiences to ours. However, because his churches were primarily gatherings of small groups, prophecy primarily occurred through informal ways as people talked about life.

In my experience, I have found that prophecy comes in many different forms, but primarily it comes in very simple ways. A few days ago, I felt impressed to tell another pastor that she should trust her heart with regard to an issue. I did not know what it meant, but she did when I told her. While leading a training of a small group of leaders, I sensed that God wanted to minister to a woman in the room. I simply called her name and said, "I feel that God wants to move through you and release your frustration." Immediately she was in tears. I have found that prophetic words need not be shared in overly spiritual ways. I just share what is on my heart. Sometimes, I don't even realize it is prophetic before I share. I only know it is prophetic because what I said edifies or builds up another person. So when I say "prophecy," I don't see such activity in the spectacular forms that are often manifested in some circles. I see it as a very ordinary sharing of a word of encouragement by ordinary people who seek God.[16]

The church needs ordinary people who will hear the truth of God and prophesy this truth to others. When the church enters the dance or the *koinonia* of the Holy Spirit, it discovers that prophecy is for the building up, the *oikodomeo*, the raising of an edifice around other individuals who form the church. Prophecy in its proper use is designed to build up members of the church, bringing Spirit-inspired truth to the point of need of another person. This results in edification, encouragement (or exhortation, as in some translations), and comfort.

Dance Lesson #2: Spiritual Gifts

When reading the New Testament, it is quite clear that the Holy Spirit worked through the early church with spiritual gifts. Paul wrote to the Corinthian church, *"Now about spiritual gifts, brothers, I do not want you to be ignorant. ... There are different kinds of gifts* [charismata], *but the same Spirit"* (I Cor. 12:4). The Greek word *charismata* is related to the word *charis*, which we translate "grace." The Holy Spirit graced the people of God with the personal empowering presence of God to enable them to act as the extension of God in the world. In other words, they were empowered by the Holy Spirit to be the body of Christ.

In talking about how the Spirit worked through individuals in the church, Paul observes, *"When you come together, everyone has a hymn, or a word of instruction, a revelation, a tongue or an interpretation. All of these must be done for the strengthening of the church"* (1 Cor 14:26). At that church, "everyone" participated. Edification of the people of the church through worship and gifting was not limited to those with special privileges, or those with official titles. Each one had something to contribute. Of course, the problem at Corinth was that the times of worship were out of order, but Paul in no way chides them on the fact that all of them were participating.

Such a model of everyone participating seems very foreign to the modern expression of church, where only the leaders have the freedom to practice their gifts in worship services. Some have taken Paul's instruction to mean that everyone in a church service should be ready to offer a gift to the body if the Spirit leads them, even if the church is quite large. But Paul did not say "you are ready to offer your gifts to others when the Spirit moves." He said, *"When you come together, everyone ... "* (I Cor. 14:26). Paul assumed that in his churches, everyone was participating in some form or fashion. Therefore, we must imagine that the instructions he provides regarding spiritual gifts specifically apply to small groups.

The most natural place for the spiritual gifts to operate is the small group. Where else can one apply the body analogy so well? Where else can people know one another well enough to be fit together as a body? Where else can "everyone" participate? Where else can "two or three" speak in a tongue or "two or three" prophesy and others test what is said? Only in a small group can the spoken Word be discussed and applied.

This does not mean that spiritual gifts should not be happening in large group worship services, counseling sessions, one-on-one discussions and in other places. It only means that the small group is the best place for people to offer spiritual gifts to the body and to test them in such a way that the group provides feedback to those who share a gift.

Dance Lesson #3: Reconciliation

Sin separates. It puts up barriers between people. The people within the power class, usually men, adults, the rich, and the dominant race (usually white), set the rules for those of the less dominant classes. These power classes establish the barriers.

To address these issues, the U.S. government established laws. Businesses cannot discriminate against certain races of people. Apartments cannot be denied to people based on their ethnicity. Professional sports leagues set rules about interviewing minorities for coaching positions. However, these rules do not change the heart of prejudice. Laws don't bring reconciliation. Laws might demand equal treatment, but we still "pre-judge" one another based upon sex, age, economic status, and race. When the Spirit comes, he tears down the barriers we have established in our hearts. As a result, the cultural and social barriers come down.

On the Day of Pentecost, the 120 followers of Christ came out of the Upper Room full of the Spirit. Peter preached to the onlookers quoting from the book of Joel:

> I will pour out my Spirit on all people. Your sons and daughters will prophesy, your young men will see visions, your old men will dream dreams. Even on my servants, both men and women, I will pour out my Spirit in those days, and they will prophesy (Acts 2:17-18).

When the Holy Spirit comes, he tears down barriers between the "ins" and the "outs." He comes to take away the privileges that are based on the power structures of the world and restores justice to this world of injustice. In the first century, the early morning prayers of a male Jew included thanks to God that he was not created a slave, Gentile, or a woman. According to F.F. Bruce, such thanksgiving was expressed because persons "were disqualified from several religious privileges which were open to free Jewish males."[17] The Spirit comes to make such barriers irrelevant. *"There is neither Jew nor Greek, slave nor free, male nor female, for you are all one in Christ Jesus"* (Galatians 3:28).

In small groups, we have the opportunity to enter into a close relationship with people that we have pre-judged. When we keep such people at a distance, we don't have to deal with the state of our hearts. But when we come into contact with a poor man, sit next to a man of another race, give a hug to a chronically ill lady—accepting these people as true friends—we are forced to deal with the parts of our hearts that cause us to push them away. When we see the truth of pre-judging, it is not pretty nor fun, but it is freeing. God's Spirit comes to us when we confess such patterns, sins of division. Let's examine a few of the barriers that create such division.

Gender Barriers

While in seminary, I attended a seminar led by Erwin McManus, the senior pastor of Mosaic in Los Angeles. Someone asked him to comment on the reasons he thought that the churches in South America were doing well. His response, "They use small groups, they embrace the Spirit, and they are not afraid to use women in ministry." Over the past three decades, the churches that have been the most effective with small groups are those who believed that women could be empowered to lead in the church. In some churches, up to 75 percent of the small group leaders are women. As more conservative churches embrace small groups, the pastors of these churches find that they must re-think the question of women being released to minister as it relates to their tradition.

Whenever there was a new move of the Spirit in the history of the church, women were empowered and released to ministry. In the Wesleyan revival and the various North American revivals, the Spirit moved through women in great ways. Yet, after the revival waned, things changed. The conservative establishment, usually controlled by men, became involved to administrate the new churches that arose out of the revival movement. One historian put it this way:

> When leadership involved the charismatic choice by God of leaders through the gifting of the Holy Spirit, women are included. As time passes, leadership is institutionalized, the secular patriarchal culture filters into the Church, and women are excluded.[18]

For most church leaders the concern is not about control, but about being true to the Scriptures. Their traditions have based much of their beliefs about women in ministry on Paul's teaching that *"women are to remain silent in the churches. They are not allowed to speak, but must be in submission"* (1 Cor. 14:34). Even more central is Paul's instruction, *"I do not permit a woman to teach or to have authority over a man; she must be silent"* (1 Tim. 2:12). On the surface, such verses point to the exclusion of gifted women in leadership; therefore, women would be excluded from leading a small group. At best, they could lead a small group of other women. But in no way would they have any leadership responsibility over other men. To get to the heart of what Paul meant, we must look at more than these two isolated verses.

I do not have room here to adequately address all of the pertinent issues concerning women in ministry (such as ordination and preaching); the following points are not meant to serve as an exhaustive proof for releasing women to lead in the church—such a task has been addressed elsewhere.[19] The theological debate regarding women in ministry wages on today and consensus on this issue does not look like it is close at hand. Instead, I only want to provide enough grounding to deal with the issue of releasing women to lead small groups.

First, to conclude that Paul did not allow women to speak or prophesy in the churches is obviously misguided. It fails to consider the full context of what he wrote. In I Corinthians 11:5 he penned, *"Every woman who prays or prophesies ... "* In this passage, he did not correct the fact that women pray or prophesy when gathered. He assumed that they did and that it was proper for them to do so. Therefore, as almost all biblical scholars conclude, I Corinthians 14:34 must have a more subtle meaning when it is set in the context of the entire letter.

Second, all passages regarding the role of women in the church should be read in light of what Paul says of men and women elsewhere. For instance, Paul wrote in Galatians that there is neither male nor female in Christ (Gal. 3:28). Bruce writes the following in his commentary on Galatians:

> No more restriction is implied in Paul's equalizing of the status of male and female in Christ than in his equalizing of the status of Jew and Gentile, or of slave and free person. If an ordinary life existence in Christ is manifested openly in church fellowship, then, if a Gentile may exercise spiritual leadership in church as freely as a Jew, or a slave as freely as a citizen, why not a woman as freely as a man?[20]

Thirdly, as was the case with all of Paul's letters, he was addressing specific situations through his letters to Corinth and Timothy. New Testament commentators are far from agreement on the exact cultural situations, but because of the ambiguity, we cannot depend upon these two verses to exclude women from leading in the church.

Fourth, when reading Acts and the other Epistles, it is quite obvious that women held leadership positions in the church and even spoke into the lives of men. Priscilla's name is listed before her husband Aquila's name in four out of six references; this is a huge break from tradition. In one reference where her name is mentioned first, Luke tells how they instructed Apollos in the way of God. One cannot minimize her role as a teacher in this passage. By listing her name first, it "suggests that she was probably the primary instructor."[21]

Fifth, it is hard to miss the prominence that Jesus gives to women in his ministry. His actions toward and inclusion of women was nothing but revolutionary. Jesus established a radical pattern of including women as partners in his ministry. This pattern is followed by the first century church. "The New Testament indicates that the gospel radically altered the position of women, elevating them to a partnership with men unparalleled in first century society. Wherever the gospel went, women were among the first, foremost and most faithful converts."[22]

J.I. Packer, one who has reservations about releasing women in ministry, stated, "While it would be inept euphoria to claim that all the exegetical questions tackled have now been finally resolved, … the burden of proof regarding the exclusion of women from the office of teaching and ruling within the congregation now lies on those who maintain the exclusion rather than those who challenge it."[23]

Whatever your tradition and theological background, if you want to mobilize people for small groups, you will have to deal with the issue of releasing women to lead. The churches that I have observed who only recognize men as small group leaders are finding growth difficult. At the very least, the women should be released to serve as co-leaders with their husbands. Some churches are dealing with this issue by releasing women to lead women's groups. Whatever approach you choose, make sure that it is one that does not block the Spirit's flow into and through the women God wants to use.

Generational Barriers

The prophet Joel also said *"Your young men will see visions, your old men will dream dreams."* (Joel 3:28). When the Spirit comes in his church, he comes on the young and the old. There are no more special privileges. The young and inexperienced can be used by God just as much as the old and mature. In Bogotá, Colombia, there are many teenagers who oversee up to a thousand small groups before they graduate from high school. Many times, a child will have faith to see God work a miracle, while an adult is trying to figure out how God might do it. Jesus welcomed the children while the adults tried to control the children. When the Spirit comes, he restores the children to completeness, full members of the church, not those who are waiting until they are older. The valleys are raised and the mountains are brought low. All are on the same plain in the Spirit.

For eight years, my wife served as the youth pastor of our church. Her most effective ministry came as she trained and mentored youth to lead groups. She met with them every week and invested in their lives; it was incredible to see how these students grabbed the vision and invested in their small group members.

Some churches do not feel comfortable giving their youth such responsibilities. Even if they are not released to lead groups, they should be empowered to perform leadership duties within groups.

The generational barrier does not just refer to physical age, but also to spiritual age. Jackie Pullinger is a missionary who works in one of the most drug-infested neighborhoods in Hong Kong. It is called the Walled City. One pastor shared at a conference how he visited a small group where she brought a new Christian who was a drug addict. During the meeting, the Holy Spirit gave him a word of prophecy. Afterwards, the pastor asked Jackie why she would let a new Christian do such a thing, with no training or Bible knowledge. She responded, "How dare you! He has just as much of the Holy Spirit as you do." Sometimes, those who are older in the Lord will seek to control immature Christians and stifle the Spirit's activity in them. Jackie was not saying that this new Christian was mature, nor was she saying that he was faultless in how God spoke through him. But God can move through any willing vessel that belongs to him because the Holy Spirit resides in him.

Economic Barriers

The Spirit will even be poured out on servants, not just the wealthy. When Jesus told the disciples that it is easier for a camel to go through the eye of a needle than for a wealthy man to enter the kingdom, he turned everything upside down. The wealthy were seen as the ones who were blessed by God and more likely to be a part of the kingdom.

One of the barriers that the Spirit destroys is the barrier that isolates those who cannot make money because of physical ailment. Often the physically impaired, the deformed, and the immobilized feel isolated and marginalized. This status is even worse for those who are mentally impaired. These people often lead lonely lives of despair because the physically and mentally healthy are either threatened by the pain or they are too selfish to give of themselves to those in need.

When the Spirit comes, the destitute can get in on God's movement just as easily—often more easily—than the financially stable. What is more, the Spirit brings the wealthy together with the needy into the same body where they can minister and accept one another in love. In small groups, these two groups come face to face and are forced to understand each other. This is much better than merely sending money off to an organization that feeds anonymous people. The Spirit brings people together to transform them, not just to provide for them financially.

Ethnic Barriers

The primary issue that Paul addresses in his letters is the division between Jew and Gentile. He observed that Gentiles were *"excluded from citizenship in Israel and foreigners to the covenants of the promise,"* but now Jew and Gentile have been made one as God *"destroyed the barrier, the dividing wall of hostility"* (Ephesians 2:12, 14). Because Paul could say there is neither Jew nor Gentile, we can say today that there is neither black nor white, brown nor yellow. The church is the one place in the world where the walls of the races should and must be torn down. In fact, the unity of the races is a manifestation of the kingdom of God and a witness to the lost world.

Church growth theorists pointed the church in a slightly different direction. They said that the best way to grow a church is to embrace the race distinctions by targeting one homogeneous unit. "Birds of a feather flock together," as the old saying goes. In a church that is based on this principle, everything it does is designed to reach one people group. Growth is the primary concern, and reaching out to people outside a singular people group hinders growth, or so it is believed.

It is true that it is easier to connect people who have common interests. In many churches, the small groups are a place where like people gather, while the larger church is comprised of people of all races. Other churches don't feel that this takes the issue far enough. They seek to develop groups that connect people across racial and ethnic boundaries. They don't have a strategy to reach one homogeneous unit. People gather in groups, whether they are white, black, brown, or yellow.

Dance Lesson #4: Creativity

Where the Spirit of the Lord resides, there is freedom. There is no one way to do church. There is no one way to do small groups. Many churches have fallen into the trap of thinking that they have found "the" biblical model of ministry. With this belief, they succumb to pride and judgment of others who do not follow their pattern. Yet, as soon as a church camps out in one place, it will find that the Spirit leaves. The Spirit is like the wind. He is always moving.

Church leaders cannot depend upon a set model that will tell them how to do church. They must follow the winds of the Spirit into the freedom that is found in creativity. When the Spirit comes, he comes with his wisdom, the gift of applying truth to unique situations. Over the last 25 years, there have been many churches around the world that have developed powerful ministries. They all share a common thread of being unique. While they share similar patterns based on a foundation of sound principles, none of them do the same ministries the same way. Instead of copying what these churches are doing, maybe other pastors should copy their pattern of being dependent upon the creativity of the Spirit.

A few years ago, I was working with my pastor in helping one of our groups to multiply. According to all of the small group principles, this group was more than ready to multiply. But during a worship service, I sensed the Lord saying that we would regret it if we moved forward. I had nothing else but this warning, which I shared with my pastor. This unction caused us to wait and pray. As we did, we changed our way of leading groups completely. Through our praying together and the time we spent listening to our leaders, we felt that we needed to relieve some of the pressure placed upon them. So we developed a pattern of leading groups with co-leaders. Because we had the freedom to think creatively, we were not locked into one way of doing things.

Dance Lesson #5: Risk

I remember going to dances as a kid and being embarrassed by my two left feet. I would lean up against the wall with the other non-dancers and look smugly upon the risk-takers on the floor, secretly wishing I could share in the fun. The words we spoke to one another were often critical of those dancing. We did not like the fact that they were enjoying themselves while we watched.

When I finally learned to dance, my two left feet did not suddenly change. I was, and still am, an awkward dancing partner. The only way I was able to learn is to admit that I did not know how to dance and get out there and try, following the lead of someone who knew the dance steps. Even more than learning the steps, I had to learn to loosen up, to let my body move with the music, following its rhythms. It isn't always pretty, but it is a lot more fun than watching others!

Following the Spirit into the dance is risky because it is as unpredictable as the wind. At the same time, there is order to the wind. The Spirit is not out of control. Because of this, we must do more than tell groups to practice the gifts. Church leaders must equip people to listen to the Spirit and follow his leading together. As groups do this, we might be surprised at the organic, spontaneous explosion that God brings to his church.

Dance Lesson #6: Pray

More than anything, prayer is central to the dance with God. Prayer is our means for communing with the Father, Son and Spirit. Prayer is the language of the church. It is the dance of all dances. It is the ultimate activity that determines whether our churches will enter into God's relational kingdom. Unless we speak the language of the kingdom, how will kingdom life enter into his people? Watchman Nee writes this about the church and prayer:

> When the church prays, it is turning on the tap; the more the tap is turned, the less the pressure becomes. If the church does not pray, it is like a tap

being turned off with pressure building up. When God wants to accomplish something, he puts a burden in a brother, sister, or the whole church. If the church prays and fulfills its duty, it will feel relieved. If the church does not pray, it will feel stuffed and burdened. If the church continues to not pray, it will suffocate to death.[24]

Prayer is what the people of God do. The church can only be the church as it prays. It is more than a ministerial program of the church. The prayer life of the church in God's relational kingdom cannot be promoted by a prayer department or by hiring a prayer pastor, although these activities are not bad in and of themselves. If we see prayer as a ministry alongside all the other ministries of the church, how will those other ministries operate? If prayer is the job of the prayer pastor and her team, then how will the small group leader lead? How will the coach invest life into her small group leaders? How will the small group overseer establish a life-giving small-group system? If we don't pray, then trying to do all the other stuff that produces relational kingdom living will fall short of the goal.

Any church that takes up the challenge to embark on this journey toward a relational kingdom vision will discover a life of prayer. The risky adventure will force leaders and pastors into a new dependence on dancing with God through prayer. When we step out into a life of following God, the journey will be full of challenges that will produce prayer. This is exactly what the Spirit of God is up to in this world, and when he finds people who have such a heart, the Holy Spirit will draw such people into further communion. Such is the grace of our Lord.

My Last Word

To say that there is a night and day difference between a groups that are drawn into the dance of the Holy Spirit and those that don't would be an understatement. When the Spirit of God is quenched in a group, life is absent. But when a group seeks the Holy Spirit, freedom, joy and peace takes residence in the midst of the group and then empowers the members to participate in God's mission in this world.

CHAPTER 7

Connect Relationships
on Four Levels

When I first caught the vision for small groups in the church, I interviewed a small groups pioneer for a college paper. At that time, he was participating in a new church plant in Houston. He was excited about the potential of the vision. He stated, "If every group multiplies at least once per year, our church will gather for annual meetings in the Astrodome in ten years." Later, I joined the leadership team of that church plant, with similar hopes.

This church was based upon a very simple organizational structure. Almost everything we did was funneled through the small groups. We focused on getting the small group unit right, planning for consistent multiplication to follow. Because of this singular focus, we learned how to do the small groups very well. Yet it led to a different problem. The small group unit was basically all we had to help people enter into community. Therefore, the small group had to carry too much weight in our growing church. The pressure and expectations on the small groups to produce everything from good biblical teaching, vision casting, leadership development and personal relationships wore me out as a leader.

By expecting the small group to provide the only venue for community, a church can become so myopic that it fails to see other factors that can increase the experience of community. While small groups are the most important way to connect people, they are not the only level on which people experience community. Life is much more than that which is experienced in a group of five to fifteen. The reality is we live in a series of relational networks or relational webs. These webs of relationships which comprise the experience of community can be sub-divided into four levels of experience or "four spaces of belonging."[1] Small groups provide a crucial context for one of these spaces of belonging, but not the only one.

Structural Myth #7:
The small group/large group structure is all that is needed to develop community in a church.

The Relational Truth:
God's relational kingdom connects people on four levels.

Jesus' Web of Connections

When one reads the Gospels, it is obvious that Jesus did not relate to everyone that followed him in the same way. Some he called to be with him. Others he told to return home. Some he ministered to up close. Others he held at arm's length. Some he ate with. Others he fed *en masse*. Some he called friends. Others he labeled as those who misunderstood him. He loved them all, but he expressed his love in different ways, depending upon their place in his web of connections.

Bill Beckham, a respected author on this topic, has recognized the various ways that Jesus ministered to different groupings of people.[2] He has applied Jesus' pattern of relating to these groups to leadership development and small group start-up strategies. There is another application, that of understanding how people relate. Jesus being the "second Adam," not only coming to redeem mankind, but to reveal to us the working definition of true life. He is the "true human," or a pattern for us to follow. Therefore, one aspect of obeying Jesus' teaching is to relate as he related.

At the most distance point of his web, he related to the crowd. These were the thousands of people he fed miraculously, those he healed, and those who heard his sermons and parables. These people were connected in the web of Jesus, but they were not close to him. They were not close enough to ask him the meaning of his parables. They were not close enough to share a meal with him, or have an intimate conversation. If one were to ask someone from the crowds if they knew Jesus or were followers of Jesus, they would respond positively. In the eyes of the masses, they were connected to his movement. Their connection was loose, but they were still caught in Jesus' web.

On another level, Jesus related to the committed. Included in this circle were the 30-70 men and women who were attached to his ministry. Some of them supported him financially. Some he touched and transformed radically, like Mary Magdalene. Luke tells us that he sent out 72 in pairs to carry the news that "the kingdom of God is near." He assembled this smaller group of people to teach them the meaning of the kingdom. These people heard his parables and were exposed to his preaching over and over.

As a subset of the 72, there were the 12, men who formed a central web. These he mentored. These men received his most concentrated relational efforts. He ate with them consistently. He stayed at their houses. He told them the secrets of the kingdom as he explained the parables. To only this small group did he share the future about the cross. The 12 were loved by Jesus on a personal level. He expressed this love by correcting them, challenging them, and even getting angry with them. They saw a Jesus that others could not see. Jesus entrusted himself to this group because he wanted to reproduce his life in them. Such investment did not only come in the form of mentoring in the ways of ministry, but also mentoring in the ways of living. Jesus showed these men how to live as he lived with them.

At the center of the web were Peter, James, and John. These three men were connected to Jesus on an intimate level. They saw things and heard things that the other nine did not. They were also the only ones who were privileged to see Jesus at his point of greatest glory, the transfiguration. When Jesus was agonizing about his upcoming Passion, he invited his intimate circle to join him apart from the nine. This act reveals something about what it means to be human. Jesus knew that he was God, but he also had the emotions of a man. He longed for his closest friends to be with him and support him in his time of trial. Even the eternal Logos did not want to be alone.

These four groups of people form four rings of a relational web. These are not concentric circles. A web is a better metaphor because each circle is connected to all of the others. The intimate three were a part of the 12, who were a part of the committed, who were a part of the crowd.

A web is a great metaphor for another reason as well. A few years ago, I was watering our flower beds with a high powered spray nozzle. Above some plants was a large spider's web. Because I was carrying my son, I did not want to knock it down with my hand. Thinking a concentrated blast of water would do it, I sprayed it for a minute or so without success. That day my son and I learned that a spider's web is incredibly strong. In the same way, a web of relationships around a person provides strength and support to one's life.

How We Relate

Jesus related to people on four basic levels of an interconnected web. This pattern of living provides insight into what it means for us to live healthy, harmonious lives. To live a strong life, we need a web that is strong on all four levels. In today's fast-paced, frenetic, overwhelming life, we often don't stop to think about our web of relationships. Therefore, for many, the web of their lives is deteriorating around them and the only time they look for support from this web is in times of crisis. By that time it is too late.

In the book *The Search to Belong,* Joseph Myers applies these four levels, or spaces, to the church and to small groups. He bases his findings on the work of Edward Hall, who developed the science of proxemics, which is the study of the use of space or territory. Hall found that there are four spaces or distances that determine how a person relates to others. Hall labeled these spaces the intimate, the personal, the social, and the public.

Of course, few of us go around labeling people whom we meet. We don't think, "This person is in my social space so I will relate to him this way" or, "I am quite intimate with this person." Friends do not necessarily talk about their relationship with one another either. Instead, true friends walk beside one another, and in the midst of the journey they realize their friendship. Hall writes in his book, *The Hidden Dimension,* "We sense other people as close or distant, but we cannot always put our finger on what it is that enables us to characterize them as such. So many different things are happening at once it is difficult to sort out the sources of information on which we base our reactions."[3]

While it is not necessary to analyze our relationships by placing each person in a space category on our web, it is important for church leaders to understand healthy patterns of relating versus how people relate in modern life. The church must help people connect in the four spaces of belonging.

At the same time, the church must deal with the fact that life today is not conducive to developing healthy patterns of relating. Most people have lots of acquaintances at the public space and a few connections in the social space. Many don't feel that they have one person in the intimate space even though they are married.

The Public Space of Belonging

First, there is public belonging. People connect on the public level when they identify with a broad movement. Such identification does not require great participation; it only necessitates association with that movement. For instance, an individual might publicly belong to a national association to which he pays annual dues but does not attend any official meetings. He is a member in good standing and supports the goals of that association, but he has not invested time and energy into the accomplishment of its goals.

Many people limit their belonging to the church on the public level. They identify with the movement of the church through periodic attendance and by the giving of some offerings, but they are little more than casual attendees. Statistics reveal that half of church attendees only come to Sunday worship fifty percent of the time. These people feel connected to the church. They cannot be forced into deeper levels of connecting; the church can only invite them further along the path of belonging.

Everyone needs to connect at this level. If the church were to ignore public belonging, people would lose a sense of being a part of something big. The public space is where people connect with the kingdom vision that carries the church forward, a vision that calls the group out of focusing on themselves and their lives to see how they can impact the world. New Testament historian Wayne Meeks writes of the first churches, "One peculiar thing about early Christianity was the way in which the intimate, close-knit life of the local group was seen to be simultaneously part of a much larger, indeed ultimately worldwide, movement or entity."[4]

The Social Space of Belonging

The second level of belonging is called the social level. Connecting on this level occurs in smaller groupings than those of the public level, usually in groups of 70-120 people. These are neighbor relationships. Myers states, "A neighbor is someone you know well enough to ask for (or provide) small favors."[5] Many times the small group literature has communicated that the ultimate goal for all relationships is that of total transparency and intimacy. However, this is not the case. We need people in our lives with whom we can share small talk. I enjoy connecting with people about surface issues. I enjoy sharing my opinions about baseball and other ordinary thoughts with people I see regularly. I might even attend a game with one of them. I need not reserve all my time and energy for close relationships.

We need not force ourselves to share deeply with everyone. While serving on a church leadership team a few years ago, the leaders would often break up into random discussion groups during the leadership huddles. Sometimes the questions required a great deal of transparency. I was not afraid to share openly with those close to me, but the random selection of these groups created an unsafe environment. One pastor could not understand my hesitancy. He was the type of person who would share deep things with almost anyone, while I felt I was being forced to share.

The relationships I formed with most of the people in that leadership group were social in nature. We knew each other well enough to share thoughts, ideas and opinions, but issues that were more personal in nature should have been left for other venues.

The Personal Space of Belonging

Human beings are created to be known by others. On the third level, people connect in the personal space. This is where people share private thoughts, personal dreams, and feelings to a smaller group of ten or twelve. Here people experience a degree of transparency, but not naked transparency. Such groups become close friends, but there is no pressure applied to open up absolutely everything to the group.

Small groups are the ideal place to facilitate personal belonging. Small groups work when the group members become close friends, when they feel comfortable to share what is going on in their lives with each other, when they care about each other enough to sacrifice time and emotional energy to see the group succeed.

At the same time, personal belonging cannot be forced. This is Myers' concern with what he has observed in many churches. He feels that pastors are forcing people to connect on the personal level in their small groups. He writes, "The likelihood that eight to twelve people in the same room all have the need—and the competencies—to find personal space with one another are slim. This is especially true if they have been forced together by random selection."[6] I agree with Myers on one level. Many people will not connect with other small group members as "close friends" only because there are some people that will not naturally connect. Dumping people into groups and hoping they connect in the personal space may be unrealistic. I also have a concern about Myers' observation. He seems to endorse self-sorting into groups around whether or not people like one another. If this is the primary criteria for joining a group, the potential for creating cliques is quite high. While personal belonging cannot be forced, neither should we opt for small groups that sort around whether the members of the groups happen to naturally connect (more on this below).

The Intimate Space of Belonging

The final level is called the intimate space. This realm of life is usually only shared with two or three other people. Here the walls come down and we become "known" at a much deeper level than what occurs at the personal level. "In intimate belonging, we share 'naked' experience, feelings, and thoughts."[7]

In chapter one, I discussed the importance of "refrigerator rights" in depth. In a nutshell, this term describes the rights given to a few intimate friends who enter one's home and go directly to the refrigerator without asking. People who live in this intimate space have absolute permission to be family. To have two or three people who have these rights in one another's lives is normal. To expect a small group of ten or twelve to get to this level is unrealistic.

Friends in Your Home

To illustrate the four spaces of belonging, think of four different people dropping by your home to visit. Janet has attended your church for about three months, but you have only had one conversation with her. She is coming by to drop off an application to help in the church nursery. Of course, this person is welcome in your home because you have seen her, but it would be awkward to invite her in for an extended conversation. However, you want to be courteous. When Janet arrives, you invite her to sit on the front porch or to stand in the entry of your home and chat for a few minutes.

You have known Jim for a few years. Your son and his son are leaders in the youth group. Last year, you sat by him at a banquet and talked about his interest in mountain biking. When he drops by the house to pick up his son, you invite him into the house. You chat for a time sitting in your living room.

Terry was in your small group last year. You grew to be good friends, sharing meals together and going out with your spouses as a foursome. Today, she is leading a group of her own. When she stops by, you invite her into the den, even though there is a pile of dirty clothes on the floor. The two of you talk for about an hour regarding her new group and what is going on in your lives.

Tracy drops by the house a couple times a week, often unexpectantly. This time, you are still getting dressed. When you come out, she is drinking coffee and finishing off a muffin at your kitchen table. As you join her for a cup of coffee, you share how God has convicted you this week about how you treat your kids. Tracy shares how she feels overwhelmed with her current work situation.

While each of these people would be considered a friend, some are new acquaintances and others are like family. Each has a different kind of access to your homes, life and heart.

Model Small Group Churches

Small group visionaries have explained models of the church (cell church model or church of small groups) by emphasizing the large group and the small group components. These components correlate with the public and personal spaces. When churches only develop the large group and small group structures, they fail to facilitate social and intimate connections. This reality places unrealistic expectations on the small group to provide a context for more types of connections than they are designed to produce.

The reality of how model small group churches operate is often very different than how the books reveal. They are not misleading; it is just that the complexities of these model churches are almost impossible to capture in a book. I started helping authors write about the small group-based church over twelve years ago. At that point, the emphasis was primarily placed on the small and large group components because these are the "visible" groupings, the most prominent points of connection, and the primary entry points into the church. In addition, these model churches use the growth of the small groups and celebration attendance as the primary standards of measurement. However, in no way should we assume that the small group and large group settings comprise the totality of what community looks like in these churches. Much like the New Testament church, we must look beneath the most obvious structures for the organic ways that people connect within these churches.

Beneath the surface of the overt large group and small group structures are covert ways to provide social and intimate connections. They don't place all the pressure on the small groups to do everything that the large group cannot do. They hold mid-sized gatherings, and they facilitate sub-groups within the small groups for accountability and intimate sharing (more on this later). At the same time, these model churches do not allow anything to compete with the primary emphasis of community through small groups. These other levels of community are designed to serve the small groups, not to serve as an alternative to them.

What Does This Mean ... Practically?

Connecting People in Kingdom Community

Many churches struggle to involve more than 30 percent of their church in small groups, even though they have a goal of 100 percent involvement. To deal with this issue, some churches water down their vision for small groups, lowering the bar of commitment so more members and visitors will join a group. Some create bi-weekly groups while others start groups around an interest. Perhaps the problem is not with the original vision of the small groups but that too much was expected.

When small groups are expected to carry the entire load of building community and belonging, it places too much pressure upon these groups. Small group leaders feel that they must attain an ideal level of intimacy with the entire group, while many individuals may have reservations about such openness in a group of 10-15 people. In addition, small group members need to connect with a wider group on a social level. They need "neighbors" outside of their small group. And of course, they need to see that what they do in the small group is a part of a much larger church vision.

In Malcolm Gladwell's book, *The Tipping Point*, he proposes that a tipping point is that magical moment when an idea, product, or pattern of behavior takes off, crosses a threshold, and spreads spontaneously. For some churches, the development of community on the four levels might prove to be such a tipping point, the idea that releases the growth of small groups to do what they are designed to do, thereby moving beyond 30 percent involvement.

Facilitate; Don't Force

The framework of the four levels of community removes the pressure that people often feel when they join a group. Some feel that they must connect with other group members on a personal or an intimate level because the pastor expects them to. Often I hear about the frustration people feel when they assume that they must have some kind of unwritten "best friends for life" contract, often with people they don't really naturally connect with or even care for. Some churches have made the mistake of assigning people to groups and expecting them to experience not only personal belonging but also intimate connections. Myers writes, "So often our small group models encourage forced belonging. We surmise that putting people into groups will alleviate the emptiness so prevalent in our fast-paced culture."[8]

People seek spontaneous connections. One person cannot force connection with another. Friendships arise unexpectedly. People meeting weekly in a small group will not necessarily connect on a personal level. Some may only connect on a social level for a period of months before they enter into the personal space. Some will never go to a small group because of the makeup of that particular group.

Groups are more likely to move into personal belonging when they are given the freedom to relate spontaneously. People desire the freedom to connect with those with similar interests, life situations, or areas of expertise. This is one of the reasons developing a social space is so important. Myers writes. "In social space we provide the information that helps others decide whether they connect with us. We get just enough information to decide to keep this person in this space or move them to another space."[9]

Herein lies a leadership tension. As I stated earlier, creating a self-sorting small group system will often result in small groups that act as cliques. Therefore, the social outcasts are left out, resulting in a small group system that resembles the high school cafeteria experience. Leadership in the church is not just about giving people what they find comfortable. At the same time, it is not about forcing them into something they will reject.

The individualistic approach to modern life can produce relationships that are contractual in nature: people develop friendships because they find them personally beneficial. When personal cost rises above the level of benefits, the friendship is dispensable. They must see people as more than easy-in, easy-out trade-ins.

To achieve relationships in all four spaces, the church must teach the difference between contractual relationships and biblical covenanting. A covenant with another is different than a social contract, where if one party fails to perform its commitment, the other party or parties have the right to break the contract. Covenant means that I commit to you with the full knowledge that you will let me down and we will fail one another. Through covenant relationships, we learn to love people through the differences, the failures, the misunderstandings and even the judgments. We discover what Jesus meant when he told his disciples that the key to their discipleship was loving one another (See John 13).

To covenant with others also means that I choose to embrace people who are not like me. Jesus gathered a small group that was comprised of people who were very different. These men possessed no natural inclinations toward connecting with one another as friends except for the fact that Jesus had called them. He did not force them into relationship with one another, but he did invite them into something different than self-sorting.

Therefore, one of the roles of church leaders is to invite people to connect on deeper levels. Myers concludes that a church should only aim to get about 30 percent of their membership into small groups because only about 30 percent actually want to connect at that level. He assumes that aiming for a higher percentage would be forcing people into groups. While many of Myers' observations about small group community are correct, his conclusion on this issue misses the point. Pastors and church leaders must not fall prey to the temptation of allowing people to settle with the kind of connection that they say they want. An invitation to participate in deeper levels of community is much different than the forced contract that Myers seems to detest. Pastors should never be satisfied with 30 percent participation. Frazee writes, "One of the biggest challenges in the effort to build community is to convince people to choose something that may not necessarily be easy, but is nonetheless good for them."[10]

Jesus invited people to follow him in his kingdom community. He never watered down his vision for life in his kingdom so that he could get more people involved. His vision involved a way of living that would lead him to death, and he invited others to follow his way. He told his disciples, *"If anyone would come after me, he must deny himself and take up his cross daily and follow me"* (Luke 9:23). As church leaders, we are inviting people to take steps. We cannot force them, nor can we orchestrate connections. However, we can facilitate the move from the broader, safer places into community with small groups that possess greater levels of risk.

Connecting People in the Public Space

Public connections in a church are primarily established through the corporate worship services. In this forum the vision of the church is established, the Word of God is preached, and people experience the presence of God together. In public worship, people attain a sense that they belong to something larger, a movement. This is where they participate in the flow and direction of God.

Some small group writers have criticized the large group worship experience to the point that they question its validity. Some see no need for it because the house church experience should be enough. I don't find such reactionary conclusions helpful. Small groups work best when they fit into the flow of a larger movement. Small groups are great for facilitating relationships and developing family, but they are prone to go astray without the vision, teaching and presence of God that flows from the public space into the life of the groups.

Instead of "throwing out the baby with the bath water," it is better to see how the public venue of large group worship might be adjusted so that it can work better to facilitate community through the small groups. The problem is not with the fact that such services occur, but with the current role of these services. Connecting people in corporate worship services must take on a different role. In many cases, the large group worship experience resembles what Kierkegaard illustrated through the use of a parable:

> Imagine that geese could talk—and that they had planned things in such
> a way that they, too, had their divine worship services. Each Sunday they

gathered together and a goose preached. The gist of the sermon was as follows: What a high destiny geese have, to what a high goal the creator—and every time this word was mentioned these geese curtsied and the ganders bowed their heads—had appointed geese. With the help of their wings they could fly away to distant regions, blessed regions, where they really had their homes, for here they were but aliens.

It was the same every Sunday. Thereafter the assemblage dispersed and each one waddled home to his family. And so to church again the next Sunday, and then home again—and that was the end of it. They flourished and grew fat, became plump and delicate. ... Although the Sunday discourse was so very lofty, on Monday the geese would tell each other what had happened to one goose who had wanted to make serious use of the wings given by the creator and intended for the high goal set before it—what happened to it, what horrors it had to endure. The geese had a shrewd mutual understanding about this. But of course they did not talk about it on Sunday; that after all, was not appropriate, for then, so they said, it would be obvious that our Sunday worship actually makes a fool of God and of ourselves.

There were a few individual geese among them who looked poorly and grew thin. The other geese said among themselves: There you see what happens when you take seriously this business of wanting to fly. Because they secretly harbor the idea of wanting to fly, they get thin, do not prosper, do not have God's grace as we have it and therefore become plump, fat, and delicate, for by the grace of God one becomes plump, fat, and delicate. ...

So also with Christendom's worship services. Man, too, has wings, he has imagination, intended to help him actually rise aloft. But we play, allow our imagination to amuse itself in a quiet hour of Sunday daydreaming, and otherwise stay right where we are—and on Monday regard it as proof of God's grace to get plump, fat, delicate, get layered with fat—that is, accumulate money, get to be somebody in the world, beget many children, be successful, etc. And those who actually become involved with God and who therefore are obliged to suffer, appear concerned, and have torments, troubles, and grief (it cannot be otherwise, nor is it, according to the New Testament)— of these we say: There is proof that they do not have the grace of God.[11]

Some have lost hope in the possibility of changing the role of the large group church experience. The tradition of the way this expression of church operates is so entrenched in the minds of church leaders and attendees that it will require consistent and intentional focus to change it. People possess strong expectations of how the church is supposed to operate. To challenge that will challenge their paradigm about how God's grace truly operates. But if people are going to use their wings, changing its role and purpose is a must. Small groups need this venue, but they need it in a different way.

Traditionally, the large group venue of church has served as the church's end game. Sunday worship attendance is the primary focus and the measure of success of a church. Getting people to attend a large group service has been the focus of the church for 1,700 years. Everything else that the church does serves and points to the large group experience.

An alternative approach would be to use the large group experience to serve the small groups. The weekly worship service, then, would not be the end game. It would be a means for the mission of the church. Mobilizing people to connect with one another and participate in relational ministry would be the focus. The weekly large group gathering would act as a time of empowering people through worship, equipping them through teaching, and casting a vision for being relational on the mission field.

Connecting People in the Social Space

A few years ago, I had a friend who felt the need to turn almost every conversation into a deep discussion about personal or intimate things that God was doing in his life. He would then ask me penetrating questions at the most awkward times. He was very genuine and caring, but intense beyond measure. I avoided this person because he was threatening and even exhausting. His intentions were good, but his heaviness turned friendship into joyless sparring.

I am of the opinion that if you want to speak into my life, you will also desire to know the ordinary interests of my life. I like to talk about baseball, reading books, and the new things that my sons are doing each day. In *How to Win Friends and Influence People*, Dale Carnegie wrote about the art of showing interest in others. He said that he could enter a room of total strangers and demonstrate friendship to someone in the room by simply asking questions about his or her interests. If a person does not show such an interest in my surface interests, I find it difficult to trust him to speak into my life or discuss deeper issues.

Social relationships provide associations whereby people can connect on the level of small talk. Connecting socially can also occur at the level of the mid-sized group. Some have labeled this the congregation, which is a sub-set of the large church. A better way to view it is a gathering of small groups. The congregation is a group of people that ranges in size from 20-150 people and provides the following advantages:

- People have the opportunity to interact with others in the church that are outside of their small groups.
- It relieves some of the pressure of group multiplication. Group members will realize that they can still relate to old group members on a regular basis after a new group has been formed with existing members.
- New people to the church can explore relationships with others and determine where they would like to connect on a deeper level and even choose a small group to join based on these social connections.
- The unchurched often find such gatherings less threatening than a Sunday worship service or a small group meeting in a home.
- Small groups that are a part of the same congregation can work together to accomplish a task that is bigger than one group can do (such as a missions trip, intercessory prayer initiatives, or outreach events).

Mid-sized group gatherings are built into the structures of some of the major small group models around the world. For instance, the Groups of 12 model holds network gatherings once per month that connect people within a network of small groups. These networks are comprised of people within the G-12 network of a staff pastor. Therefore, the pastor overseeing the women's network would hold a monthly women's meeting. The same would be the case for the men, youth and other networks. As a church grows, there would be more than one staff pastor overseeing women's groups, therefore more than one women's network. The same would be true of the men's network or the youth network or the like. This would mean that a large church would hold multiple women's network meetings every month to maintain the ability to connect people socially at this level.

Pantego Bible Church in Fort Worth, Texas is another example of a church that connects people socially. In this model, groups of 50 to 75 people gather every week on Sunday mornings during the Sunday school hour. At this level, people from different small groups connect with one another as neighbors. Many of these people will have been in previous groups together. Therefore, groups that multiply have a place to connect socially, and they don't feel the sense of loss compared to those groups that don't have such a venue. This strategy works well in churches that emphasize Sunday school.

Other churches connect networks of small groups on a less frequent basis, usually quarterly. They might have a special baptismal service, a picnic, or do a mass service project for the community. Some have a regular men's and women's prayer breakfast, a youth service, and a college service. All of these meetings accomplish the goal of connecting people socially.

Congregational or mid-sized group meetings are most essential in churches of more than 200 because people in small churches connect on a social level every week. The problem is that most small churches stop at this level. They don't go any deeper than "small-talk" relationships. They don't open up about their personal and intimate lives, sharing their hidden struggles or covered fears. These churches feel good because no one pries into anyone's business. In addition, people step up and support one another during times of celebration (marriage and birth) and crisis (sickness and death). But they don't get involved with one another in the mundane daily stuff of life. Social relationships are important but they are not nearly enough.

Connecting People in the Personal Space

Small groups are the most logical place for people to move into personal connections with others. However, the reality is that most small group members will only connect socially, especially during group formation. Group members will gather each week looking to make friends. They want neighbors and they are checking out the other group members to determine if they want to open up their lives to one another and become more personal. Some groups remain at the social level because the group members, for whatever reason, do not want to move into the personal space with one another.

At the same time, as people are given the freedom to connect socially with others in a small group, some—if not many—will enter into the personal space and become family for one another. For a group to move from the social space to the personal space, the group members must move through the stages of group development. No group will immediately jump into the personal space of community. At first, it will need to form as a group. It will go through a process where the group members get to know one another. During the forming stage, people assume that they like each other because they have not spent enough time together to reveal any faults.

Then comes the storming stage, or as M. Scott Peck calls it, chaos. After a group has been together for six to eight weeks, the group members will start rubbing each other the wrong way. Jim will tell an offensive joke or Tom will show up late to the meeting repeatedly. Cathy will whine and complain repeatedly about the same issue while Tammie is just "too happy" all the time. When people rub up against one another, they will rub the wrong way. Group members have a choice. They can ignore what they feel and stuff their feelings. This is the only option for many Christians in small groups. They ignore the personal issue at hand and the group cannot enter into the personal space. Or they can be offended and hold a grudge against the offender. This only heightens the chaos, and many times it leads to gossip and slander. The best solution is for the group members to deal with the issue, to talk it out, and to forgive one another.

When group members choose to work through the chaos of the storm, it will enter into the norming stage, which is a period of community. This is the time a group becomes family for one another. Members become comfortable and lower their defensive postures. They share more openly and reveal their needs. Transparency that is found in community feels good, but it does not come naturally. Therefore, the group leader must model the kind of transparency that he or she wants the group to experience. Group members will rarely become more transparent than the leader.

Connecting People in the Intimate Space

Naked intimacy requires such a high level of trust that small groups don't often attain it. While such sharing at this level is encouraged in small groups, it is not always appropriate. For instance, if a man reveals his struggle with lust in the presence of women, it can cause a great deal of discomfort. I was leading a group with a member who struggled with homosexual patterns. He shared his secret with me and one other person, but he did not reveal his pain and shame to the entire group. He was not ready to share his struggle that openly and the other group members were not ready to learn of his struggle. In this situation, confiding in one or two other men in the group was appropriate.

Many churches facilitate intimate connections through the use of accountability partners. Some churches provide mentors for new or immature Christians where they can share intimate struggles. Ralph Neighbour has addressed this issue in his book, *Mentoring Another Christian*. Another common pattern is to help group members form prayer triads. Neil Cole calls these Life Transformation Groups in his book, *Cultivating a Life for God*. One church has adopted this prayer triad pattern, labeling them mini-groups.

However a church might facilitate intimate connections, it must be recognized that intimacy like this cannot be forced or contrived. It must occur naturally. The reality is that my intimate connections might not be with others within my small group. I might lead one group but share intimate space with a leader of another group. Someone in my group might be best friends with a member in another group. The ideal would be for these people to be in the same small group, but this is not always possible.

How Webs Are Constructed

When a person is connected on these four levels, she creates a web of relationships. Spiders are meticulous about how they construct their webs. They should be; it is where they live. When a spider locates a good place to build a home, it will string a series of lines marking the outer limits of the web it wants to create. Then it will work toward the center from the outside. It is impossible to work from the inside out because the center of the web is supported by the anchor lines that form the outer limits of the web. At the same time, the center of the web is the most crucial. It is the point where the spider has strung the lines with the most density, therefore being the place where it receives its sustenance.

The same is true of a relational web that a church wants to create. The center of the web—personal and intimate relationships—are the spaces of life where we receive the greatest support and spiritual nutrition. At these levels, we are able to deal with specific issues in our lives, whereas at the public and social levels, the issues are more general. At the same time, the center is dependent upon the building of strong outer limits and support lines. Effective personal and intimate relationships in the church depend upon the relationships established at the public and social levels.

What does this mean for the development of small group community? The public experience of the large group worship should focus on inviting. By inviting people into deeper connections, the large group worship service becomes a venue for mobilizing people as opposed to serving as an end to itself. As people are mobilized to connect, the web will be constructed and filled in. At that point, people will enter the web through all four levels of connection. In fact, spiders catch most of their flies at the center of the web, not the edges.

My Last Word

Entering community in a culture defined by individualism can be quite risky for people. And telling these individualists that community only comes in the form of small groups can actually drive them away from the journey into community. However, when we see how we connect on four different levels, churches can then facilitate the journey so that individuals can take gradual steps that will allow them to redefine how they view church and rethink what participating in church looks like.

Invest Relationally in Group Leaders

During my third year of college, I served as an overseer of seven different small group leaders, playing the role of their coach. Because I had recently repented and was baptized, I was in a great place of humility before God and others. I started off humbly, but what kept me there was the student minister who met with me every week. I looked forward to those meetings with her because she prayed, encouraged, and listened to me. As a result, I had a lot of energy to minister to my small group leaders, and I was never short on resources.

During the following year, I served as the student president of the ministry with about twenty-nine other students on my team. My overseer that year had some significant medical problems and was only able to meet with me about four times during the entire year. I did not receive the same kind of prayer, encouragement, feedback and direction I had before. I did not have someone listening to my heart and guiding me. As a result, that year of ministry was very frustrating. I felt alone and I made some significant mistakes that could have been easily avoided if I had someone guiding me.

These two years of ministry illustrate two ways of overseeing group leaders. Fortunately, as I have led groups since this experience, I have had someone personally investing in me. I never want to repeat the frustrating experience of being thrown out into a leadership opportunity with little more than a hope and a prayer. And I don't want those I oversee to miss out on the power of relational investment and the positive impact it can have on one's ministry.

Structural Myth #8:
Small group leaders will flourish when they are managed
properly by coaches and pastors.

The Relational Truth:
In God's relational kingdom, small group leaders need
someone who invests in them to empower them for mission.

A Management System

When you visit your local McDonald's and order your favorite French fries, your main concern is with the speed of delivery and the taste of your fries. You don't really care about the steps involved to cook those fries or even who cooked them. As a customer, you are only concerned about the end product. But if you were to purchase a McDonald's franchise, your concerns would change. You would discover that the quality of the fries and the speed in which they are delivered depends on things that the customer cannot see. There are written procedures in official manuals for cooking fries that must be followed. On a more important level, there are team leaders who oversee those who cook the fries and then store managers who make sure that all of the elements are in place to deliver the best possible food as quickly as possible. Without these team leaders and managers, the front line workers will get sidetracked, lose sight of the vision, or just get tired and quit. They need the support, direction and encouragement of the team leaders and managers.

The management of small groups is clearly of greater significance than the cooking of French fries. Yet, fast food companies understand its importance while the church seems to miss the point. I am quite concerned about what is happening across North America in the small group world. Churches are jumping on the small group bandwagon, buying up curricula to start as many groups as possible. Some of the pastors of these churches have called me saying, "I have 30 groups as a result of a recent 40-day small group focus; what do I do now?" The question is based on the assumption that they only need to instruct the group leaders in what to do and what to teach. The question ignores the development of team leaders and managers to oversee and support these group leaders. It is easy to start lots of groups. It takes much more effort to establish a support infrastructure of team leaders and managers that will ensure that these groups will still be healthy and growing a year from now.

Same Song, Fourth Verse

This pattern is nothing new. When pastors traveled to South Korea in the 1970's to learn about Yoido Full Gospel Church, they returned to America with a clear understanding that small groups should be a priority. They started as many groups as possible, expecting to see the miraculous growth like they saw in Korea. A few years after starting the groups, the church decided that small groups were nothing but a failed experiment. The same thing happened in the 1980's with the home Bible study movement and even in the 1990's as pastors jumped on the cell church wave. I followed the journey of one church of 1,500 that retooled everything around small groups. They developed over 160 groups expecting continued growth. However, they failed to raise up enough coaches (overseers of three to eight groups) and pastors (overseers of 20-50 groups with three to twelve coaches) to support these leaders. As a result, they lost almost 100 groups due to leader burnout and frustration.

Searching for the Right System

Groups of 12, 5x5, the Cho model, Purpose-Driven groups, Meta-church, Free-market groups. How do you know which one works best? In 1512, Ponce De Leon came to the new lands of America, looking for the fountain of youth. He sold a bunch of men a bill of goods, convincing them of the existence of a nectar that would restore youthful vigor. In the church today, the search for this magical nectar has continued. Many have touted their small group model as the church's proverbial fountain of youth. They make claims that they have found the New Testament model, promising everything from transformation of one's church to unlimited exponential growth. The multitudes of Abraham will be yours!

Sadly, many fall for such a sales pitch because they want to see the kingdom come. But there is no fountain of youth, no silver bullet, and no oceanfront property in Arizona. The "perfect" small group model is nothing but a myth.

Regularly, pastors ask me, "Which oversight structure should I adopt? Which one is the best?" Such questions assume that there is a predetermined oversight model that they can lay over their churches and implement with little difficulty. When they find such a model, they will fill positions with capable people. However, these people will probably not possess the skills or the experience to fulfill the role they have been given. As a result, they do their duties and manage the people they oversee, making sure they do their jobs. In this situation, the management duties are being fulfilled but the system lacks life or what may be better described as direction.

Just because a small group management system works in one church does not mean that it will fit elsewhere. In no place in the Bible do we see a one-size-fits-all oversight system. The closest we come to such a system is in Exodus 18, where Moses is overwhelmed meeting with the people all day long. His father-in-law, Jethro, observes the lack of wisdom of such leadership given by Moses and he advises him saying,

> What you are doing is not good. You and these people who come to you will only wear yourselves out. The work is too heavy for you; you cannot handle it alone. Listen now to me and I will give you some advice, and may God be with you. You must be the people's representative before God and bring their disputes to him. Teach them the decrees and laws, and show them the way to live and the duties they are to perform. But select capable men from all the people—men who fear God, trustworthy men who hate dishonest gain—and appoint them as officials over thousands, hundreds, fifties and tens. Have them serve as judges for the people at all times, but have them bring every difficult case to you; the simple cases they can decide themselves. That will make your load lighter, because they will share it with you. If you do this and God so commands, you will be able to stand the strain, and all these people will go home satisfied.

Moses then set up a management system for the people of Israel based on Jethro's advice. But we cannot assume that this system is transcultural and that it is the only oversight system that will ever be effective. At best, it highlights that Moses established four levels of leadership under his direction (more on these four levels below).

Beyond Management

On a trip to Illinois to train small group leaders, I stayed in the home of a small group coach. In his former role, he led a very successful small group and had been promoted to oversee five other small group leaders. He shared, "I feel quite frustrated with my new role. I don't feel that I am touching people any more. I am only managing others who touch people."

This man's frustration is not unique. Good small group leaders don't particularly like playing the role of middle management. They are expected to check up on leaders and make sure that they do their jobs, secure reports and attend middle management meetings. In this role, they feel that they have been removed from the front lines of ministry.

The role of a manager of group leaders can feel disempowering, especially when one saw God do incredible things every week. While there are definitely aspects of a coaches role that require management, the most important aspect of the coach's role is not management in orientation. Instead, a coach has a different kind of "front-line" ministry. She is called to invest relationally into the lives of small group leaders. This is true, regardless of the organization structure that a church adopts. Whether you adopt the 5x5 oversight structure of the Elim Church in El Salvador with over 140,000 people, the G-12 structure of the International Charismatic Mission with over 20,000 small groups, or any of the other creative oversight structures across the globe, it is effective not because of the structure or because of middle management. It works because of relational investment by pastors and coaches in the lives of the group leaders.

Why is such relational investment so crucial? Small group leaders will care for their people in the same way that they are being cared for. If the pastor trains and appoints leaders and only talks with them when they see a problem, how do you think those leaders will care for their groups? Barring exceptions, they will lead their groups every week, perform their minimal duties and only address issues of concern as they arise. They won't be actively involved in the lives of their group members, because no one in leadership is actively involved in their lives.

I recently spoke at a church's small group leader's meeting where we asked all of the uncoached leaders present to raise their hands so that we could meet with them in another room. Only two were present, and this church had about 40 small group leaders that were uncoached. We assumed that the uncoached leaders would attend the meeting because they were not getting help from a coach. Just the opposite is true. Those who receive relational investment want more of it. They seek out wise counsel, follow direction better and work as a team voluntarily. Those who don't have a relationship with a coach or pastor feel that they must lead in autonomy.

Relational investment is a broad term that includes many different aspects. At times, the one investing might serve as a mentor, providing very practical instructions on how to do ministry. At other times, he or she might play the role of spiritual advisor, giving godly counsel about personal situations. Sometimes, this kind of investment calls for life coaching, which comes in the form of practical life guidance. Primarily the role is that of listening to what God is doing in the leader's life, trying to facilitate what God is already doing and helping the leader listen to God.

We don't learn how to do life in a classroom. Jesus did not teach the disciples the kingdom of God through one-hour lectures. He demonstrated the kingdom and then mentored them in the ways of that kingdom. These men then repeated the process after Jesus ascended and the Holy Spirit filled them. While the communication gifts of teaching and preaching are crucial in the church, we cannot depend upon them as the sole means of equipping the church for ministry. The lecture model of teaching is a Greek concept, one based upon the eloquent communication of abstract principles to a broad range of people.

The Hebraic concept of teaching has a much broader application. While it includes verbal communication to masses of people, it is focused much more on mentoring or the passing down of a spiritual heritage to those less mature in the faith. This is illustrated in Moses' relationship with Joshua and Elijah's tutelage of Elisha. Paul instructed Timothy, *"And the things you have heard me say in the presence of many witnesses entrust to reliable men who will also be qualified to teach others"* (2 Tim. 2:2). Without the mentoring component, the teaching will have no practical meaning. Therefore, those being taught without a mentor will lack the ability to implement the truths spoken.

Paul writes, *"Even though you have ten thousand guardians in Christ, you do not have many fathers, for in Christ Jesus I became your father through the gospel. Therefore I urge you to imitate me"* (1 Cor. 4:15). The Greek word *paidagogos*, translated in the NIV as "guardian," has no direct translation into English. It was a word used for a slave or paid attendant who had the responsibility of caring for the children as they went to and from school.

They had the paid duty of overseeing their education, but not the investment of a father. The *paidagogos* corrected the children, but many different people could play this role. In this passage, Paul writes that the Corinthian church has had thousands upon thousands of such "educational guardians," but his relationship with them is different. He had birthed something in them becoming a father to them. Fathers set an example in life and deed for others to follow, mentors of a way of living. For this reason he called them to imitate him and not get distracted by the many Christian "educational guardians."

Point to Christ

When Paul said, *"Follow my example, as I follow the example of Christ,"* he was not seeking to connect his spiritual children to himself. They were to imitate him only as he imitated Christ. They were not to become like Paul; they were to be like Christ as Paul had set the example.

When I first started learning about mentoring, I interpreted Paul's statement in I Corinthians 11:1 this way: *"Be like me; do ministry my way."* I falsely assumed that I had to become like those who mentored me and those I mentored had to become like me. In my life, this resulted in frustration. I could not tell stories as good as one of my mentors. I could not talk to lost people as naturally as another. And I only placed unrealistic expectations upon the leaders I mentored.

Then I remembered something I overheard my father say while growing up on a farm. In my early teens, I remember him telling a friend, "I will support Scott in whatever he chooses to do in life." That was a very freeing statement for me. While it would have been very natural for me to enter my father's vocation, I realized that I did not have to follow him into his profession in order to receive his love and acceptance, or to learn how to do life from him. He demonstrated the truth that parenting is about helping the children become who God created them to be.

The job of a spiritual father or mother is to point children to Christ. Many mentors falter or fail at this point in the relationship. They become advice givers to their spiritual children or the experts, making the children dependent upon them. This hinders the spiritual development of the children. Such mentoring tries to connect the leader to the mentor, rather than equip the leader to hear from Christ.

The way God moves through me to minister in a small group is not the same as the way he moves through others. I cannot force my personality and giftings on someone just because it works for me. My job as a mentor is to help a future leader discover how God moves through him or her. Fathers and mothers rejoice in the uniqueness of their children. Small group pastors and coaches must empower group leaders to walk in the ways God made them. This plan gives the leaders the freedom to be themselves without an expectation to follow some ideal model of leadership.

Elijah mentored Elisha, helping him move from being a farmer to a mighty prophet. In fact, Elisha asked for a double portion of the spirit that was on Elijah. Such a request did not threaten Elijah because he had the heart of a father. He wanted his spiritual son to advance further. As a result, Elisha performed exactly twice as many miracles as Elijah.

While at times spiritual parenting will include the giving of specific instructions and even advice, more important is the impartation of spiritual know-how, which releases the Spirit of God to move through the one being mentored in even greater ways than the mentor has seen or known. Small group leaders need someone who will invest in their lives with the pure desire to see that leader succeed in both life and ministry. The excellent mentor will show them the ways of living and leading in Christ, not just give them advice or share how it has worked in the past.[1]

Life Investment

Fathering and mothering involves much more than showing people how to do something. Many small group pastors and coaches miss this point. They become trapped in a performance mode, thinking that the key to successful small group ministry is to focus on the practical how to's of leadership. This would be like a natural father only talking to his son about making money without concern for his personal well-being.

Spiritual parents have a heart for the whole person. They are not just concerned about how well the small group meetings are going. Their scope of care extends beyond the numeric attendance at the small group each week. They ask questions about the person as much as they ask about the person's ministry. Without such an investment, the small group leader will eventually feel used and become used up. Their reservoir will run dry and they will lose the ability to be spiritual parents to their group members.

This does not mean that the small group coach who oversees the small group leader must become the only mentor of that leader. No one person can mentor another in all the skills they need. This would connect that leader to the coach, not to Christ. God might use the investment of a coach to help a leader through one problem, a pastor to deal with another issue, and a friend for yet another. I have had many spiritual parents in my walk with Christ. But the most effective ones demonstrated a primary concern for me personally followed by a secondary concern for my ministry. Those who were only concerned about what I was doing in my ministry fell short of true spiritual parenting.

A few years ago, I met with my pastor and shared what was going on in my life. I assumed that I was meeting with him to share how I could contribute to the church, as I had considerable small group leadership experience. Instead, he focused on what God was doing in my life and recommended a time of personal reflection and retreat with God. I thought he would suggest ways to plug me into a new role in the church. Instead, he listened to my heart and listened to how God wanted to minister to my heart. He then said I should take a personal prayer retreat and even organized the venue for me.

To help facilitate this experience with the leaders within the small group system at the church where I serve, we have developed four questions that act as guidelines of interaction between pastors and coaches with their leaders. These questions are:

1. How is your time with God?
2. What has God been showing you in his Word?
3. What is going on in your leadership life?
4. How can I support you in your life?

These questions seek to demonstrate interest in both the life of the leader as well as her leadership and ministry activities. It should go without saying that we do not use the questions ritualistically or ask them verbatim. Instead, we printed these questions on a card and gave them to our coaches and leaders. As a result, they know to expect that our conversations with them will get around to talking about these four topics.

Missional Investment

Beyond leader management and personal investment into leaders is a God-centered, missional investment. God's mission for the leaders we mentor is the ultimate purpose. After all, people are the end goal of his mission. In Jesus' ministry, God's kingdom reign reveals that people are more important than rituals and rules.[2] Therefore people are not a means to an end. People are not a means to the demonstration of the kingdom. The kingdom comes to restore people into communion with the king, thereby restoring community with one another and contagion within the culture.

Therefore, leaders should not be developed for the maintenance or continuance of the church with all of its programs and rituals and rules. Leaders participate with God in leading because they matter to God. God seeks deeper relationships with people and invites people to walk with him in leadership roles so that he might commune with them on deeper levels. This is the heart of our relational God.

The purpose of relational investment is to release people into a missional partnership with God. When leaders join God in his mission, they get in on the God life in entirely new ways. They discover what God is doing in this world and how it does not always fit into the confines of the rules and rituals established by the church. David Bosch writes, "Mission therefore means being involved in the ongoing dialogue between God who offers his salvation, and the world, which—enmeshed in all kinds of evil—craves that salvation."[3] The job of those who oversee other leaders, then, is a much more expansive and grander calling than growing the small group ministry. It is a call to invest in leaders so that they might enter the dialogue with God on more intimate and deeper levels.

Recently, a coach stepped down in our church to re-think her life. She asked me and another pastor, "If I were to step back into a role of leadership, where would you see me fitting?" I replied, "I am not concerned about filling positions. The need for more leaders will always be present. I am much more concerned about helping you listen to what God is doing in your life during this season. While we value your contribution, we value you more. As pastors, we want to help you listen to God's call on your life. And for some reason that does not happen as quickly as we would like."

I don't have a predetermined small group plan that everyone must fit into or a long list of jobs to fill. I have a vision for groups that live out the vision for Upward, Inward, Outward and Forward. What this looks like can take many different forms. I want to hear what God is doing in the hearts of our church's leaders. When I help our leaders discover this, it is then easy to facilitate their entering a new mission with God.

What Does this Mean ... Practically?

Most churches launch their small group system with fewer than ten groups. Because most churches in America have fewer than 100 people, they often start with one or two groups. In such cases, the senior pastor acts as the mentor of these groups. If he adopts the relational principles outlined in this book, he will bear much fruit from his investment. The groups will grow numerically and spiritually. Two groups become three, which become five, which become seven and even ten or twelve.

Then something happens. Growth plateaus. The groups struggle. Leaders report back that they are tired and frustrated. The pastor hears stories about group members falling away and attendance is now decreasing.

At this point, the senior pastor often hires a small group pastor. This often helps, as he or she can invest more time into the lives of the leaders. The groups turn around and they start growing again, reaching about 18 in number. But then the growth plateaus again and the spiritual struggle repeats itself.

When a church has a small number of groups, relational investment can occur in ad hoc, random ways. The pastor has time to be the primary mentor for all of the leaders. But as the groups grow, he has to spread the same amount of time across a greater number of leaders. Therefore, a relational investment system is required. If a church waits until they need such a system, they are already losing the game. The development of this system must be considered from the very beginning.

Leadership Power

Many organizational oversight systems are based upon a philosophy of leadership that exudes power over the people at lower levels. "Power-over" systems are based upon the ability to inflict some kind of pain or punishment upon those who challenge or defy the authority of the overseer.[4]

This is the basic power presupposition of the kingdom of this world. World governments and secular organizations operate within the paradigm that one must gain power over others in order to attain one's goals. In some cases, church leadership systems adopt this approach. The pastor is clearly the one who controls the ship. He makes the decisions about how things will work and those who work on the staff or serve as volunteers are expected to follow his command. If this is the only kind of relational investment provided for a church's small group leaders, then the impact will be limited. In fact, the leaders will see their service as a duty to perform to please God and their pastors.

Jesus taught a different perspective, one that could be labeled "power-under." He explained to his disciples about how they were to relate to one another in Matthew 20:25-28. It reads as follows:

> Jesus called them together and said, "You know that the rulers of the Gentiles lord it over them, and their high officials exercise authority over them. Not so with you. Instead, whoever wants to become great among you must be your servant, and whoever wants to be first must be your slave— just as the Son of Man did not come to be served, but to serve, and to give his life as a ransom for many."

Jesus modeled a philosophy of power that understood where true power is realized. Jesus, as the image of God, demonstrated the way God works with people. He did not lord over the people, demanding that they align themselves with his agenda. Instead, he chose to serve and sacrifice himself so that people might realize the true source of power, thus demonstrating the nature of power within the kingdom of God. Power-under addresses the need for a change of heart, where someone changes from the inside out, while power-over only has the ability to address a change in actions.

Clearly, Jesus lived the philosophy of power-under in dealing with the kingdom of this world. This is demonstrated in his relationships with the Pharisees and Sadducees, others who rejected him, and the political leaders of the time (Herod and Pilate). He never forced his agenda upon them. They operated from a power-over perspective while he lived out a power-under worldview.

At the same time, when the metaphor of power-under is applied to

Jesus' leadership of the disciples and his other followers, there is potential for misunderstanding this principle. Some might apply the power-under to leadership and assume that a leader's duty is to cater to the whim of those he or she leads. In other words, the leader's power-under role is to be nice and supportive, never challenging, nor confronting. Some have misapplied this view of power under to their expectations of a pastor or volunteer leader in the church. For instance, if a volunteer leader proposes an idea to a pastor that does not fit the vision, that pastor has the duty of redirecting the idea or even rejecting it totally. If the volunteer leader misunderstands the power-under principle, this pastor could be labeled as being controlling or accused of playing the power-over game, even though the pastor was trying to serve as a steward of the vision of the church.

When we examine Jesus' leadership of his followers, we find that he too sought to protect the vision of the kingdom. The disciples had ideas about how he could lead the coming kingdom. They did not understand why he would go to Jerusalem. Yet Jesus did not allow them to dictate how he led them. He was no pushover. In fact, if we examine the passage from Matthew quoted above we will find three parallel clauses:

1. Those who want to be great will be a servant.
2. Those who want to be first will be a slave.
3. The Son of Man came to serve and be a ransom for many.

If we take the first two in isolation and interpret the meaning of "being great" and "being first" according to modern cultural definitions we'd miss his point. In most cultures, to be a servant or slave means that there is a boss. When combined with the power-under principle, some would interpret this to mean that a leader's role in the church is to lead people in the direction they already want to go, to facilitate what they already want to do.

However, when the third clause is added to the mix, it defines what Jesus meant by servant and slave. "The Son of Man came to serve and be a ransom for many." Jesus filled these words with his meaning as he demonstrated servanthood. He did not serve those he led the way they wanted to be served. He challenged. He confronted. He led them to Jerusalem. He made a fool of himself in their eyes. And then he went to the cross. Those who followed Jesus had an agenda for him. They tried to steer him clear of the direction he knew that he had to go. Nevertheless, he led them where they did not want to go. This type of leadership could be labeled "power-before."

When pastors and coaches practice relational investment with their small group leaders, their role is to lead that leader and his or her group down paths that they would not necessarily go on their own. Traveling these paths can be done through power-over, but the long-term impact will be limited. Instead, leaders are called to operate in a power-before approach. Leaders go before those they lead, demonstrating the way into the kingdom of God. Yes, they support others the way Jesus did through power-under, but they also call people into a new life by setting the standard and proposing new ways to enter into that life. They don't wait for people to suddenly discover that they want to embrace a new vision. They invite small group leaders and small groups into this new life and show them how to live it. This is power-before leadership.

Four Investment Roles

Power-before leadership establishes a way of living for others to follow. It sets a course toward the manifestation of the kingdom of God. Previously we read Exodus 18, which outlined how Moses organized the oversight of the people of God. He appointed four different roles, leaders of 1,000's, 100's, 50's and 10's. While there is no supernatural power in this structure, all of the major small group oversight structures are organized around four basic roles. The specific numbers overseen in each structure vary from church to church, but the roles are very similar. To illustrate how these four roles work, let's use a diagram that demonstrates movement toward the kingdom of God.

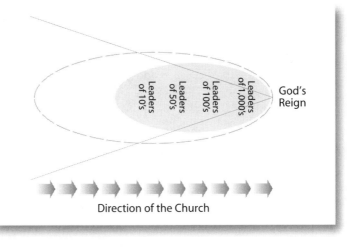

Direction of the Church

By visualizing leadership roles as moving before the people into the life of the kingdom, we can imagine leaders within a church are called to practices and disciplines that exemplify life in the kingdom. The grey circle in the diagram represents those who have committed not to leadership positions, but to a way of living that puts the kingdom on display. While the entire church is called to this, those who are in leadership are called to demonstrate a model of leadership, one that emulates the way Jesus demonstrated leadership to the disciples.

While there is no space to do a thorough explication of these four leadership roles—and I have written about the practical ways these roles are best practiced elsewhere[5]—it is important to provide a basic outline of how people in these roles go before the people to live out the kingdom of God. (To do this, I depend upon Bill Beckham's summary of these roles in his book, *Redefining Revival.*)

Most churches do an effective job of performing the role of vision and direction because that is what the senior pastor does. Most are also doing a good job of recruiting and training group leaders to implement that vision. But the roles of the small group coach and the small group pastor are the most misunderstood and neglected in the church.

The Role of Missional Direction

At the front of every vision is a visionary. For visions to become reality, it requires leaders who will facilitate the vision. Small group leaders follow visions that arise from leaders who seek the face of God. When a church lacks a clear vision of their mission, the small group leaders will lack a sense of direction. As a result, they will wander aimlessly, doing what is right in their own eyes. The missional leader—described in chapter four—provides this sense of vision of what the church is supposed to be. Bill Beckham finds that those who play this role do the following things:[6]

1. Coordinate the administration of the church.
2. Cast the vision.
3. Birth the concepts.
4. Model the basic task.
5. Mentor the small group pastors.
6. Provide vision for growth.
7. Facilitate the five-fold gifts.
8. Oversee celebration.

The Role of Small Group Pastoring

The small group pastor supports and guides small group leaders. (How many they oversee depends upon the structure the church adopts. More on those options below.) This person provides a big umbrella of spiritual covering for the small groups, leaders, and members. This covering allows them to fully enter into the vision God has given the church. Practically speaking, this person recruits and trains new leaders, raises up small group coaches, and helps groups and leaders deal with their problems. He or she—some of the best small group pastors are female, by the way—acts as a shepherd to all the people within the groups under his or her care. The coaches and group leaders are under-shepherds, helping him or her pastor and direct the sheep in the direction of the vision. Bill Beckham observes that a person in the role of small group pastor will:

1. Lead the flock.
2. Plan for expansion in an area.
3. Counsel leaders and members.
4. Train leaders.
5. Equip members (through special equipping encounters).
6. Shape growth in the designated area.
7. Mentor the leaders over 50's.
8. Serve as a link to the whole church.

Because most churches are under 100 people, the senior pastor will play both the visionary role and the small group pastor role. As a church grows over the 200 mark, the senior pastor should pray that the Lord would raise up someone to fill the role of the small group pastor. The best place to find such a person is within the congregation: a person who has proven himself as an effective group leader and coach. It is very difficult to hire someone from another church or from a seminary and make it work. Small group pastors that serve in such capacities in other churches are fulfilling their callings in their current churches. They know the importance of long-term investment and are not looking to go somewhere else. In most cases, seminary students learn how to lead churches in patterns that do not fit the kind of ministry required to pastor people in small groups. Seminaries are great for preparing preachers and teachers, along with administrators of programs such as Sunday school. But few seminaries provide the practical experiences or the course work that would equip students to step in to a church and effectively serve in this role. (See my book, *How Do We Get There From Here?*, pp. 350-359 for more information on this role.)

The Role of Small Group Coaching

The small group coach is called to invest life into a few leaders, usually no more than five (the G-12 system promotes 12). This person has proven himself to be an effective small group leader and has the heart and skills to pass on his experiences to other group leaders. Dr. Jim Egli performed extensive statistical research to determine what kinds of things actually impacted the health and growth of small groups. He found that no other action, including training and prayer, had the kind of impact that coaching has when he mentors and supports a small group leader. Joel Comiskey writes in his book *How to Be a Great Cell Group Coach*, "A cell coach equips cell leaders with the tools, knowledge, and opportunities they need to develop themselves and become more effective. A cell coach encourages, nourishes, and challenges cell leaders to grow and multiply their cell groups."[7] Beckham outlines the role of a coach as:

1. Shepherding two to five small group leaders.
2. Providing quality control for small group life and ministry.
3. Providing trouble shooting as needed by group leaders.
4. Being the eyes and ears for the small group pastor.
5. Mentoring small group leaders.
6. Affirming the selection of small group assistants
   (interns or apprentices).

The best place to find coaches is to look at the best small group leaders in a church. Appointing those who currently hold a position like "elder" or "deacon" rarely works. If they have not experienced success by actually leading a group through multiplication, they will not know what to give those they are coaching.

Excursus: The Groups of 12 Model (G-12)

Before proceeding, I must digress and address a popular myth that is being promoted about the G-12 model of small group oversight. Many highlight it as being quite unique compared to the other small group models. While it is true that it does include some distinctive practices, it is built upon the same principles of all the other effective small group models around the world and contains all four levels of leadership.

For example, the Groups of 12 model emphasizes the development of groups of small group leaders, which form a "Group of 12." A Group of 12 is not an open small group, but a closed leadership group comprised of leaders of open small groups. The G-12 leader then performs the role of a small group coach, a role that is also present in all other models. The difference is that, in the G-12 model, small group leaders attend their G-12 meeting every week, meaning that they lead an open small group every week and attend a leadership meeting every week. This weekly coach's meeting is a practice or method. The principle, however, is quality coaching—and there are many different ways to effectively coach group leaders.

Another difference in the G-12 model is the emphasis placed on the number 12. All small group leaders are encouraged to develop a group of 12 leaders by helping their small group members start their own groups. This emphasis places special significance on the number 12, claiming to follow the model that Jesus established. While the number 12 does carry special significance in biblical theology, it was never established as a practice of the New Testament church. We have no evidence that Peter, Paul, or John ever developed 12 disciples under them. The focus on the number 12 is a practice, not a principle.

At the same time, this practice does point out two important principles. First, small group leaders can become coaches of the small group members they raise up to start new groups. Second, the coach should work with as many leaders as he is able to support successfully. In some cultures, 12 are possible, but in many contexts to ask busy volunteer leaders to oversee 12 small groups (120 people) is too much. Three to five is much more manageable, resulting in G-3's or G-5's.[8]

Developing an Investment Model that Fits Your Church

Relational investment is passing down the life of God from fathers to sons, from mothers to daughters. It is the impartation of the Spirit to faithful men and women who can care for other people. Relational investment flows through the four roles of an effective small group system—vision direction, small group pastoring, small group coaching, and small group implementation. When a church first starts small groups, developing an extensive oversight structure won't be crucial because there will only be a handful of groups. The senior pastor can provide the mentoring and spiritual parenting. But when a church starts five to ten groups, it will prove crucial to begin formalizing an oversight structure.

If a church launches its small group initiative with more than five groups, it is paramount to develop an oversight structure from the beginning. The problem churches encounter in such situations is that the people in oversight positions won't have the experience of actually leading a small group, and therefore find it difficult to speak into the lives of those leading the groups. Determining the structure is crucial, but if the people in that structure don't understand how to mentor others, then it matters very little what kind of structure you develop.

Most churches venture into small groups with an affinity toward one model or another. Some prefer 5x5 as exhibited by the Elim Church. Others prefer the oversight structure of Cho's model that is similar to the 5x5 but slightly different. Many are embracing the G-12 model developed by International Charismatic Mission. Still others are following the principles of the G-12 model and developing a hybrid like the G-12.3 model. The question of the day is: How do you know which model will work best for your church, in your culture, and with your leadership style?

Key Questions for Understanding the Models

Many become confused when they study the different oversight models and get lost in the details. To describe the fine points of each model and compare the methods of operation would require a 200-page book. As an introduction to this topic, I will describe the basic oversight structure, and then I will break down the differences with a few key questions. This discussion may prove more helpful to you than trying to figure out the exact differences between the models. If you understand these questions, you will be able to develop your own oversight structure, following the leadership of the Holy Spirit.

These questions come in two categories: core and peripheral. The core questions define the essential differences between the models. The peripheral questions are those that often characterize a model but are not required to follow. For instance, some have assumed that the 5x5 model is the geographic model and the G-12 model organizes groups around affinity. While this is typical, by no means is it true for all churches organized with these models. It is a category mistake to say that 5x5 must organize groups geographically and the G12 must do so around affinity or gender. This is illustrated by the fact that the Meta-Church model embraces a 5x5 structure which is not based on geography but on the type of group (task group, service group, choir group, just to name a few). Therefore, when establishing your oversight structure, start with the core questions and then move to the periphery.

Three Basic Structures

While there is a great deal of creativity within churches as to how they organize group oversight, there are three basic structures that guide most of the creativity.

Five by Five (5x5)

In the structure illustrated below, a coach oversees five group leaders and a staff pastor oversees up to five coaches. Therefore, a full-time staff pastor would oversee up to twenty-five groups. In larger churches, another level is added, sometimes called a district pastor. This person would oversee up to five staff pastors or 125 groups.

	People	Groups	
District Pastor	1250	125	
Small Group Pastor	250	25	
Coach	50	5	
Group Leader	10	1	

Groups of 12 (G-12)

The International Charismatic Mission in Bogotá, Colombia developed the structure illustrated at the top of the next page. It is called "Groups of 12" because the goal of each coach—called a G-12 leader—is to develop 12 small group leaders. When this goal has been reached, this coach then reports to an overseer—usually a staff pastor—who has developed a network of 12 coaches. Therefore, a coach (G-12 leader) would oversee up to 12 groups or 144 people and a pastor up to 144 groups or 1,728 people.

	People	Groups	
District Pastor	20,000	1,728	
Small Group Pastor	1,728	144	
Coach	144	12	
Group Leader	3-12	1	

G-12.3

This structure illustrated below is an organic combination of both the 5x5 and the Groups of 12 models. In this structure, the coach would develop three small group leaders, while reporting to a staff pastor who oversees up to 12 coaches. This structure does not fixate upon numbers the way the G-12 model dictates. If a person has capacity to coach more than three groups, then they are freed to do so.

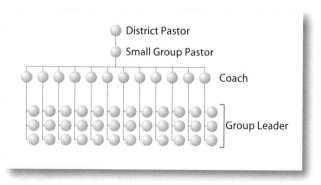

Core Questions

How many leaders does the coach oversee?

In the G-12 model, the coach will mentor up to 12 small group leaders. In the 5x5, he will mentor up to five. In the G-12.3, three is the goal. The principle: raise up coaches who have experience leading groups and allow them to coach as many groups (up to 12) as they have the time and skills to coach. The more groups the coach oversees, the greater the commitment and time will be required for success. Therefore, in busier metropolitan cultures, it is wise to limit the number that a volunteer coach would oversee to no more than five.

How often do they meet in coaching huddles?

Frequency of coaching huddles varies from once per week to once per quarter. The pure G-12 model requires the coach to meet with his 12 leaders every week to model what they should do in their open cell groups that week. In other models, the frequency is not fixed. The most effective models meet at least once per month. The principle: Discover what your people need. Leaders that require lots of hands-on mentoring will appreciate weekly meetings.

Does the coach continue to lead a small group?

This is a crucial distinctive of the G-12 model. The G-12 leader, who plays the coaching role, also continues to lead a group. In the 5x5 model, the coach typically hands his group over to another leader. In other models, both options are viable. The principle: Talk with the leader and ask him what he wants to do. Many effective small group leaders have been promoted to the role of coach and are now frustrated because they so enjoyed leading a group. Good leaders are often able to lead a group while coaching two or three additional leaders.

How many coaches does the small group pastor oversee?

The number of coaches directly under a small group pastor is a key differential between the various models. The 5x5 model dictates that the small group pastor oversees up to five coaches (up to 25 small groups). In the G-12, the small group pastor will oversee up to twelve coaches (up to 144 small groups).

In the G-12.3 model, the pastor for small groups oversees no more than 12 coaches and 50 groups. Other creative models have various numbers between five and twelve coaches under the small group pastors (See Joel Comiskey's book *From 12 to 3*).

Peripheral Questions

How do the groups multiply?
Traditionally, the 5x5 model embraces the split approach where 14 people divide into two groups of seven. The G-12 model practices small group planting, a process where one small group member is launched out to start a new group, leaving the old group intact. The reality is that there are many ways to multiply a group. Three people can launch out to plant a new group. The old leader might start a new group, handing off the old group to an apprentice. Two groups might work together to start a third. All of these are used in the different oversight strategies.

Are groups homogenous or heterogeneous?
For churches that follow the G-12 model as outlined by International Charismatic Mission, groups are organized homogeneously (by gender or age). In most 5x5 churches, the groups are heterogeneous family groups. But there are also many churches using the G-12 model to oversee heterogeneous family groups, and the same is also true for the 5x5 model. Some churches have a mixture of both.

Are groups organized geographically or by affinity?
It has been assumed that the 5x5 model is the geographic model and the G-12 model is the affinity-based model. While this is often the case, it is false to assume these connections as a basic principle. Many 5x5 churches have groups based around affinity, such as youth small groups, groups that meet at lunch breaks, or men's and women's groups. In the same way, many G-12 churches organize their small groups around geography. Once again, in some churches, the small groups are organized around either type, depending on the passion of the small group leader.

Organic Development of an Oversight Model

Most pastors would love to have a prescribed model that works in all situations. To have a clearly articulated destination, a final product directly from the hand of God would be most comforting. However, no such model is given in the New Testament. Instead, the Bible only lays out principles that overseers and shepherds are to follow. The Bible seems to emphasize the journey more than the final destination. It seems to encourage the church to live out the principles of following God and allowing him to organically develop his church as he sees fit.

The popular small group oversight models were not predetermined structures that pastors received from God in a vacuum. They arose through the journey of trial and error, through following God's leading in the messiness of ministry. In such organic development found on this journey, God shapes his people into the Bride he desires. You can and should learn lessons from these models; you don't have to recreate the wheel. But you cannot short-circuit the journey and arrive at a perfect oversight model without going through the process of following God to see what kind of model he wants to create in your church.

Use these questions as guideposts on your journey. See what kind of oversight structure he is developing in your church, one that works in your culture at this time. It will share characteristics of other models, but as it organically develops, it will possess unique traits given from God's heart to you.

My Last Word

The oversight model should develop out of the relational investment that is provided to the group leaders. The model must be a servant of the relationships, not the other way around. As soon as the model becomes the focus, we miss the point. God does not move through models; people are his preferred conduit for life. As an oversight model emerges in your church, you must recognize that it must continue to emerge and change. The Spirit of God calls us on a journey of experimentation and risk, not one of stagnation and risk. And as soon as we think we can settle on one way to structure groups, we will miss out on the new shift that God wants to introduce.

CHAPTER

Equip the People
for Kingdom Relationships

Recently, I had a minor car accident. The police officer who drove up to sort it all out offered me a sheet a paper that no one in my situation wants to receive—a traffic ticket. On it he wrote, "inattentive driving." Not exactly what I like to read about my driving when I think about my family sitting in the car.

As a pastor and consultant, I have observed a pattern that probably deserves some kind of pastoral citation. If there were such a thing as the "pastor police," there would be a category on the citation that reads, "inattentive equipping."

I did not pay attention to what was happening on the road. As pastors, we often do not pay close enough attention to how the people we lead are being equipped. Thereby, we continue with patterns of equipping that have been handed to us from the past, ways of equipping that may have worked previously but fail the church today in preparing people for relational kingdom living.

The equipping tradition that has been passed down from previous generations assumes that the primary goal of equipping is to create a people who think correctly. With this assumption, we adopt communication strategies that impact people's cognitive processing skills—specifically preaching and teaching—with the expert communicator informing people in what they do not know.

I have found myself opting for this pattern in my equipping of people. I preached and taught people in large group settings. I have organized classes that served as elective training for individuals including a new member's class, apologetics, and prayer. I have written Bible study materials to shape how people think. All of this is important, but at the same time incomplete. I have not been fully attentive to the effectiveness of this methodology. This pattern of equipping keeps us as pastors busy, but the way we do the equipping inadvertently ignores key issues needed for effectively equipping people. As a result, unnecessary pressure is added to the job of small group leaders because they have to handle the equipping of their small group members, something that they feel ill-prepared to do.

Instead of equipping a people who are only marked by right beliefs, the relational way equips people in the ways of belonging and the practices of faith. Beliefs, belongings, and behaviors form a three part foundation for the life of what Peter calls "strangers and aliens in this world."

Structural Myth #9:
Equipping that solely addresses 'right Christian thinking' will adequately prepare people for relational kingdom living and fruitful small group life.

The Relational Truth:
In God's relational kingdom, equipping the people must prepare them to walk as aliens and strangers in this world.

Equipping for Alienship

When someone migrates from another country to the United States, he must complete the process of naturalization in order to change his status from an alien to a U.S. citizen. This process includes the completion of an application, demonstration of a basic command of the English language, and the passing of a civics test on the history and government of the United States. In other words, for an alien to become a citizen, he must go through training for citizenship.

As members of the church of God, *"Our citizenship is in heaven"*

(Phil. 3:20). We are aliens and exiles according to the apostle Peter. We do not belong to the kingdoms of this world but the kingdom of our God in heaven. The church is in the business of training its people to be good aliens in this world and therefore good citizens of heaven. God has charged the church with the task of equipping people for kingdom citizenship, people who stand out as having something radically different than the citizens of this world.

Because we Americans tend to view ourselves as belonging to a Christian nation, the church becomes a means for improving ourselves to be better American citizens. Therefore, church is a place to hear a sermon for the purpose of spiritual recharging. After the service, we can then go out and live our "real" lives the other six days of the week. We see church as a meeting with preaching and singing that serves as a spiritual gas station, something that is necessary when needed, but not central to the journey of life.

Many church leaders have fallen victim to this "better citizen" mentality. They seek to provide the best church services possible to attract these people so that they can try to shape their spiritual lives to some degree, even though they know the impact will be limited. They are satisfied with attracting people and trying to make them into "good church members," as if church were a hobby or a club. Of course, no one would ever use such language, but the way we treat the church reveals more than words.

Through our inattentiveness to equipping people for alienship, church leaders have inadvertently allowed their people to settle for what Dietrich Bonhoeffer calls "cheap grace." By this, Bonhoeffer is not proposing that the church should espouse browbeating legalism, but the church need not settle for a Christianity whereby the culture dictates the role that church plays in shaping how people live. In the opening sentences of his book, *The Cost of Discipleship*, Bonhoeffer writes,

> Cheap grace is the mortal enemy of our church. Our struggle today is for costly grace. Cheap grace means grace as bargain-basement goods, cut-rate forgiveness, cut-rate comfort, cut-rate sacrament; grace as the church's inexhaustible pantry, from which it is doled out by careless hands without hesitation or limit. It is grace without a price, without costs. ... Cheap grace means grace as doctrine, as principle, as system. It means forgiveness of sins as a general truth; it means God's love as merely a Christian idea of God.[1]

Cheap grace fails to offer alternative ways of living that stand against the norms of the culture. Instead, it only offers information, doctrines, and principles. It offers beliefs and systems of beliefs, but it does not necessarily challenge the patterns of living. Cheap grace allows people to remain within the assumptions of culture instead of inviting people on a radical journey to become aliens to this world. Such is costly grace. Bonhoeffer explains, "It is costly, because it calls to discipleship; it is grace because it calls us to follow Jesus Christ. It is costly, because it costs people their lives; it is grace because it thereby makes them live."[2]

Putting people into small groups will not necessarily address these entrapping norms. Instead, as has often been the case in cultural Christianity since the day that Constantine made the church the official state religion, the norms of the culture shape the small groups. If we are going to equip the people of God to live the relational kingdom life, we must deconstruct the assumptions of today's norms. We cannot ignore them as if they don't exist. Bonhoeffer states, "Staying in the old situation and following Christ mutually exclude each other."[3] To summarize, if we fail to identify the old situation accurately, its ways will creep into the ways of Christ.

Norms that Shape Life Today

In a culture of individualism, people come to Christ having been schooled in these norms. If they go unchallenged, we may have Christians who have correct doctrine and live moral lives, but they will have failed to fully enter the journey of communion with the triune God of community. There are many norms that must be challenged by the church. The subtle, hidden life patterns are often ignored.

To identify some of these hidden patterns, I use four basic questions. These are questions that everyone asks when they take the time to ponder life. They may not ask them in these ways, but these questions and how people answer them form the bedrock for how people live their lives.

Question #1: Where do I belong?
Question #2: Who am I?
Question #3: What do I have to offer?
Question #4: What is my destiny?

Cultures around the world answer these questions in different ways at different times. There are no universal answers to these questions. I provide an example of one way to answer each of these questions. In your situation, you could provide three or four different ways that people in your church answer these questions. Ask these four questions of the culture in which your church sets and see what you discover.

"I work to create an image so that I can attain acceptance."

This norm is one way many answer the question, "Where do I belong?" Our world categorizes people into social classes according to their financial worth and their possessions. The kind of car we drive, the size of house and the plethora of other toys we work hard to purchase put us in a category. As a result, we end up belonging to our things more than we belong to other people. We dispose of relationships far more quickly than we throw away what we have paid for.

People work to make more money so they can attain a level of belonging that they believe will give them some level of satisfaction. Sadly, no one ever finds it. While pastoring in Vancouver, one of our college small groups often met in the 6,000 square foot home belonging to the parents of a college student. It sat on the side of a hill providing the owners with a view of an inlet from the Pacific Ocean, downtown Vancouver and the Lion's Gate Bridge. It was spectacular. The student's father was successful, but his success rarely allowed him to enjoy the view. He left for work before the sun rose, and would only come home for about an hour for dinner before returning to the office until 10:00 p.m.

The church is not immune to this malaise. I have seen pastors that are more proud of their buildings than they are of their people. When asked about how God has moved through their ministry, they first talk about their building programs and other physical changes to the church property. Other pastors are even more proud of how hard they work (until they suffer from burn out). They think that they are giving everything to God, but they are doing things in their own efforts at the expense of their health, their families and their joy. At a conference a few years ago, a pastor felt the Lord's prompting that there was an alcoholic in the audience. He invited anyone with this struggle forward for prayer. While waiting for a response, he said, "Don't worry about it. Some of us are workaholics."

Is one worse than the other?

"I must make a name for myself."

A Christian song refers to the lives of great men of faith in the history of the church. They are held up as icons to be emulated as the song states, "I want to be a man that you can write about ..." While I cannot speak of the motivation of the men who sing these words, I find it hard to believe that Martin Luther, John Wesley, Billy Graham, or the Apostle Paul had the aim of becoming great so that future generations could read about them. I see them as having more concern about obeying God in the moment, not about personal greatness.

This song illustrates a need to answer the question, "Who am I?" In the culture of individualism, some assume that the way to answer this question is to become somebody significant, to attain a level of individual significance in the eyes of other people. Self-promotion and self-development become central to one's life. This question drives people to take care of "me" and "mine," to look out for "number one," because no one else will.

As a result, we are trained to be competitive. People get into college because they have test scores that are better than others. Athletes are venerated because they defeat other athletes. Pretty girls feel pretty until a prettier one moves to town. We live in a world where there are winners and losers built upon comparison. Winners attain significance. Losers sit back and watch the winners.

Such an attitude has been imported into the church. In high school, I thought I would become a doctor or a veterinarian, two professions of perceived significance. When I decided to get serious with God, I looked around to see how I could become a significant Christian. I heard a clear message—although implied, but nonetheless clear—"if you want to be a great Christian there is a hierarchy of commitment. On the top rung is the missionary; the second the pastor; the third a youth pastor or some other associate pastor role; the fourth a deacon; and the fifth a Sunday school teacher. Therefore, if I wanted to be somebody in the church world, I needed to become a missionary or a pastor."

It was quite easy for me to import the norms of the wider society into how I perceived roles within the church. Of course, no one in the church ever stated that pastors were more important than the deacons ... the unspoken norms of hierarchy and control surely communicated this fact.

"I escape reality by being entertained."

We are entertaining ourselves to death, just as Neil Postman argued years ago. With more movies than anyone can afford to see, more channels than anyone can surf, and more web sites than anyone can imagine, who needs reality? We have chat rooms where people create imaginary identities, video games where eight-year-olds become mercenary soldiers, sexual fantasies at the click of a mouse, and drugs that will ease our strife. We look at our daily lives and wonder, "What do I have to offer?" Our world provides ready-made activity combined with false realities that keep us from giving or sharing life with others. Therefore, instead of dealing with life, we just cope with the entertainment of our senses.

I have never seen a television show where the characters sat around for thirty minutes watching television. Why? That would be boring. Great television is about life, and we are intrigued by a good story about people's lives. Many vicariously live through such stories because they are so bored with their own. They don't have friends like the people on *Friends*. They want to "do nothing" with a few confidantes like the four characters on *Seinfeld*.

Many times, pastors become frustrated because of the lack of involvement by church members, concluding that they need to be challenged to commit their lives to Christ again. But as they listen to the call to commitment, they silently tell themselves, "I don't feel that I have anything to contribute to the church because I am so overwhelmed with the rest of my life. I need to escape reality when I come to church, not deal with it."

This point of view can cause pastors to stop challenging people, abdicating to the culture of entertainment (after all, if you can't beat 'em, join 'em). Sermons become little more than a motivational speech to become a better person. In some cases, the subtle message becomes something like, "It does not really matter if you are addicted to television, gossip, or eat too much to cope with your life. Don't worry; God loves you. It will all be okay. Just believe and it will all get better."

"I am trapped by situations out of my control."

This last norm tries to answer the question, "What is my destiny?" Many people have been told that the future is an extension of today. Tomorrow's picture is more of what they have today without possibilities. They don't possess within them a vision of what they can be or how their life can change.

Although America is the land of opportunity, opportunities primarily come to those who already have them.

What does this look like in a practical sense? Young men and women grow up saying that they will be different than their parents. They proclaim that they won't make the same mistakes. But 20 years later they struggle with the same patterns of behavior, the ones they most despised as a child. They might have better jobs and live in bigger houses, but they often perpetuate the same life modeled by previous generations.

People need more than personal salvation and a promise of a mansion in heaven. They need hope that God is active in this world today and that he can change lives now. Some need a vision of life free from previous struggles. Some need assurance that God can heal damaged emotions. All need affirmation that their current depression need not last forever.

Does the church fall into this pattern? I wish my answer was different. It is so easy to meet a person at church and size up their potential in the first conversation. As church leaders, we are tempted to only have hope for those with obvious potential. The rest are relegated to roles that are behind the scenes. They don't have the markings of a leader or exhibit the traits of an influencer. Quite often, these beliefs become self-fulfilling. People often are limited by the labels others put on them.

Equipping for Alienship

Jesus instructed the church to baptize disciples in the name of the Father, the Son and the Holy Spirit. In the early church, baptism was a sign that the Christian was choosing to enter an "extraordinary thoroughgoing resocialization" so that the church "would become virtually the primary group for its members supplanting all other loyalties."[4] Baptism is much more than a sign of where the believer would go when he died or an act of obedience. It is a statement to those outside the church and those inside the church that the Christian is joining a movement of aliens.

Equipping for alienship is the process of inviting and then preparing people to advance along a journey, which is a walk with the triune God and a walk with others in his church. In Peter's first letter, he calls God's people, "aliens and strangers in the world." I also see how this letter can be used to answer these four questions and help shape our lives around this call to alienship.

Where do I belong?

God's categories of belonging don't follow the categories of modern class or socio-economic distinctions. He is building something much different than a nice house in a new neighborhood. His building project is one of spiritual construction. He is connecting his people together into a spiritual house. Peter writes, *"Coming to him as to a living stone, rejected indeed by men, but chosen by God and precious, you also, as living stones, are being built up into a spiritual house, a holy priesthood, to offer up spiritual sacrifices acceptable to God through Jesus Christ"* (1 Peter 2:4-5).

God is shaping his church to manifest his glory as we learn to love one another. Church is not a spiritual drop-off point where we recharge our souls so we can go out and live our individual lives. Church is people who belong to one another. The New Testament uses the image of "the family of God" to illustrate this point, a family not based upon race or blood or even experience. It is a race founded upon the redeeming act of Jesus and the filling of the Holy Spirit. The family of God is more than meetings; it is belonging, connecting in an intertwined life.

The people of God need equipping in this principle because even the most faithful of churchgoers often miss this point. To most people, church is not a place to belong. It is a place to receive spiritual food. When that food becomes less than tasty, it is time to go elsewhere. There is little to no understanding of entering covenant relationships as a people and with a people. Most churchgoers enter into contractual relationships with a church. As long as the church upholds its side of the contract—providing the right spiritual food—then people will continue warming a seat and contributing tithes. This is even true of volunteer leaders. They too belong to a church around a silent contract. As long as things are working well, they will serve.

Covenant relationships stand as a contrast to contractual relationships. In covenant, God vows his faithfulness to his people even in their unfaithfulness to him. The story of Hosea and Gomer demonstrates the stark difference between God's covenant and contract. If he were a contractual God, he would have bowed out of the relationship with man long ago. When we discover the heart of covenant relationships, we assume a different position within the church. In covenant, we vow not to an organization called church but to be a part of a people called church. When I am called to a vision of a church, I covenant to participate in that vision, even through the difficulties.

Who am I?

From belonging flows belief. From our beliefs we discover who we are in Christ. Some will argue that beliefs come first, but beliefs are much more than cognitive points. Beliefs are learned as they are passed down from one generation to the next. We learn spiritual truths from spiritual parents just like we learned about life from our physical parents. For instance, a small group leader who prays and knows the voice of God may not be able to teach a seminar on prayer, but group members will discover how to pray like the leader as they connect with her in prayer.

I learn who I am as a person, set upon the living stone of Jesus Christ, as I belong to others. It is in church that I catch the mystery of who I am in Christ. Many times, the best way I receive truth comes through the voice or actions of another. Sometimes it is just through the consistent presence of the other. In this context of life with others, cognitive teaching takes on the role of providing direction, pointing the way to truth. This truth provides the foundation that becomes real as I live it out in experience with others.

What do I have to offer?

Peter writes, *"But you are a chosen generation, a royal priesthood, a holy nation, his own special people, that you may proclaim the praises of him who called you out of darkness into his marvelous light; who once were not a people but are now the people of God, who had not obtained mercy but now have obtained mercy"* (I Peter 2:9).

The church is a chosen people. Chosen for what? God's people are not set apart to stand against the world as an enclave of isolation. Part of being chosen means being sent to proclaim his praises. The chosen nation of Israel was called to be a light to the nations. Abraham's seed were to be a blessing to all peoples. The church is chosen to be God's means of blessing the world, not for hoarding his riches. He desires to move through his people. This means that participants must realize that they are members of the royal priesthood, people who have the potential to connect people to God.

The priesthood of the believers is a foundational doctrine of the Reformation. Every individual can go to God without an official member of the clergy as an intermediary. As members of this priesthood, each individual has the ability to commune with God and hear his voice. Each individual has the potential to hear his calling and his instructions. This potential is not due to the individual, but to the reality and power of the Holy Spirit at work in this world. As a royal priesthood, the Holy Spirit is speaking to his church, directing as to how to minister and calling people forth to share the praises of God with the world.

The church must equip people to move from pew-sitter to priesthood-walker, inviting them to give away the life of God. To adequately answer the question "What do I have to offer?" we need to learn the art of listening to the voice of God's leading in our lives. Each person has a vocation, a calling to impact the world. Small group members who serve as accountants, grocery store clerks, or elementary school teachers have just as much a calling to impact their world as does the small group leader. Each one possesses a unique vocational calling whereby the Spirit of God seeks to move through them to bring light into darkness. To hear this calling, we need to create space in our hearts to listen to this voice. To find this space, we need to make room in our lives by doing less so that we can hear God's leading to do what he desires for us to do.

What is my destiny?

Peter tells the church that at one time we were not God's people, but now we are the people of God. We were not included, but now we are. We were sitting on the outside, but now we are children of the great and only King of the universe. We have been released from the things of the past that held us in bondage and limited the potential freedom of our future. The King has set us free from those sins and patterns of life that control us. Before we did not have mercy, but now we do. We have a destiny.

What a person imagines today will directly impact the possibilities of the future. If a man can see himself free from anger, he will discover how to walk in it no matter how difficult the struggle. However, if his imagination is filled with a future that is only a continuation of today, he will lose hope. If a single mom can imagine how she can minister to others despite her time limitations, she will be open to the Spirit's leading. Yet, if she only sees a life of perpetual stress, lack of time, and stacks of bills, her problems will hide the reality of what God wants to do in and through her.

Leaders in the church have the call and the responsibility to shape the imaginations of ordinary people who have failed in life. I recently heard a missionary from China share how he felt a call on his life as a child to serve the people of China. Later, he lost that imagined destiny and walked away from God. After divorce, disappointment, and finally desperation, he returned to Christ and had the appearance of a seemingly successful and settled man in his early fifties. Then God put China on his heart again. Fifty-year-old men don't start careers as missionaries…but God does! Today, he leads an orphanage, working with abandoned children. While all are not called to overtly spectacular ministries, for each member of this chosen generation, God has a destiny, a huge dream that will bring utter fulfillment and joy.

Stanley Hauerwas and William Willimon wrote a book entitled *Resident Aliens*, calling the people of God into a life in the Christian colony. They challenge the assumptions of a secularized church that buys into the norms of the culture. They write, "Through the teaching, support, sacrifice, worship, and commitment of the church, utterly ordinary people are enabled to do some rather extraordinary, even heroic acts, not on the basis of their own gifts or abilities, but rather by having a community capable of sustaining Christian virtue. The church enables us to be better people than we could have been if left to our own devices."[5] Life in small groups will start this process of doing something extraordinary. A process of equipping will reinforce the potential for heroic acts.

What Does this Mean…Practically?

Equipping Aliens

Equipping the people of God and developing new small group leaders form two sides of the same coin. I have yet to encounter a pastor with a surplus of leaders. In fact, the greatest impediment to the multiplication of new groups is not the lack of people to fill these groups. The greatest impediment is the shortage of Spirit-equipped leaders who can effectively minister to people. Far more new groups could be started if such leaders were available.

This problem is not new. Jesus also found it a limiting factor. At the end of chapter nine of Matthew, Jesus goes throughout the villages preaching the good news of the kingdom and healing every disease. Then Matthew wrote something very interesting: *"When he (Jesus) saw the crowds, he had compassion on them, because they were harassed and helpless, like sheep without a shepherd."* While reading this passage one day, I thought, "If Jesus, the Good Shepherd, is performing miracles with these people, how can they be like sheep without a shepherd?" Then Jesus explained why in the next verse, *"The harvest is plentiful but the workers are few. Ask the Lord of the harvest, therefore, to send out workers into his harvest field."* Even Jesus recognized that he had limitations. He could not minister to the whole world by himself. The problem is not a lack of harvest, but the lack of workers who can minister to the harvest.

How then does the church raise up workers for the harvest? We begin with Jesus' instruction. We pray. Prayer allows us to tap into the mysterious part of following Christ as a disciple. Larry Crabb writes of the practice of *Soul Talk,* which he uses to describe relationships that result in discipleship. He says, "There are some things we can understand, some truths we can know because God revealed them to us in the Bible. But what we can know will never serve as a manual for helping people change. Mystery will always exceed knowledge. There's no formula for Soul Talk, but if there were, it would be ten parts mystery to one part knowledge. Did we really think it would be different?"[6]

Prayer is our door into the mystery. Discipleship is caught not because someone reads a book or processes new content. We can control what we read or what we process. The mystery occurs when my spirit opens to the Holy Spirit, and I see things differently as I read a book or process new content.

The rest of this chapter deals with the one part of knowledge. These are forms that can facilitate the mystery, assuming that prayer is underlying their implementation.

More than Leadership Training

The most direct approach to raising up workers is leadership training, specifically small group leadership training. This component is important, and there are many sets of good curricula available.[7] Training of new leaders should be held consistently and often. At least twice per year, potential small group leaders should be given the opportunity to be trained in a local church. Even if only two or three are interested, this is two or three more than the church had before, so it's worth the time and energy.

Finding people who are spiritually mature and ready for leadership training is the key to starting new groups. They won't just arrive magically at your door hoping to serve as small group leaders. Tomorrow's small group leaders are today's small group members. Providing regular leadership training will train those who are ready for leadership, but there must also be a way of equipping group members so that they will move from immaturity to maturity, with the hope that some of them will be ready for group leader training at some point in the near future.

Resistance to Equipping

For every one church that has developed an effective process for equipping members, I find that at least five have tried and failed. They just cannot get their people to embrace discipleship and receive the spiritual direction that such a process will provide. Dallas Willard locates the problem:

> Nondiscipleship is the elephant in the church. It is not the much discussed moral failures, financial abuses, or the amazing general similarity between Christians and non-Christians. These are only effects of the underlying problem. The fundamental negative reality among Christian believers now is their failure to be constantly learning how to live their lives in the Kingdom Among Us. And it is an accepted reality.[8]

Attending the classes for the 101, 201, 301, and 401 series and receiving a certificate of completion will not transform anyone or provide an alien status. Many churches have implemented such processes only to have graduates who possess a little more information, but lack the ability to resist the culture norms that they have inherited. Making disciples is a much bigger undertaking than putting people through classes or checking to see if they read the assigned pages for the week.

Because the church often concedes to the demands of consumer Christianity, the church is seen as a place where people come and worship while para-church organizations or Bible schools are better designed to disciple and train people. The local church then settles for playing the role of a holding pen—by keeping the group happy—until those who are "called" to ministry step forward and are sent off to be trained. Such an approach is troubling. God did not give the Great Commission to para-church organizations and Bible schools. He gave it to the church, his kingdom agency on the earth. The church needs more than inspiring worship services and effective small groups. It needs a way to equip people for alienship, to prepare the army of the Lord to be the people of God.

Limitations of Public Proclamation

To accomplish this equipping, most churches depend most heavily on public communication in the forms of preaching and teaching. Within the established church, the gift of public communication is held in high esteem. While we should not denigrate how God uses the speaking gift, neither should we elevate this gift to the degree that we depend upon it too much as the means for equipping.

Public preaching and teaching primarily impacts the cognitive domain of learning, or the center of mental processing that stores information and facts. "The cognitive domain involves knowledge and the development of intellectual skills. This includes the recall or recognition of specific facts, procedural patterns, and concepts that serve in the development of intellectual abilities and skills."[9] The lecture format of the sermon and the classroom primarily focuses on the communication of facts and concepts that one must process on a cognitive level. As a result, a person will develop the ability to comprehend biblical truth and analyze theological nuances based upon the sermons and teachings heard in the church. I am thankful for the years of such sermons that have shaped my thinking about God.

At the same time, there are some concerns about the church that overly depends upon the sermon and the classroom for equipping. It requires everyone in the church to learn through auditory presentations. Auditory learning is only one of many different learning styles. For many people, they can hear something ten times and it will not register. However, if they see it visually they will retain the information quickly. Others are tactile learners, as they need to touch or do something physically to learn something new. Some are verbal processors and require talking through the information with others to learn effectively. To assume that people are equipped because the preacher taught a lesson on a subject will lead a church down a quick road to frustration. The pastor will become frustrated with the people because they don't get it; the people will get frustrated with the pastor because he does not get them.

The most significant problem with an overdependence upon public proclamation for equipping people is the fact that it has a limited impact upon the affective and social domains of learning. While it can have a huge impact on the cognitive domain, its impact on these other two domains is limited.

The affective domain "includes the manner in which we deal with things emotionally, such as feelings, values, appreciation, enthusiasms, motivations, and attitudes."[10] For instance, someone can hear about the theological truth that they are forgiven by God for their sins, but this fact alone often fails to impact how one feels about their failures because the person struggles with rejection. As a result, cognitive information about the fact of God's love and forgiveness hits a brick wall when it comes to how the person feels about receiving love.

The social domain of learning relates to one's ability to interact with others in healthy ways, including communication, teamwork and management of people.[11] In the relational way of the church, this domain of learning is crucial. I have interacted with many church leaders who know how to pray by themselves, but do not know how to lead others into prayer. They know how to communicate what they want, but they don't know how to listen to others who need to share their desires. These pastors also know how to run a program, but they don't know how to guide people into a new vision.

Breaking Free from Redundancy

The heavy reliance upon public preaching and teaching also results in another deficiency in equipping. Most churches become redundant in the messages that they preach. Different traditions within the church at large seem to focus on different streams of spirituality. This is the thesis of Richard Foster's book, *Streams of Living Water*. He finds that churches tend to focus on one of six traditions that have permeated church history. These include: contemplative, holiness, charismatic, social justice, evangelical, and incarnational. He observes how these six traditions identify six different aspects of the ministry of Jesus.[12] At the same time, when a church focuses on one of these six traditions, the equipping can become myopic in nature, limiting the exposure to the other five traditions. For instance, some churches within the evangelical tradition emphasize the initial conversion experience. Every sermon will creatively transition to an invitation for people to give their lives to Jesus, even if it is clear that everyone in attendance is a committed Christian. Another example is found in charismatic churches that focus on

Spirit empowerment. In some of these churches, almost every service somehow relates to a call to receive a fresh touch of the Spirit or to be filled with the Spirit for the first time.

This is not the place to critique any of these traditions. The problem is not found within the focus of any of them, but in the myopia that can result by focusing on one of them. Because almost every tradition depends upon the public proclamation of the Word as the primary form of equipping, the passions of the primary speaker, most likely the senior pastor, will dominate the messages. Some preaching professors state that most preachers only have three messages, no matter what biblical text they use. Even if this number is too low and your preacher has fifteen sermons, he will tie almost any text to his passion, whether a call to salvation, the filling of the Holy Spirit, or an invitation to holiness.

As a result, people will enter a church immature in that particular tradition or aspect of the tradition that the pastor finds most interesting. They will sit under his teaching for a few years and internalize that passion. Often, these people will become frustrated and confess that they need to move on to another church because they feel that they have received as much as they can from that pastor. Those who stay and continue to grow in a church tend to go to deeper levels with the passions of the pastor's tradition by getting involved in sharing the same message. For instance, if the passion is leading people to Jesus, those who remain for the long haul in a church have a similar passion and will get involved in leading the church further into that tradition.

As a result of the redundancy of a specific tradition, a church will exclude people who have the ability to lead people into the other traditions. Foster clearly outlines how the Gospels reveal the life of Jesus as displaying all six of the traditions. Each church should explore ways to promote all six streams of living water. This will most likely mean having multiple voices providing speaking to the people. It will also require releasing the gift of the teacher to creatively facilitate experiences whereby the church can reveal all of Jesus.

The Gift of the Teacher

The gift of the teacher as outlined in the fourth chapter of Ephesians (see chapter four for more on this topic) has the purpose of equipping people for works of service. This extends beyond the provision of cognitive information and enters into the domains of affective learning and social learning. As a result, teachers are those unique individuals within the church who have been called to establish and facilitate learning experiences. This format releases people to live in the truths of the kingdom, which requires knowledge as well as new values and practices.

As a result, the teacher is not necessarily the one who can eloquently verbalize the nuances of the faith. He or she may have this ability, but other abilities are required to effectively impart the freedom of kingdom living within individuals. In order to equip today's people for kingdom living, it will require the ability to provide learning experiences along with the skills to establish new learning systems whereby the people of God equip one another by the power of the Spirit. Such equipping will establish a people who are set apart as aliens and strangers to this world.

The gift of the teacher is manifest when someone or a group of people acts as architects for the creation of a culture of equipping for life within a church. Dallas Willard writes, "I am learning from Jesus how to lead my life, my whole life, my real life."[13] Cognitive teaching alone will not make a true disciple of Jesus. Training in beliefs is crucial, but the social domain requires equipping in belonging while the affective domain demands equipping in behaviors.

Belonging involves the resocialization of the believer into the body of Christ. It is not enough that one gets saved and attends church. When one makes Christ Lord, he is stating that he desires to establish himself within a new community. This is the only way a body can work. One cannot be a body part if he is not connected socially to the other body parts. Life works this way. We are social beings and if a believer does not belong to the body, then he is nothing more than a body part twitching in a ditch.

In addition to beliefs and belonging, holistic discipleship includes equipping in behaviors. Most faithful church members are very clear on what they are not to do, but if you ask them what they are to do, they would say things like, pray, go to church, and read the Bible. Beyond that, things get quite blurry. They have little understanding of the spiritual disciplines that Richard Foster and Dallas Willard describe. They lack an ability to practice their spiritual gifts. They need equipping in the practice of hearing God for others and edifying others as Paul instructs in I Corinthians 14. While believers must rid themselves of the stuff that is on the not-to-do list, if they don't understand what they are to do, they will not have anything to replace the old stuff with, giving permission for that old stuff to come back even stronger.

A Holistic Discipleship Strategy

Discipleship strategies vary from one church to another.[14] The purpose of the following is not to prescribe a one-size-fits-all strategy because none exists. Instead, I aim to introduce four patterns that seem to help churches break free from the cognitive patterns of discipleship that have plagued Christendom.

Pattern #1: One Message

I grew up in a church that had three weekly services, Sunday school and the Sunday afternoon training hour. If someone were to attend every meeting each week, she would be exposed to five different messages and biblical texts, all delivered in lecture style and thereby ignoring the affective and social domains of learning. I received a lot of Bible knowledge for which I am thankful, but three to five different messages per week resulted in too much information to internalize, let alone apply to my life. In addition, most of these presentations were given by our senior pastor, preventing him from lending much of his creativity to any one message. As a result, we settled for mediocrity.

One or two topics per week are more than enough. Repetition is good. A person must be exposed to something six or more times through various approaches before they actually learn it. Without repeated exposure to a biblical principle, the average person will never wrestle with it enough to embrace it.

Therefore, the discussion in the small groups works best when it is an application of the message given during one of the large group services. This format keeps things simple and allows people to process what they are hearing. There seems to be great resistance to this practice in North America. People don't want to be told what to study. Yet, if church leaders can help people understand the principle of one message through different forms, the small group lesson can focus on Bible application rather than Bible study.

Most people do not actually apply a sermon to their lives just because they heard it preached. They need to process the topic before they can apply it. Therefore, the large group provides a forum for preaching and teaching and the small group for processing and application. To put pressure on the small group leader to present a compelling teaching every week can prove quite daunting. Too often, this results in boredom. It is much easier and more effective to facilitate in a group that focuses on processing and application of a text than to teach a text.

Some churches have adopted a pattern whereby a second service (Sunday night or Wednesday night) focuses on the same text which is preached on Sunday morning. In these secondary services, the text is presented in a different way or by a different person. A gifted teacher might delve into the background of the text, thereby equipping people to effectively interpret the Word of God. Another pattern uses the Sunday school hour for the same purpose, where teachers teach the same text which was shared with the entire church by the pastor.[15]

Another way to communicate the same message is through the written medium. Pastors encourage their people to have a time with the Lord everyday. What if the pastor or a group of gifted writers wrote daily devotionals on the topic of the week? Such will keep the people thinking every day about the message. They need not be long or even professionally written, and with the availability of the Internet, distributing such devotionals is not difficult.

Pattern #2: 40-Day Spiritual Adventures

Another pattern that equips the entire church for ministry is the use of short-term adventures. *The 40-Days of Purpose* campaign has demonstrated how effective this can be when done properly. Many have assumed that the magic is found in the content of the *40 Days* and *The Purpose-Driven Life* book. While Rick Warren has tapped into a powerful message, the linchpin to its success is an underlying principle of focusing a church around a thematic campaign for a six-week period.

During those six weeks, the pastor preaches on that theme, the small groups discuss that theme, and individuals read daily devotionals on the same theme. In addition, people are encouraged to participate in a special project or a seminar during that six-week period.

Some churches hold such a campaign every year based around different themes—usually in September or January. This practice invites the entire church to rally around a singular focus and raises the level of maturity of that area of focus. *The 40 Days of Purpose* rallies people around the question of "What is my life focus?" Others include *Walking Out Your Spiritual Gifts, Learning to Reach Out to Your Friends, Finding Hope in a Dark World, Connecting to God,* and many more. Church leaders should seek the Lord as to what he is saying to the church at that season.

The primary key to such an adventure is to include the four elements: the sermon, small group discussion, devotionals, and a corporate project. This will promote the campaign to the church, inviting everyone to participate in an experience that is different than what happens during the rest of the calendar year.

The second key to success with this pattern is proper promotion. A church cannot pull a spiritual adventure together in a couple of weeks. This should be a central thrust on the church calendar so that people realize its importance.[16]

Pattern #3: Parallel System

Small groups provide a great place for people to connect with God, apply the Bible, share life together, and even reach the lost. They are also a natural place for people to process what they are learning from the Lord as they journey with God. Some small group systems have relied upon the small groups to also be the place for discipleship. But the test of time has proven this approach lacking in effectiveness. It is now recognized that an equipping track or path must run parallel to the small group system. The small group leader cannot carry the sole responsibility of leading the group to be a spiritual family and be the primary equipper of each group member. The church leadership must develop an equipping process that addresses the needs of individual Christians: it must take a person from baby Christian, to a growing Christian, to maturity, and then into ministry and leadership. If the pressure is placed on the group leader to walk every member through this process, he will become overwhelmed.

Therefore, running parallel to the small group system is an equipping system, one that provides clear steps that promote progressive maturity from new believer to mature minister. This track is separate from the small groups, but not independent. People don't choose between them. The small group is the place of spiritual family. The equipping track is the place where they receive teaching appropriate to their level of maturity and their unique needs.

Whatever the form of the equipping, whether a discipleship book used a protégé/mentor relationship, class, or retreat, it must have a purpose: one of helping a person grow from point A to point B. The purpose is not to pump people full of information about God and the Bible, but to equip them in beliefs, belonging and behaviors. This means that the first part of the equipping journey should lead into part two, then part three, and so on. There is a natural graduation from one to the next. Common steps in this equipping process include:

- New Christian Equipping
- Growing Christian Discipleship, which might include:
  - Prayer
  - Worship
  - Studying the Word
  - Identity in Christ
  - Servanthood
- Freedom from Hidden Sins (See Next Section, Pattern #4)
- Learning to Minister to others, which would include:
  - How to pray for others
  - How to reach the lost through relational evangelism
  - Discovering and using spiritual gifts
- Training for Group Leadership

This parallel track is different than a Bible school within a church. The Bible school paradigm seeks to provide classes that resemble the curriculum of a seminary or Bible college. The class offerings would be too wide and most likely not integrated. In other words, each class stands on its own. This parallel track is much more limited in nature. Fewer steps are involved, they may not even include classroom experiences, and they are integrated. Each step on the track connects to the others, seeking to move people from one point to the next.

These equipping steps would be provided repetitively so that everyone in the church can go through them. Beyond these basic elements, elective equipping may also be provided that might address more specific needs, such as marriage and family class, worship leading, apologetics, or how to study the Bible. But you must be very careful that these electives do not take priority over the basic elements that are necessary for everyone to grow in Christ.

Pattern #4: Spiritual Freedom Experience

Craig had served God for many years. He was faithful to church, paid his tithes, and had given his life to God in every way that he knew how. He had even seen people healed through his ministry of praying for others. After a few years of being a strong small group member, he went through the leader training and became a relatively effective group leader. But there was something holding Craig back from being fully free to minister the way God wanted him to minister. Later, he shared with a leader how he had a secret sin that was causing him great guilt and stress.

I wonder how many times this story could be repeated. We will never know because they are "secret" sins, those sins that cause shame, fear, and doubt. Faithful men and women of God struggle with things that they don't want anyone to know about.[17] Society tells them that they should not expect freedom from every bad habit and hurt that they have experienced...after all, everyone has a dark side. Even streams of the church have bought into this lie, often because those streams don't have anything to offer their people that would bring them freedom. Other streams of the church try to manipulate people into freedom through guilt and condemnation. This approach has never worked, either.

The best equipping leads people through a process to deal with those nagging sins—paralyzing fears, overwhelming guilt, and other secrets of the heart—allowing them to walk in true freedom. Many churches call these "encounters." In these retreats, group members gather for a time of worship, a teaching on how strongholds limit freedom, and times of confession and prayer in small groups or between pairs of men or women. Things like unforgiveness, bitterness, resentment, compulsive behaviors, sexual sins, and relationships with parents are dealt with.[18]

My Last Word

Imagine your church full of people on a journey toward maturity. Imagine people who are hungry to learn, hungry to meet with God and hungry to live their lives in radical ways. Imagine people who are initiating radical practices like fasting, silent retreats, and random prayer meetings in their homes (not on small group meeting night). No matter how wild your imagination becomes, let yourself dream and then let those dreams lead your church into a different kind of equipping, that kind that will prepare people for kingdom relationships.

Mobilize
for War

In the early 1990s, I participated in an experimental church plant that was based on small groups. After serving as a co-leader of a group that multiplied, I led a new group which I expected to grow and multiply in similar fashion. However, the group struggled. One couple determined that they could not continue in their marriage. Another member wavered over whether he wanted to return to former patterns within a homosexual lifestyle. I had been taught that small groups would organically grow and multiply every six months to one year, but my group was not living up to those expectations.

After a number of months, I realized that the call to God's relational kingdom is a call to war and that the enemy would not give up easily. The satanic hold upon people's lives has been woven deeply into their patterns of thinking and living. These patterns are not changed just because people talk about the Bible and develop a few friendships with other Christians. Satan loves to lull people into the thought that simply gathering in a small group will radically transform their lives. He realizes that, unless people confront his lies, that there will be no lasting change.

The enemy of our souls fears little more than soldiers who recognize the reality of war and are mobilized for victory. Sadly, Satan has little to fear from the American churches because so few recognize the war that we face. Most go through life ignorant of the war that surrounds them, even those who attend church. C. S. Lewis wrote of this malaise in *The Screwtape Letters*, a series of fictional letters from an experienced demon,

Screwtape, to his novice nephew, Wormwood. When a Christian starts to think about the reality of demons, Screwtape instructs,

> Our policy, for the moment, is to conceal ourselves....If any faint suspicion of your existence begins to arise in his mind, suggest to him a picture of something in red tights, and persuade him that since he cannot believe in that (it is an old textbook method of confusing them) he therefore cannot believe in you.[1]

Because many Christians are blinded to the reality of the spiritual war, they settle for a kind of mediocre life that feels right and may even look "Christian." They even gather for meetings every week and study the Bible. They can laugh together, pray that God will bless each person, and support one another during the rocky times. Yet there is little that is truly remarkable about their lives, and nothing exceptional about their groups. In fact, when group members realize the mediocre state of the group, they often find another small group or something else to do. Lewis writes these words through the voice of Screwtape about churchgoing, "Surely you know that if a man can't be cured of churchgoing, the next best thing is to send him all over the neighborhood looking for the church that 'suits' him until he becomes a taster or connoisseur of churches,"[2] or small groups. On the other hand, small groups that enter the war are never mediocre because group members realize that they are confronting lies that have controlled their lives and they are doing something to change how they live.

Structural Myth #10:
Small groups will grow and multiply if they simply serve as a place to discuss the Bible and connect people in relationships.

The Relational Truth:
In God's relational kingdom, groups and individuals are mobilized into units for spiritual warfare.

To War

While in college, my life was defined by two things. First, my relationship with God was dynamic and new. Every day was a new adventure. I was desperate for God and nothing was going to get in the way of that relationship. I fought for my life with God and sensed this deep within my heart.

Secondly, my relationships with other Christians can be described as nothing less than a deep penetration into my soul. It was hard to determine where my life as an individual stopped and where my life with my friends started. We met in small groups every week. We prayed for God's protection, dealt with difficult issues, and had a ton of fun together. But there was more to our lives that that. We were deeply connected to the point of deep knowledge and dependence upon one another. We were more than a small group. We were family. And as such, we were mobilized for war.

My time at war with these friends in the Lord was not new to that ministry. We were walking in a heritage of students who had pioneered new ways of ministering. I heard stories that sounded much like ours, stories of risked adventures, and warlike efforts. Testimonies of stepping out in faith, leading people to the Lord, sacrificial giving, and costly missionary trips were common. From time to time, one of these pioneering graduates would return for a visit and talk of their post-college lives. Their stories were not the same. Yes, they were going to church and had become leaders in churches. Some were even small group leaders. I just did not hear stories that depicted the war they had once fought. Their lives were no longer risky or adventuresome.

Dion Robert is the senior pastor of a church in the Ivory Coast, a stronghold of the Rosicrucian cult. His church planned a crusade in Bouake, the second largest city in his country, requiring hundreds of church leaders to board buses for a three-hour drive on treacherous mountain roads. Just before the event, he received word that the event was under a curse and that he should consider delaying or canceling the crusade.

While buses were transporting the leaders to Bouake, a lumber truck lost control and destroyed one of the vehicles, killing all 28 people aboard. When Pastor Dion came upon the scene, he grieved for an hour or so with the other leaders, then gave some instructions to some of his pastors as to what to do in his absence and proceeded to the crusade to preach. Thousands found Christ at the crusade in the days to follow.

An American pastor present went to him after the service and said, "I don't know how you could get up like that and preach after coming through the shock of the deaths of your small group leaders!" Pastor Dion put his thumb into the chest of the American pastor and said, "That's the difference between the kind of Christianity you have in America and the kind we have here. For you, there is black and white and a lot of gray in between. You are so confused by the gray, thinking that some of the events of life do not have to do with the battle between God and evil. For we Christians in Africa, there is no gray area. There is only the power of God and the presence of Satan and his evil deeds."[3]

The spiritual war is not confined to Third World countries or to pre-Christian cultures. In fact, spiritual warfare is a biblical perspective of what is transpiring on the earth. In his book, *God at War*, Greg Boyd provides a thorough analysis of the biblical view of spiritual conflict. He concludes, "In this view the whole of the cosmos is understood to be caught up in a fierce battle between two rival kingdoms. This view entails that the earth has, quite literally, become a fierce war zone and a desecrated battlefield."[4]

North America is just as much a battlefield as the Ivory Coast. However, the project of Christendom has lulled the Western church into a state of comfort with the so-called Christian culture. We have rock stars that stand in semi-transparent dresses at award ceremonies thanking God for his blessings. We have country music performers who proclaim their allegiance to God and country while singing of things that would make most people blush. We fight for the right to pray before high school sporting events, as if this is a manifestation of God's kingdom.

We participate in a culture that has been inoculated to the Gospel. The Gospel language is embraced but the Gospel life is quietly set aside. The church does not feel the need to fight because the war is not obviously against the church. Satan's strategy to undermine the Western church has been to quietly and subversively weave the lie into the church's self-understanding, that the battle against evil is much smaller in Western culture than it is in countries around the world.

Believing such a lie results in a life of spiritual mediocrity and below-average small groups. People gather every week to help each other feel better about their lives, but there is no call to war, no call to enter into the spiritual battle to lead men and women from captivity. Instead, small groups become enclaves for what Eugene Peterson calls the spirituality of narcissism. He writes,

> Self-spirituality has become the hallmark of our age. The spirituality of Me. A spirituality of self-centering, self-sufficiency, and self-development. All over the world at the present time we have people who have found themselves redefined by the revelation of God in Jesus' birth, death, and resurrection, going off and cultivating the divine within and abandoning spouses, children, friends, and congregations.[5]

If this is true, then we need go no farther than our small group meetings to fight the war because this "spirituality of Me" stands against God's relational kingdom every time we gather.

Numbers Focus Leads to Mediocrity

For decades, church growth experts have told the church to set goals for growth. Small group specialists have shifted the emphasis from counting heads to counting groups and setting goals for group growth. Around the world, the fastest growing churches set ambitious goals for small group growth. Some even display these goals at the front of their worship auditoriums.

While setting goals for group growth is not evil, it can lead pastors and leaders down the wrong path. Many of the model churches have set ambitious goals and have done whatever it took to accomplish these goals. Pastors feel compelled to work harder and they embrace workaholic patterns at the expense of their own relationships with God and their families. Small group leaders feel pressure to multiply their groups even if they are not healthy. People who are new to the church feel that they have become just another cog in the wheel. The focus has shifted from discipling people to meeting growth goals. This does not mean that a church should not set growth goals, but it does provide a clear caution from focusing solely on these goals as a measurement of success.

When Dr. Yongii Cho saw astronomical group growth in the 1970's, he found that setting goals for group growth helped them move in the right direction. However, we must take some facts into account about the culture of South Korea before assuming that American churches can adopt the strategy of setting goals for growth.

Yoido Full Gospel Church is set in a traditionally Buddhist country. To become a Christian and join a small group and attend a weekend service every week is a statement of radical commitment. The same is true of other countries like El Salvador where the Elim Church sets radical goals. To join the Elim Church and become part of a small group is as much a cultural break as it is a spiritual break.

By contrast, cultural Christianity has subtly reshaped church in America. If the spirituality of narcissism is not confronted, it can infiltrate small groups and even help them grow numerically. We can build entire group systems on the foundation of self-sorting, which often results in what Peterson identifies as the enemy of community: sectarianism. He states, "The sectarian impulse is strong in all branches of the church because it provides such a convenient appearance of community without the difficulties of loving people we don't approve of, or letting Jesus pray us into relationship with the very men and women we've invested a good bit of time avoiding."[6] Therefore, we inadvertently facilitate the propagation of groups of like-minded individualists who reinforce the focus on "me." Often, such groups grow because they reinforce the goals of individuals and, of course, we look at this growth as a mark of success.

Therefore, numbers are not enough. God may be more pleased with the work of a church of 70 with five small groups that are impacting the world than he is with a 5,000-member church that is growing by 25% each year. We are so enamored by numbers that we assume that growth is the manifestation of God's blessing. It is the way to get recognized by the wider church, to sell books, and get on television.

On the other hand, growth does not mean that God is not in it, either. There are many large churches that are growing because they have embraced a radical call to follow God into radical service and enter the war to change lives and social structures. (I hope this is the case. I am a staff pastor in a large church that is aiming to do this very thing.) There is nothing wrong with a megachurch, but church leaders must turn their focus from the glory of a large church back to the simplicity of just following the Spirit of God.

What, Then, is the Goal?

If not group growth, then what should be the goal? The church is not in the business of getting big for the sake of getting big. The church has been charged with the goal of creating a place where God's relational kingdom is practiced. Life in the kingdom is established by the King. The way that life in the kingdom is lived is modeled for us by the one we worship. The church is to create an atmosphere where this kingdom life is the norm, where people's minds and lives are shaped by the ways of the kingdom. Paul states that church leaders are to equip the saints *"until we all reach the unity in the faith and in the knowledge of the Son of God and become mature, attaining to the whole measure of the fullness of Christ"* (Eph. 4:13).

Pastors that have adopted the small group vision to accomplish visions of grandeur will be sorely disappointed. While they have great dreams of impacting the world like Yongii Cho or another great church leader, they don't want to go through the process of breaking that God often uses to prepare leaders. They want the resurrection power without the experience of the cross. They want the thrill of victory without going through the pain of struggle. So they try to bypass the cross by adopting the practices, structure and materials of another church without going through the God-shaping process that led the original church to those practices, structures, and materials. This is ministry in the flesh, and the motive of this kind of pastor is all wrong. The goal of growth and success is not God's aim. He is shaping a people, and the way he shapes his people is through the process. His aim and that of those looking for church success is different.

The Gospel of Mark illustrates this for the church. Three times Jesus informs his disciples that he is going to Jerusalem to suffer, to die and to rise again. The first of these is found in Mark 8:31-33, immediately on the heels of Peter's recognition that Jesus is the Messiah. The disciples—like all first century Jews—expected a Messiah who would restore the political power of Israel and drive out the Romans. The disciples missed the point in this passage and in the subsequent announcements of the cross because they did not understand Jesus' concept of success. They did not see that true power comes not through force, like that of a great strategic plan. They did not see that the power of God only comes on the other side of the cross, upon the death of the dream, and the realization that all is lost without God's intervention.

God does not lead his church to the pinnacle of success without first leading his people to the hill of Golgotha. Church growth without death is nothing more than man's good efforts to do something for God. The life of David Yongii Cho illustrates this. Before he embarked upon the journey of small group development, his church was a growing, thriving group of 3,000 people. Cho failed to see that he was working himself into a grave, literally. He had worn himself out to the point that doctors told him he could no longer pastor. The stress of the job was too much for his body. This sent Yongii Cho into a deep brokenness before the Lord. He could only lie in bed and pray and read his Bible. Flat on his back, he caught a vision for how people could be mobilized for the work of ministry through small groups. It is clear in reading his story that the key to success is not his small group strategy, but the brokenness that led him to the strategy. This death to self for Cho generated a new dependence upon God. Today, Cho prays for three hours per day, realizing that his hope is not found in what he can do or the kind of strategy he can develop, but only in the realized presence of the Almighty.

If most church leaders are like me, they avoid this experience like the plague. No church leader wants to find himself in a time that is less than successful. Yet, such an experience shapes us for the coming blessing. Without it, we don't have the strength to handle the success.

The goal, then, is not growth, but allowing God to shape the people of God into a kingdom people who reflect his glory through humility, servanthood, and prayer. We must develop warriors who are on mission with God to live in a way that contrasts the ways of the world and live risky lives. This will serve as a witness to the world that there is a God who is bigger than the present reality.

The Church's War

The church in America has a long history of being at war. Sadly, most of these conflicts have been civil wars focusing on internal disputes, causing division and shame to God's body. Whether it is the battle over inerrancy, disagreements over the use of spiritual gifts, questions about gender-inclusive translations, disputes over women in ministry, or debates over divine foreknowledge, American church leaders have adopted a practice of allowing disagreements to stand in the way of loving each other. We choose to position ourselves as the judge of others who don't agree with us.[7] We find it hard to fellowship with people with whom we are debating. As a result, we make judgments about others and start verbal sparring matches. In some instances, the disputes have generated rumors causing church members to question the credibility and morality of their pastor. All of this occurs within the body of Christ!

The church has often missed the larger war. The enemy knows that, if he can keep us entrenched in the battle with one another, we will miss the true battle for life. The church is God's means for demonstrating the God-life to the world. It is his way of communicating how life can be different from the rat-race pursuit of our culture. *"His intent was that now, through the church, the manifold wisdom of God should be made known to the rulers and authorities in the heavenly realms, according to his eternal purpose which he accomplished in Christ Jesus our Lord"* (Eph 3:10-11). We are in a spiritual war against very real powers in the heavens that directly impact and destroy lives of people every day. There is a war out there, and the Lord is waiting for his church to recognize its reality and become his warring partner.

Later in Ephesians Paul writes, *"For our struggle is not against flesh and blood, but against the rulers, against the authorities, against the powers of this dark world and against the spiritual forces of evil in the heavenly realms"* (6:12). If we are to understand the nature of the Church's war, then we must seek to understand what Paul labels as rulers, authorities, powers and spiritual forces. If we don't understand our enemies, then we will fight the wrong war.

Typically, interpreters treat Paul's words in one of three ways. The first is they are dismissed as a point of view of the first century. Some argue that because of the modern scientific worldview, we need not worry about realms that are not physical. The modern world only places value on the material, that which can be experienced by the senses. When churches choose to live only in the material, the fight does become one of flesh and blood. They only deal with what they can see, often resulting in a battle of wit and will. All the while, the powers of this dark world laugh at the havoc they can wreak due to this dismissal of spiritual warfare. Few churches actually admit to such a view, but their practices give them away. They do not place a high value on prayer and fasting. They don't seek God for the impossible. They rarely ask for a miracle. Instead, they only look at the physical side of doing church, focusing solely on things like organization, training, curriculum, and oversight structures.

The second is called the spiritual view. This approach sees the spiritual forces as real and active, demons that were once angelic beings but rebelled against the Lord. These demons have a leader the Bible calls Satan. They can inhabit people, cause sickness and create scandal and division. Their primary tool against the believer is to whisper lies. They know that if they can get people to believe that a lie is actually true that they can undermine almost anything.

Those who look for a demon behind every rock have adopted this extreme spiritual view. They blame demons for everything instead of trying to see how people also participate in the deception. Extremists will even command demons to leave multiple times in what seems like a power struggle or a shouting match. Such extreme actions have caused some to dismiss the reality of spiritual forces altogether.

At the same time, there is plenty of evidence that demons exist in this world.[8] In some countries around the world, when the name of Jesus is lifted up, demonized people will scream uncontrollably in fear. Americans look at such displays as disruptive. The people of those countries take such people into prayer rooms and cast out the demons in the name of Jesus. There are spirits that lie to us and cause us to live in blindness to the truth of this matter.

The third view is called the systems view, as it interprets the powers as being cultural patterns or societal habits that create foundational life structures for a people group. Walter Wink describes this view,

> We might think of 'demons' as the actual spirituality of systems and structures that have betrayed their divine vocations. When an entire network of Powers becomes integrated around idolatrous values we get what can be called the Domination System. ... From this perspective, 'Satan' is the world-encompassing spirit of the Domination System.[9]

These powers are not concrete demons that disrupt individual lives; rather they are structural forces that have been corrupted by the fall. Examples of such forces would be Western materialism, which has helped foster a credit-card society in which people spend on average 10% more than they make every year; extreme poverty, where the poor find themselves more and more destitute while those with the money continue to earn more and more; and individualism that leads to isolation, depression, and the dependence on coping mechanisms.

This systems view can take the structural interpretation too far, but when combined with the reality of the spiritual view, we can see how demonic beings work through these cultural and societal patterns to destroy lives and paralyze churches. The Bible clearly assumes that state of cosmic evil in the world, that there is an enemy who is fighting against the advancement of the life God intends for the world. He aims to kill, steal and destroy, and he does this by establishing lies and patterns of lies. These patterns become so prevalent that they become systems of thinking and living. These systems then develop into cultural assumptions. To attack these assumptions is to attack the powers of hell that come against the freedom of God.

If the church fails to realize the extent of the war—that it is not just dealing with personal attack upon individuals, nor is it just addressing social problems, but it is coming against demonic lies that the culture assumes true—then it will fail to reveal the manifold wisdom of God. The war is much bigger than we can imagine.

Christus Victor

The war that the church wages today was won through the cross and the empty tomb. *"Since the children have flesh and blood, he too shared in their humanity so that by his death he might break the power of him who holds the power of death—that is, the devil—and free those who all their lives were held in slavery by their fear of death"* (Heb. 2:14-15). Jesus is the Christ, the Messiah who came to fight and win the war that Israel could not win. He came to fulfill the call that God had given Israel and embody what it means to be a faithful covenant people, the true Israel. This led him to the cross, and as a result he opened the door of freedom so that all nations might enter into the victory that he achieved.

At the same time, complete victory has not been manifested. Victory has been accomplished, but it has yet to become evident. The principalities and powers of this world are defeated but they remain, lying and setting up patterns of lies for all who will believe them. This is the already/not yet eschatological dichotomy.[10] Christ is already the victor, but this victory is not yet fully manifested. The kingdom of God was inaugurated with his first coming, but it will not be completed until his second. George Ladd writes,

> Its [the church's] witness to God victory in the future is based on a victory already achieved in history. It proclaims not merely hope, but a hope based on events in history. ... The church can never be at rest or take her ease but

must always be the church in struggle and conflict, often persecuted, but sure of the ultimate victory.[11]

The church lives in between the two comings of Christ. We live as an in-between people. Some look to the first coming and focus too much on the already. They expect God's total blessing to be realized right now. Sickness, poverty, struggle are not part of their vocabulary because they only see the already. Others focus so much on the not yet that they become dispersers of depression rather than hope. They expect nothing good to happen until Jesus comes back. Both of these emphases are ways to escape the responsibility of entering the war. The optimist "already" focus sees the battle as complete, while the pessimist "not yet" focus only sees defeat until the return of Jesus.

The way has already been cleared for the church to live the kingdom life as an alternative society. We must remember this fact because the circumstances that surround the church—and in some cases within the church—loudly proclaim that victory is impossible, that it is too difficult and that biblical community is an impossibility in the context of Western individualism. The temptation to give up on the vision beckons pastors to quit and just do church as everyone knows it.

The church is the bride of Christ. In the ancient world of first century Judaism, marriage had two stages. The first was betrothal. Once betrothed, the couple was more than engaged; they were fully committed to one another except for marriage, which would also include living together and consummating the relationship. They were already a couple, but not yet fully manifested. For about a year, the man would work to construct a house and prepare a home for his bride. During that same year, the bride would prepare herself for the bridegroom's return. She had to be ready at all times because she did not know exactly when he would come for her. After about a year, the groom's father would decide when his son was ready and would send him to go get his bride. The bride and bridal party had no idea when this day would be. They had to remain prepared at all times.

The Son will return for his bride one of these days. Our calling as the church is to fight for our preparation for the one we love as his waiting bride. If we quit fighting, we won't be a bride prepared for the wedding consummation. If we press on, waging war to enter into this kingdom life, we will be ready, a bride not wearing the garments of this world, but adorned with beauty for the coming King.

What does this mean...Practically?

While writing this book, the Lord led me and my family through a major transition. During this time, I found myself watching quite a few war movies. I did not plan this. It looked coincidental until I asked the Lord if there was any significance to this pattern. Then the correlation became clear. Just as these movies depicted war in the physical, I realized there was a spiritual conflict over the decisions my wife and I were making about our future. In the heavenlies, a war was being waged against us to bring confusion, fear and doubt to derail us and lead us to destruction. Against these warring spirits were heavenly emissaries who were seeking to lead us into the next place of God's blessing. Once I saw the war for what it was, Shawna and I devised a different plan to confront this attack.

The church's war is greater and has far more impact than the battle over one family; therefore, each church must have a plan for war, a set of battle tactics that will guide it to victory. No doubt, Satan has a clear plan of attack to immobilize the church of God. He is not short on tactics to immobilize, confuse, and even destroy churches. He knows how to fight.

If the church does not develop a clear battle plan, then it can only expect to experience more of the same, mediocrity. Albert Einstein defined insanity this way: "doing the same thing over and over again and expecting different results." The kind of community described in this book cannot be done through great strategic planning, the establishing of an efficient oversight structure, or the use of top-notch materials. Those approaches have already been tried and fell short. We can only expect different results if we are willing to fight for those desired results. And it will be a fight. The enemy of our souls hates a church walking in community. He knows that biblical community is a manifestation of the kingdom that destroys his kingdoms.

How Then Do We Fight?

Much has been said on how the Christian and the church should enter the spiritual war. Explanations of the spiritual armor in Ephesians six was a favorite topic of sermons when I was a child. But to tell you the truth, I never understood how to live out the teaching on the spiritual armor. It sounded interesting during a sermon, but I could never connect it to a practical context in the way we lived as a church body. If a person or a church never ventures out into anything radical for God, there is little need for putting on the armor, much less knowing how to use it.

To possess a need for spiritual armor, one needs to understand not only how it is used but also where it is used, creating a context for the war. The context for spiritual warfare is quite different than the context of modern life. It is like a house with three levels. On each level of the war there is a distinct story that parallels the stories on the other two levels. The story on each level is unique to the factors of that level, but they reflect and interface with the other two levels.

The church cannot fight on one or even two levels. It must allow the Spirit to lead the church into the war on each level. The first level is that of the physical, the realities of what happens within the people of God, how they are led, or how people respond to the vision. The second level is the spiritual battlefield, the heavenly war zone, where angels and demons do the bidding of their commanders. The third level occurs in heaven itself, where God's mission is declared and done. Let's look at these three levels, starting with the top and working our way down.

Level #3: God's Mission

Jesus instructed us to pray *"Our Father in heaven,...Your kingdom come, your will be done, on earth as it is in heaven"* (Matt. 5:9-10). God has a mission, one that flows from his heart without end. It is a mission to bring forth the kingdom of God—often called the kingdom of heaven in Matthew—or the manifestation of God's will. God desires to do so much more on this earth than we can ever imagine. His resources to fulfill his mission to restore the fallen creation are unlimited. Ever since Adam sinned, God embarked upon his missional faithfulness to reconcile fallen life back to his kingdom order.

Because God's mission flows from his heart, we must allow the Holy Spirit to lead us into communion with the Father to understand that mission. This is the first calling of the church. We are invited into a way of being with God before we are to do ministry. Without a prayer-filled walk, we do not have a clear sense of God's mission and all we have is what we see on the level of the physical, hence, the importance of the role of the Holy Spirit. His job as a part of the Trinity is to connect man to the heavenlies, revealing the will and the kingdom mission. Peter, quoting the prophet Joel in Acts, preaches, *"In the last days, God says, I will pour out my Spirit on all people. Your sons and daughters will prophesy, your young men will see visions, your old men will dream dreams"* (Acts 2:17).

Old Testament prophets understood the need for visions. This reality is especially true of Ezekiel. He spoke to the exiles in Babylon who were waiting for God's deliverance. They were caught in the war zone of their daily physical existence that made it difficult for them to understand what God was doing. To speak into this reality, God revealed what was going on in the day-to-day life of Judah's captivity. This is the nature of revelation. The captives could not see God's perspective because their circumstances clouded their understanding. Likewise, the church today is surrounded by such chaos and change; feelings of confusion and disillusionment hinder our ability to see what God is doing through the church. To understand God's missional heart, we must prayerfully wait on the Spirit to open our eyes to what God is doing in our day. Such praying takes time, but in this time of the church where there are no quick fixes or magical answers, we must take the time to allow God to reshape us around the mission that flows from his heart.

This is the story of God. The Bible is his story of how the covenant-keeping God revealed his nature and plans to his people who were limited by their first level point of view. It is his revelation, his action toward his people and the world that redeems the people of the first level.

The vision for the church must come as we commune with God. It cannot come from books or from other churches. It cannot come through consultants or new pastors. It cannot come in strategic planning or special speakers. It can only come from seeing God and hearing his word to the church. The Spirit comes to open our eyes to the potential of the power of God in the church. The Spirit is already at work in his churches. Most churches assume that the Spirit will manifest from the outside in, that they must seek God's will through a specialist who will come with a magical answer to get them on track. Churches don't need any more grand schemes or ready-made plans. What happens after the scheme or plan is completed? God has called his people, and the redeeming Spirit is moving in his churches. When churches learn to listen to the Spirit and recognize his life and will within them, then they learn to depend upon the Spirit of God. Here the will of heaven is revealed.

Level #2: The Spiritual War Zone

For 21 days, Daniel prayed and fasted, seeking God for understanding of a vision. Then a being the Bible calls a "man" came and said to him, *"Do not be afraid, Daniel. Since the first day that you set your mind to gain under-standing and to humble yourself before your God, your words were heard, and I have come in response to them. But the prince of the Persian kingdom resisted me twenty-one days. Then Michael, one of the chief princes, came to help me, because I was detained there with the king of Persia"* (Daniel 10:12-13). This "man" is clearly an angelic being who was sent from heaven to interpret the visions that Daniel had seen. He states that his delay was a result of a spiritual war that was going on between heaven and earth. The prince of Persia was a ter-ritorial emissary of Satan who was charged with the duty to hinder the will of heaven.[12]

The Bible presupposes that there is an unseen realm where spiritual war transpires. Since the Enlightenment, many biblical scholars have interpreted passages that identify such a war zone as part of the mythological view of ancient societies. They see no need for angels or demons, even though the Bible says that Satan is like a "roaring lion, seeking whom he may devour." The second level is collapsed, thereby only leaving the will of heaven and the physicality of the world.

If this is the case, then why did Jesus, the revelation of truth, not correct this "mythological" worldview? Why would he leave the church with a faulty paradigm for prayer and the realm of the Spirit? To highlight one example, Luke explains,

> Jesus was driving out a demon that was mute. When the demon left, the man who had been mute spoke, and the crowd was amazed. But some of them said, 'By Beelzebub, the prince of demons, he is driving out demons.'...Jesus knew their thoughts and said to them: 'Any kingdom divided against itself will be ruined, and a house divided against itself will fall. If Satan is divided against himself, how can his kingdom stand?' (Luke 11:14-18).

Jesus does not refute the reality of Satan or demons. He does not undermine this worldview. Instead, he embraces it and enters into the war to defeat the enemy by stating, *"But if I drive out demons by the finger of God, then the kingdom of God has come upon you"* (Luke 11:20). He argues that victory in this spiritual war is a manifestation of the kingdom of God. It is one way that the will of heaven (the third level) is revealed on earth (the first level).[13]

The church can learn a few things about how to follow God into the will of heaven. First, the second level has bearing on how pastors lead their churches, not just on the lives of individuals. Most of the spiritual warfare literature applies the struggle between God and evil to the victory experienced by individuals, to demonic bondage and spiritual deliverance. The story of Daniel does not correlate to personal spiritual freedom. The spiritual battle narrated there centers around the spiritual bondage and freedom of the people of God. There is a battle over the church. To place an individual in bondage stops one person. To bind an entire church stops an army. Therefore, pastors must recognize that through the second story, Satan stands against their grasping (in the first level) the revelation of God's mission (the third level).

Secondly, God's mission will only be seen and understood through prayer. Daniel illustrates this. He saw visions and then he waited in prayer for their interpretation. Church leaders are tempted to jump to vision conclusions without hearing God's interpretation and direction. Because we are pragmatists by nature, we assume that God is only interested in results via action. Rather, he is more interested in the relationship that is developed as we walk the journey with him. If we fail to wait on him in prayer then we miss him and we often miss the meaning of the visions we have been given.

Such a vision need not be dramatic or symbolic as those in Daniel. Many pastors have received God visions through reading a book promoting the vision of the church. For example, I have heard countless pastors relate how their hearts pounded with a resounding "yes" as they read one of the many books on the small group vision. When I first started consulting with churches as a part of a non-profit ministry, pastors would call and ask, "How do I do this?" In those days, we assumed that if we provided them with practical steps and tools, these churches could effectively develop small groups. Now I realize we overlooked a crucial step. We did not help churches discern God's interpretation of the vision. We gave them a model to follow. We did not help them listen to the Spirit and allow God to develop his unique relational life through the churches. Many leaders understood that they could not just adopt a ready-made program, and they waited on God's clarification. These are the churches across North America that are manifesting God's relational kingdom, and they are doing it in many different creative forms.[14]

Third, seeing and understanding the will of heaven takes time. We cannot dictate to God how he will provide his vision and his understanding of those visions. In addition, because there is a war zone between the third and first levels, there are powers that resist the revelation to us. In addition, the revelation of God's mission is revealed by the Spirit through is people. Many pastors today take a different approach. They catch a vision for community and they begin proclaiming the new direction of the church at every venue. However, a pastor is not the Spirit. A man or woman cannot be the revealer. The leaders of a church must see the vision and attain its understanding together, often adding varying nuances via their gifting and perspective. Such takes time and prayer. It requires patient communion with the relational God who is not in a hurry. He has been on mission to redeem creation for thousands of years and is not interested in short cuts.

I worked with one church that had received God's visions for its calling and direction progressively over a period of about ten years. The visions primarily came to one of the lead pastors during times of corporate prayer. As these visions were shared with the overseers and the other pastors, they waited and prayed together so that the Lord might reveal his understanding. During this time, the senior pastor preached what he saw in the Bible. After about 10 years of praying, talking, and receiving more visions from God, another pastor began to put the series of visions together and share them with the other leaders. Through lots of sharing and dialogue, it became clear that the interpretation fit the themes in which the senior pastor had been preaching. The understanding did not come quickly. The team of leaders was forced to wait on God together before the understanding came.

Level #1: The Physical Manifestation of a Kingdom

The Enlightenment interprets the world as purely physical. That which can be seen, heard, felt, or smelled determine what is real. In some ways, the Enlightenment worldview was a reaction to an over-spiritualized reality.

Traditionally, the church since Augustine has denigrated that which is physical in favor of a spiritual reality that lies behind the physical. For instance, praying that God would bless the food before one eats it originates in a belief that food must be cleansed and made holy by God because it is physical. The same it true about sex. Because sexual intercourse is physical, it was viewed by the church as suspect.

An over-spiritualized reality is not the worldview reflected in the Scriptures. While the Bible recognizes the God of mission (level #3) and the realm of a spiritual war zone (level #2), it in no way de-emphasizes the reality of the physical. In fact, it sweeps the physical reality up as a subset of the spiritual. Therefore, the first level is just as much a part of the spiritual war as the other two.

We see this clearly in the ministry of Jesus. He was concerned about more than the spiritual welfare and the eternal destiny of individual's souls. He attended to their physical well-being also. He understood that hunger, disease, mental illness, social oppression, poverty and the like were physical manifestations of a kingdom, a kingdom ruled by the enemy of our souls. They were not purely physical. The physical had spiritual connections. He addressed such issues in ways that recognized the value of the physical life. The miracles, or the "signs" as they are called in the Gospel of John, illustrate this fact. The first sign was the turning of water into wine at a wedding. Such an act not only endorses the physical; it celebrates it. Jesus did more than just claim to be the bread of life; he fed the 5,000. He is the light of the world, and he healed the man born blind. He is the resurrection and the life, and he manifested this reality by raising Lazarus from the dead. The physical world was the realm where he manifested the reality of the kingdom of God. He did not leave it to the world of "spiritual" talk. He demonstrated what it means for the will of heaven to confront the kingdoms of this world.

The spiritual battle of the church has a physical reality. Spiritual warfare cannot be relegated to prayer strategies alone. The actions that church leaders take have spiritual ramifications that impact how people respond in third level visions. Spiritual leadership is spiritual warfare. It is on this first level that the will of heaven (third level) that has been envisioned and interpreted by the Holy Spirit (second level) is manifest. The actions taken by leaders on this first level have a direct impact on whether or not the will of heaven is manifest.

Let me illustrate. Many pastors have received a clear vision for biblical community. They have even waited upon the Spirit's understanding so that they might apply this vision to their local situation. The excitement of the vision overwhelms them to the point that it is all they can talk about. Every sermon seems to weave aspects of the new vision. The pastor publicly pronounces the new vision as a modern-day prophet. The pastor develops new training materials and promotes the vision at every turn. Initially, the people support the new vision, but after six months, the excitement wanes. The pastor still has the vision, but the people just don't get it. So he increases the communication of the vision. He becomes more direct about what God is calling the church to be. As a result, some of the people leave. Leaders get frustrated and tired because of the stress, but the pastor knows that he has heard God's vision.

Over the past ten years, I have seen one mistake consistently made by pastors who have attended conferences on biblical community. They become so enthralled with the prophetic vision they have received that they communicate the vision to their people in the same prophetic manner in which they received it. They often communicate with black and white contrasts, setting up the traditional ways of doing church as an antithesis of the new vision, criticizing the old ways to which many possess emotional attachments. They enforce this critical message on their people over the period of weeks in the same way they heard them over a couple of days. As a result, people are forced to make a quick decision among three options: 1) get excited about the prophetic calling; 2) leave; or 3) resist in a passive-aggressive manner.

Pastors assume that the way to lead people into the new vision is to talk about it. They proclaim the new vision as prophetic voices because they see the new vision clearly. As a result, the message gets out too quickly, forcing people to make a premature decision to enter into the vision. Therefore, they only understand the forms or the external nature of biblical community and fail to see the spirit or the internal life of it. They only see the small group as a weekly meeting and miss the relational kingdom life that makes these small groups vibrant. Thus, they import the life they had in the previous forms into these small groups, and they end up being just as mediocre.

When a new vision is launched, people respond with predictable emotional patterns. At first, the reaction is generally optimistic. As time progresses, people realize the potential of the new vision and the optimism increases. Then reality sets in. The ups and downs of trying to live out a new venture manifest, resulting in the dark night, the point when the leaders wonder if the will of heaven will ever become a reality. It is during this dark night that God shapes his leaders and his people for the new vision.

The valley (dark night) is a necessary part of how God shapes his people to live out the new vision. The vision of heaven is more than a new strategy. It is the call to be a new people. Without the dark night experience, the people will not be reshaped for the new structure. They will just have a new form of church without being the kind of people who can live out the values and heart of that structure.

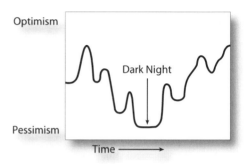

During this dark night, the church has a choice. Will it return to the old ways or will it press on, allowing the Spirit to shape them, trusting that the will of heaven will manifest? Somewhere during this time, the church must break with the past. This is called discontinuous change. Up until now, change has been progressive or incremental. Incremental changes help maintain and improve the church. Such changes include adaptation to new situations and fine-tuning what has already been done. It also includes the testing out of new ideas without fully committing to them. With incremental change, the new vision can be mixed in with the old. The two run simultaneously. During the dark night, the choice must be made to enter discontinuous change and break from the past, or remain in mediocrity and return to what the church knows.

Discontinuous change is the re-creation of the life of the church. It is the shift to walk in the mission of God. It is the point of no return that requires full commitment of the entire church, not just those interested in small groups, and not just the small group advocate. It especially requires the full investment of all the pastors and key volunteer leaders. Without this investment of those who lead the church, the journey will result in conflicts that will immobilize the church, generating more status-quo mediocrity.

In other words, the church must make a decision if it will live out the relational kingdom or be a church that provides small groups as one of many offerings. Will it determine a way to lead people into an alternative life of right relatedness with one another, or will it just create nice wholesome small groups for the pleasure of individuals? Will the church embody the mission, or will it just experiment with structures that seem to fit the vision? Will it let go of old ways of doing church so that it can fully enter the connected life? Will it seize the vision that has been proclaimed or will it just go through the motions? Questions like these take time to answer and require much dialogue among leaders. It is tempting to answer them positively and move on to the questions of how a church can move forward. But quick answers by one or two leaders often results in the rest of a church feeling left out and misunderstood.

Communicating God's Mission on Plains of Earth

God's mission is exciting stuff. God's third-level visions are radical, inspiring and life-changing. There is nothing ordinary when God makes his will in third level clear to those of us living in the first level, earth. Jesus taught us to pray *"Thy kingdom come, thy will be done, on earth as it is in heaven"* (Luke 11:2, KJV). The realities of life found on the plains of earth do not match up with God's kingdom will. Jesus instructs us to pray that this will not continue to be the case.

If public proclamation of God's mission forces people into premature decisions, we must seek out other ways of communicating what God is doing in this world. I believe some answers can be found in what biblical scholars have named the Messianic Secret. Jesus modeled a way of communicating his meaning of the kingdom and the true nature of the Messiah that did not force people into premature decisions. He allowed people time to catch his meaning and his mission as they followed him.

In the Gospel of Mark, Jesus begins his ministry by proclaiming, *"The kingdom of God has come near. Repent and believe the good news"* (Mark 1:15). Mark's Gospel progresses without providing a clear definition of what Jesus meant by the kingdom of God. Jesus did not explain his mission to his audience. He used terms that any first century Jew would understand, but he did not refute their understanding of the kingdom with propositional statements. When he calls the first disciples immediately after making this proclamation about the kingdom, Jesus does not lay out a ten-page proposal of what it meant to be a disciple. He just said, "Come, follow me."

Does this mean that Jesus did not have a clear vision for the kingdom of God or that he was discovering it along the way? Doubtful. He knew his vision was so radical that it would lead to the cross, that it would cost him everything. Yet he did not reveal these things to those who followed him up front. Some today might call this a "bait and switch" strategy. Jesus was not being fully honest because he did not lay out his vision for the kingdom with three propositional points, a poem, and an illustration.

Instead, Mark tells us that Jesus repeatedly talked about the *musterion* of the kingdom. R. T. France states that:

> [The use of the Greek word *musterion*] can easily mislead English readers who naturally think of a 'mystery' as something which is inherently hard to understand, and which can be unraveled only by unusual cleverness— if it is not totally incomprehensible. But the true sense of *musterion* is better captured by the English 'secret', which denotes not incomprehensibility but hiddenness. A secret is that which is not divulged—but once known it need not be hard to grasp. It is privileged information rather than a puzzle.[15]

Jesus cloaked the meaning of the Messianic kingdom in a secret. After the Parable of the Four Soils (Sower), Jesus told the disciples and a few others close to him, *"The secret of the kingdom of God has been given to you. But to those on the outside everything is said in parables"* (Mark 4:11). Jesus purposely revealed the meaning of the kingdom through the use of encrypted language or parables. He hid what he was up to. This hiding was not done through covering up the vision, but through the creative display of actions and parables that would redefine the meaning of the kingdom without the use of propositions.

The Parable of the Four Soils highlights how people respond to the true kingdom message in different ways. Jesus explained to those close to him that the secret of the kingdom has been made available to those who have ears to understand. To those who cannot understand it, he is just telling interesting stories. If he were to take a propositional approach, they would understand the meaning of the kingdom too quickly, forcing them into a premature decision about Jesus. If he had defined the meaning of the vision to the masses in propositional terms, he would have had too many followers and too many enemies. Eugene Peterson writes of Jesus' use of parables:

> Jesus continually threw odd stories down alongside ordinary lives (para, 'alongside"; bole, thrown') and walked away without explanation or altar call. Then listeners started seeing connections: God connections, life connections, eternity connections. The very lack of obviousness, the unlikeness, was the stimulus to perceiving likeness: God likeness, life likeness, eternity likeness. But the parable didn't do the work—it put the listener's imagination to work. Parables aren't illustrations that make things easier; they make things harder by requiring the exercise of our imaginations, which if we aren't careful becomes the exercise of our faith.[16]

The artistic use of parables allowed Jesus to share the vision with everyone who was willing to listen, without giving the masses too much information about the mission. He needed time for those close to him to understand and embody the mission of the kingdom. He had to demonstrate his radical vision through his actions. He had to teach them over and over the meaning of what he was doing. He had to provide experiences for them so that they might be able to touch and see how the relational kingdom worked. The use of the alternative to propositional teaching gave the disciples and others close to him the space to process the meaning of the kingdom without requiring premature discontinuous change.

Of course, Jesus' followers experienced their own dark night when they saw their leader hanging on a cross. This faith crisis stripped them of all their preconceived definitions of the kingdom. Jesus had told the disciples three times that he was going to Jerusalem to die, but they did not understand what he was saying. It was only after the resurrection and the ascension that all of Jesus' teachings started making sense. We see in the second chapter of Acts how the Holy Spirit empowered the 120 to understand God's mission and powerfully share that with others.

What does this mean practically for how church leaders disseminate a vision for biblical community? Here are a few principles that can be drawn from the Markan Messianic Secret:

1. The larger the group, the more cryptic and secretive the message should be. The vision must be communicated to the church-at-large, but it

should be done through the telling of stories, dropping hints of alternative approaches, and the sharing of testimonies. Propositional presentations that define the vision explicitly will force the crowd into a crisis of decision, resulting in a premature dark night experience. Repetition and creativity is crucial for vision casting to the crowd. The kingdom life will not be embraced through a sermon series. It will take years to get this into the imaginations of the crowd.

2. Use a variety of non-propositional teaching methods with those in leadership. Jesus told more parables to his disciples than he proclaimed to the crowds. Understanding requires experiences and mentoring. Repetition is crucial for leaders to redefine what church means. Leaders need time to process the vision and dialogue around its meaning. Share books and tapes with them. Hold discussion groups around what they are learning. Take them to conferences. More than anything, enter into relationship with them so that you build enough trust with one another to process what you are learning together.

3. If your church has multiple levels of leadership, there must be a different vision dissemination strategy for each level. For instance, those who are the core leaders of the church (3-7) will need to come to a place of understanding that demonstrates absolute commitment and lifestyle embodiment of the vision. Vision dissemination at this level will be much more prophetic and intense and it will require less time. For each level of leadership out from the core, the strategy will be more cryptic and more experiential.

4. Vision dissemination and embodiment through the levels of leadership requires time—lots of time. One intense retreat or a series of sermons will communicate the information, but it will not give people the space to initiate the embodiment of the vision. They will not truly understand what God's relational kingdom looks like. They will only be able to define it. Longevity is essential. And the further out from the core of leadership, the longer it will take for people to understand the vision. Therefore, visionary leaders must be willing to slow down the vision, without losing sight of it.

5. Facilitate dialogue around the scriptures. Create space in leadership team meetings to reflect on and share about some key scriptures that define what it means to be the church. For instance, my leadership team has often used Luke 10:1-12, Matthew 9:35-38 and Ephesians 4:7-16. We will read one of these scriptures aloud, sit in silence for a few minutes and then share what we see. We do this with the same scriptures over and over, allowing them to reshape our imagination. In this way, the entire team taps into God's vision, and I need not feel the pressure to persuade people into the vision.

6. Pray. The mission of God is mysterious stuff. We cannot expect to control it or own it. As we seek God, the Holy Spirit will include us in this mystery and the mission will take hold of us. It will consume God's church. As his mission consumes us, the holy fire of God will consume everything that does not fit with that mission. Oh God, let this be.

My Very Last Word

The fall of man occurred thousands of years ago. Upon the expulsion of Adam and Eve from the Garden, God initiated a war plan for the redemption of man. Through Genesis, we read about the ups and downs of man's response to God's war plan. Abraham is invited to start something that he never saw. Hebrews 11 tells of the great men and women of the Old Testament and of their faith to trust in a God at war to redeem man. They saw that it was God's war, not theirs; his timeline was different than man's. As men and women of action, we attach success to the principle of speed. We want to see God's glory quickly and victory now. We want biblical community sooner rather than later. If we were to apply the principle of speed to those listed in Hebrews 11, all the heroes of the faith would be classified as failures because they died waiting for the fulfillment.

We live in the day that the prophets foretold, the day when God is manifesting his presence around the world as never before. At the same time, God is not in a hurry. He has been at war for thousands of years on behalf of his creation. It is time that we learn to fight according to his rhythms and his speed. Realizing the vision may not occur in this generation, I pray that I am a part of a war effort that will take the church one step further toward its realization so that the next generation might live in it.

Acknowledgements

This book took far longer to write than expected. During the four years of research and writing, it seems that God has led me and my family on a journey into what I wrote about, a journey that has included two job changes and a move from Houston, Texas to Saint Paul, Minnesota. As a result, the list of people that have influenced my heart and my words during this time is entirely too long.

However, I must first thank Randall Neighbour for believing in me enough to allow me to venture down this path even though I did not quite know where it would lead. To James Bell, my father-in-law and pastor for eight years, thank you for challenging me to break out of the love affair I had with church structures and into an understanding of relating to the God of the church. To Alan Roxburgh, you have been a friend, mentor and a breath of honest air about life and the church. To the Executive Team of Woodland Hills Church, Greg Boyd, Paul Eddy and Janice Rohling, for trusting me enough to move my family 1,200 miles to live out the ideas of this book and for your feedback on this book, I cannot express my depth of gratitude.

This book would have been impossible without the editorial feedback of Mark Collins, Tyler DeArmond and Joey Beckham. Thank you for your input. To Sue Yonker, you made me sound better than I really write.

Finally, I must thank my parents. We do life quite differently, but you showed me the relational way. You lived in one house for 38 years. I cannot count the number times my family has moved over the last few years. You like farming and tradition. I like my Apple® laptop and hope to own an iPhone when they are released later this year. My hope is that I am half the relational parent to my children as you are to me.

Notes

Introduction

[1] See Eric Scholosser, *Fast Food Nation* (New York: Harper Perennial, 2002).

[2] *"Super Size Me By the Lb."* www.supersizeme.com

[3] James Brownson, *Stormfront: The Good News of God* (Grand Rapids: Eerdmans, 2003), 9.

[4] Alan Roxburgh, unpublished manuscript, 44.

[5] Alan Roxburgh, unpublished manuscript, 45.

[6] Tod Bolsinger, *It Takes a Church to Raise a Christian* (Grand Rapids: Brazos Press, 2004), 15.

[7] David Bosch, *Transforming Mission* (Maryknoll, NY: Orbis, 1991), 390.

Chapter 1

[1] Will Miller, *Refrigerator Rights*, (New York: Perigee Trade, 2002), 11.

[2] Ibid, 34.

[3] Ibid., xii

[4] Ibid., 81.

[5] Miller, 11.

[6] Gregory Nazianzen, *Oratoines*, 40.41 in T.F. Torrance, *The Christian Doctrine of God: One Being Three Persons* (Edinburgh: T & T Clark, 1996), 47.

[7] Lynn Anderson, *They Smell Like Sheep* (West Monroe, LA: Howard Publishing, 1997), 29,30

[8] Henri Nouwen, *Adam* (London, UK: Darton, Longman & Todd, Ltd., 1997), 52-3.

[9] George Barna, *Turn-Around Churches* (Ventura, CA: Regal Books, 1993), 68.

[10] Miller, 130.

[11] Barna, 68.

[12] Henri Nouwen, *The Way of the Heart* (New York: Ballentine Books, 1981), 11-12.

[13] Brownson, 54.

[14] Robert Coleman, *The Master Plan of Evangelism, 30th Anniversary Edition* (Grand Rapids, Baker Book House, 2993), 34-5.

[15] Paul Zehr and Jim Egli, *Alternative Models for Mennonite Pastoral Formation* (Elkhart, IN: Institute of Mennonite Studies, 1992), 43.

[16] D. Michael Henderson, *John Wesley's Class Meeting: A Model for Making Disciples* (Nappanee, IN: Evangel Publishing House), 138.

[17] Karen Hurston, *Breakthrough Cell Groups* (Houston, TX: TOUCH® Publications, 2001), 125

Chapter 2

[1] Alan Roxburgh and Fred Romanuk, 25-26.

[2] Trevor Hart, *"Revelation," in The Cambridge Companion to Karl Barth*, edited by John Webster (Cambridge: Cambridge University Press, 2000), 37.

[3] This interpretation is supported by modern biblical scholars. In his commentary on Matthew, Eugene Boring writes, "One of the achievements of contemporary ecumenical scholarship, however, is that both Protestant and Roman Catholic scholars generally agree that the original meaning of the text is that Jesus builds the church on Peter as the foundation (contrary to previous Protestant views) rather than on Peter's confession or Peter's faith, and that the position Peter held was unique and unrepeatable (contrary to previous Roman Catholic views). *New Interpreter's Bible*, *"Matthew," volume 8* (Nashville: Abingdon Press, 1996), 347.

[4] Dietrich Bonhoeffer, *Christ the Center*, 27.

[5] George Barna, *Revolution: Finding Vibrant Faith Beyond the Walls of the Sanctuary* (Carol Stream, IL: Tyndale House, 2005), 31-32.

[6] Contrary to popular teaching, it does not make sense for this passage to be about binding and loosing demons. For someone to pray that a demon be bound and then loosed is contradictory and just plain unthoughtful. I have heard more than my fair share of prayers where demons with names like murder, rape, and child molestation were bound over a city, but the crime rates did not change. Jesus' instructions are not related to spiritual warfare from a macro perspective. Specifically, this passage in its context relates to the authority given to Peter, and to the other disciples in chapter 18, to teach and lead the church. Boring writes, "The language of binding and loosing is rabbinic terminology for authoritative teaching, for having the authority to interpret the Torah and apply it to particular cases, declaring what is permitted and what is not permitted.

[7] Donald Hagner, *Matthew 14-28* (Dallas: Word Publishing, 1995), 533.

[8] N. T. Wright, *Jesus and the Victory of God* (Minneapolis: Fortress, 1996), 297.

[9] Paul S. Minear, *Images of the Church in the New Testament* (Eugene, OR: Wipf and Stock Publishers, 1998), 192.

[10] N.T. Wright explains, "Many writers on Paul in the last two hundred years have paid no attention whatever to the concept of Messiahship, assuming that when Paul wrote Christos he thought of it simply as a proper name. (Many non-scholars today, I discover, hear the phrase 'Jesus Christ' in that way, with 'Jesus' being as it were his Christian name and "Christ' being as it were his surname, as though Jesus' parents were called Joseph Christ and Mary Christ.) Equally, there are many writers, both in New Testament studies and in systematic theology, for whom the word 'Christ' has been taken to mean, more or less straightforwardly, 'the incarnate one', 'the God/Man', 'the one who reveals God', or something else down those lines, without regard either for the Jewish meanings of "Messiah', to which such ideas were foreign, or for Paul's own actual usage, which was both derived from Judaism and interestingly innovative" (N. T. Wright, *Paul: A Fresh Perspective* (Minneapolis: Fortress Press, 2006), 40-1.).

[11] Bonhoeffer, 46.

[12] James Dunn, *The Theology of Paul the Apostle* (Grand Rapids: Eerdmans, 1998), 559.

[13] For more on this type of group system see Ted Haggard, *Dog Training, Fly Fishing and Sharing Christ in the 21st Century* (Nashville: Thomas Nelson, 2002).

[14] Dietrich Bonhoeffer, *Life Together*, translated by Daniel Bloesch and James Burtness (Minneapolis: Fortress Press, 1996), 42.

[15] Ibid., 44

[16] Miller, 145.

[17] This is not a statement that all of the homes in the cities where Paul ministered were the same. Archeological evidence has revealed that they are vastly different. But the capacities of these home were very similar. See Roger Gehring, *House Church and Mission* (Peabody, MA: Hendrickson, 2004), 141.

[18] Dunn, 538.

Chapter 3

[1] See Christian Schwarz, *Natural Church Development* (Saint Charles, IL: ChurchSmart, 1996).

[2] There have been many interpretations of the kingdom of God. I recognize that not every tradition applies the kingdom in the particular interpretation that I present here.

[3] Jurgen Moltmann, *The Way of Jesus Christ*, translation by Margaret Kohl (Minneapolis: Fortress Press, 1990), 31.

[4] I am thankful for the generous permission of Randy Frazee to adapt his illustration of how public life is acted out in America. See his excellent book, *Making Room for Life* (Grand Rapids: Zondervan, 2004).

[5] Stanley Hauerwas, *A Community of Character: Toward a Constructive Christian Social Ethic* (Notre Dame: University of Notre Dame, 1981), 81.

[6] Dallas Willard, *The Divine Conspiracy* (San Francisco: Harper, 1998), 214.

[7] N. T. Wright, *Jesus and the Victory of God* (Minneapolis: Fortres Press, 1997), 206

[8] Leslie Newbigin, *The Gospel in a Pluralist Society* (Grand Rapids: Eerdmans, 1989), 203.

[9] Newbigin, 204.

[10] Alexander Solzhenitzyn, address at Harvard University; *Harvard Gazette*, Jun 1978, 2, quotes in Hauerwas, 248.

[11] Randy Frazee, *Making Room for Life* (Grand Rapids: Zondervan, 2003), 187.

[12] Robert Putnam, *Bowling Alone* (New York: Touchstone, 2001), 193.

[13] Putnam, 264-5

[14] Frazee, 74.

[15] Frazee, 130.

[16] *"The Epistle to Diognetus"* in *Early Christian Writings,* translation by Maxwell Stamforth (New York: Penguin Books, 1987), 144-5.

[17] Moltmann, 103.

Chapter 4

[1] Everett Rogers, *Diffusion of Innovations* (New York: The Free Press, 1995), 263.

[2] I am thankful for the work of the Gospel and Our Culture Network for the image "providing spiritual goods and services." The work that these authors have reported in Darrell Guder, *The Missional Church* (Grand Rapids: Eerdmans, 1998), James Brownson, *Stormfront* (Grand Rapids: Eerdmans, 2003), and Lois Barrett, *Treasures in Jars of Clay* (Grand Rapids: Eerdmans, 2004) provide a foundation for what I write in this chapter.

[3] Brownson, *Stormfront,* 7.

[4] David Yongii Cho, *Successful Home Cell Groups,* 107.

[5] Peter Senge and his team clarify the definition of a system as "a perceived whole whose elements

'hang together' because they continually affect each other over time and operate toward a common purpose....Some people think the 'structure' of an organization is the organization chart. Others think 'structure' means the design of organizational work flow and processes. But in systems thinking, the 'structure' is the pattern of interrelationships among key components of the system. That might include the hierarchy and process flows, but it also includes attitudes and perceptions, the quality of products, the ways in which decisions are made, and hundreds of other factors." Peter Senge et. al., *The Fifth Discipline Fieldbook* (New York: Currency Doubleday, 1994), 90.

[6] These stories are intentionally simplified for the sake of communication. Systems theory taken to a much greater level would identify just how complex the stories are. See Peter Senge, *The Fifth Disciple* (New York: Currency Doubleday, 1990).

[7] While only 5% of Protestant pastors are female, I do want to recognize the fact that there are many women who serve churches, seeking to lead people into the life of the kingdom. In addition, there is a much higher percentage of women who serve as church leaders as volunteers and as pastors in large churches. I am honored to be married to a woman who has served as a youth pastor for eight years and to serve with many women in my current position who are called to lead people.

[8] Kent Hunter, *Move Your Church to Action* (Nashville: Abingdon, 2000), 122.

[9] George Barna, *A Profile of Protestant Pastors in Anticipation of "Pastor Appreciation Month,"* Sept. 25, 2001, http://www.barna.org/FlexPage.aspx?Page=BarnaUpdate&BarnaUpdateID=98

[10] Guder, 80.

[11] Paul Fiddes, *Participating in God* (Louisville, KY: John Knox Press, 2000), 7.

[12] Roxburgh and Romanuk, *The Missional Leader: Equipping Your Church to Reach a Changing World* (San Francisco: Jossey-Bass, 2006), 123-124.

[13] See Alan Roxburgh, *The Sky is Falling: A Proposal for Leadership Communities To Take New Risks for the reign of God* (Eagle, ID: ACI Publishing, 2005).

[14] Roxburgh and Romanuk, 159.

[15] Phyllis A. Tickle, *God-Talk in America* ((New York: Crossroad, 1997), 126.

[16] Roxburgh and Romanuk, 124.

[17] This "add water and stir" analogy comes from a conversation with Alan Roxburgh.

[18] Alan Roxburgh, Unpublished manuscript.

[19] Alan Roxburgh and Fred Romanuk, *The Missional Leader* (San Francisco: Jossey-Bass, 2006), 118.

[20] Robert Quinn, *Building the Bridge as You Walk on It* (San Francisco: Jossey-Bass, 2004), 24.

[21] Ibid., 21.

[22] Ibid., 24.

[23] Robert Greenleaf, *Servant Leadership* (Mahwah, NJ: Paulist Press, 1977), 15.

[24] See Ron Myer, *Fivefold Ministry Made Practical: How To Release Apostles, Prophets, Evangelists, Pastors and Teachers To Equip Today's Church* (Lititz, PA: House to House Publications 2006).

[25] William Isaacs, *Dialogue*, 9.

Chapter 5

[1] Cho, 67-70.

[2] Bruno Bettelheim, *Home for the Heart* (Thames and Hudson, London, 1974), quotes in Vanier, 90.

[3] Jim Egli, *Upward, Inward, Outward, Forward* (Houston: TOUCH® Publications, 2000), 10.

[4] Bill Donahue and Russ Robinson, *The Seven Deadly Sins of Small Group Ministry: A Troubleshooting Guide for Church Leaders* (Grand Rapids: Zondervan, 2002), 129.

[5] Robert Wuthnow, *Sharing the Journey*, (New York: The Free Press, 1994). 3-6.

[6] Statistics from Barna Research Online at www.barna.org (2002), quoted in Steve Sjogren,

Irresistible Evangelism (Loveland, CO: Group Publishing, 2004), 38.

[7] Leonard Sweet, *Post-Modern Pilgrims: First Century Passion for the 21st Century World* (Nashville: Broadman & Holman), 162-163.

[8] Rebecca Manley Pippert, *Out of the Saltshaker and Into the World* (Downers Grove, IL: InterVarsity Press, 1979.) NP.

[9] Win Arn and Charles Arn, *The Master's Plan for Making Disciples* (Grand Rapids: Baker Books, 1998).

[10] Steve Sjogren, *Consipiracy of Kindness,* 10th Anniversary Edition (Ventura, CA: Regal Books, 2003), NP.

[11] Quotes in Randy Frazee, *The Connecting Church,* (Grand Rapids, Zondervan, 2001), 85.

[12] D. A. Carson, *The Gospel According to John* (Grand Rapids: Eerdmans, 1991), 569.

[13] Stanley Grenz, *Renewing the Center,* 213.

[14] William Beckham, *Redefining Revival,* (Houston: TOUCH® Publications, 2000), 46.

[15] Putnam, *Bowling Alone,* 237.

[16] Vanier, 34

[17] Vanier, 99-100.

[18] Alan Torrance, class notes, May 5, 1997, lecture at Regent College.

[19] Rick Richardson, *Evangelism Outside the Box* (Downers Grove, IL: InterVarsity Press, 2000), 100.

[20] Charles Ringma, *Catch the Wind: The Shape of the Church to Come* (Sydney: Albatross, 1994), 61.

[21] Henri Nouwen, *Reaching Out,* 98.

[22] Nouwen, 99.

[23] Putnam, *Better Together,* 291.

[24] Steve Sjogren, *Irresistible Evangelism,* (Loveland, CO: Group Publishing, 2003), 91.

[25] Sjogren, *Conspiracy of Kindness,* (Ann Arbor, MI: Vine Books, 2003), 29.

Chapter 6

[1] If interested in this topic, see Wayne Grudem, *Are Miraculous Gifts for Today?: Four Views* (Grand Rapids: Zondervan, 1996).

[2] Alister E. McGrath, *Christian Theology: An Introduction* (Oxford: Blackwell, 1994), 240.

[3] Gordon Fee, *God's Empowering Presence* (Peabody, MA: Hendrickson, 1994), 6.

[4] Jurgen Moltmann, *The Spirit of Life,* (Minneapolis: Fortress Press, 1997), 40.

[5] Jurgen Moltmann, 10-11.

[6] Gordon Fee, 363.

[7] Clark Pinnock, *Flame of Love* (Carol Stream, IL: InterVarsity Press, 1996), 31.

[8] Gordon Fee, *Paul, the Spirit and the People of God* (Peabody, MA: Hendrickson, 1996), 40.

[9] Billy Graham, *The Holy Spirit* (Waco: Word Books, 1978), 121.

[10] Martin Luther, *LW: Sermons, Lenker edition,* 12.190; preached on Ascension Day, 1523, quoted in Douglas Oss, *"A Pentecostal/Charismatic Response to Robert L. Saucy"* in Wayne A. Grudem, *Are Miraculous Gifts for Today: Four Views* (Grand Rapids: Zondervan, 1996), 167.

[11] R. T. Kendall, *The Sensitivity of the Spirit* (Lake Mary, FL: Charisma House, 2002), 37.

[12] R.T. Kendall, *The Anointing* (Nashville: Thomas Nelson, 1999), 146.

[13] Moltmann, *The Source of Life,* 79.

[14] Pinnock, 30.

[15] Colin Gunton writes, "The need here is to avoid the western tendency to conceive the Spirit as the one who closes the circle of divine love, replacing it with an orientation outwards, so that corresponding to the Spirit's constitution of the otherness in relation of the Father and Son in the eternal Trinity is an orientation to the other which is the created world." Colin Gunton, *Act and*

Being (Grand Rapids: Eerdmans, 2002), 120.

[16] See Jack Deere, *The Beginner's Guide to the Gift of Prophecy* (Ann Arbor, MI: Vine Books, 2001).

[17] F. F. Bruce, *Commentary on Galatians, New International Greek Testament Commentary* (Grand Rapids: Eerdmans, 1982), 187.

[18] Maria L. Boccia, "Hidden History of Women Leaders of the Church," *Journal of Biblical Equality,* September 1990, 58, quoted in Stanley Grenz with Denise Muir Kjesbo, *Women in the Church* (Downers Grove, IL, InterVarsity Press, 1995), 37.

[19] See Grenz and Kjesbo, *Women in the Church,* and Ronald Pierce, *Discovering Biblical Equality* (Downers Grove, IL, InterVarsity Press, 2005).

[20] Bruce, 104.

[21] Grenz, 82.

[22] Grenz, 78.

[23] J.I. Packer, quoted in Grenz 141.

[24] Watchman Nee, *The Prayer Ministry of the Church: God Does Not Work Alone* (Anaheim, CA: Living Stream Ministry, 1993), 16.

Chapter 7

[1] See Joseph Myers, *The Search to Belong* (Grand Rapids: Zondervan, 2004).

[2] See Bill Beckham, *The Second Reformation* and *Redefining Revival.*

[3] Edward T. Hall, *The Hidden Dimension,* (New York, Anchor Books, 1969, 1990), 115.

[4] Wayne Meeks, *The First Urban Christians* (Yale University Press, 2003), 75.

[5] Joseph Myers, *The Search to Belong* (Grand Rapids: Zondervan, 2004), 143.

[6] Myers, 70.

[7] Myers, 143.

[8] Myers, 68.

[9] Myers, 143.

[10] Randy Frazee, *The Connecting Church,* 135.

[11] Soren Kierkegaard, *Soren Kierkegaard's Journals and Papers,* Volume 3, L-R, Edited and Translated by Howard and Edna Hong (Bloomington, IN: Indiana University Press, 1975), NP.

Chapter 8

[1] See Larry Krieder, *The Cry for Spiritual Mothers and Fathers* (Lititz, PA: House to House Publications, 2000).

[2] Bosch, 36.

[3] Bosch, 400.

[4] Greg Boyd contrasts power over with power under, applying it to political and national agendas. He argues that the Kingdom of God assumes a power-under approach. At the same time, the context of his book does not apply this principle to church leadership. Therefore, I am building upon his contrast of power over vs. power under and fleshing out how this principle might look within the church leadership world. See *The Myth of a Christian Nation: How the Quest for Political Power is Destroying the Church* (Grand Rapids: Zondervan, 1996), 18.

[5] M. Scott Boren, *How Do We Get There From Here?* (Houston, TX: TOUCH® Publications).

[6] William A. Beckham, *Redefining Revival* (Houston, TX: TOUCH® Publications, 2000), 111-114.

[7] Joel Comiskey, *How To Be a Great Cell Group Coach* (Houston: Cell Group Publications, 2003), 13.

[8] See Joel Comiskey, *From 12 to 3* (Houston: TOUCH® Publications, 2004).

Chapter 9

[1] Dietrich Bonhoeffer, *Discipleship* translated by Barbara Green and Reinhard Krauss (Minneapolis: Fortress Press, 2001), 43.

[2] Bonhoeffer, 45.

[3] Bonhoeffer, 62.

[4] Meeks, 78.

[5] Stanley Hauerwas and William Willimon, *Resident Aliens* (Nashville: Abingdon Press, 1989), 81.

[6] Crabb, 232.

[7] See my *Cell Group Leader Training* which is available from TOUCH® Outreach Ministries at 1-800-735-5865 or online at www.touchusa.org.

[8] Willard, 301.

[9] Bloom B. S. (1956). *Taxonomy of Educational Objectives, Handbook I: The Cognitive Domain.* New York: David McKay Co Inc. http://www.nwlink.com/~donclark/hrd/bloom.html

[10] Krathwohl, D. R., Bloom, B. S., & Bertram, B. M. (1973). *Taxonomy of Educational Objectives, the Classification of Educational Goals. Handbook II: Affective Domain.* New York: David McKay Co., Inc.http://www.nwlink.com/~donclark/hrd/bloom.html

[11] http://pcrest.com/social.htm

[12] Richard Foster, *Streams of Living Water* (San Francisco: Harper Collins, 1998), 3-22.

[13] Dallas Willard, *The Divine Conspiracy* (New York: Harper Collins, 1998), 283.

[14] See *How Do We Get There From Here?* and the *Navigation Guide for Making Cell Groups Work.*

[15] See *The Connecting Church.*

[16] See my article in *Group's Body Building Guide for Community* (Loveland, CO: Group Publishing, 2006), chapter 14.

[17] See Stephen Arterburn, *Every Man's Battle* (Colorado Springs: Waterbrook Press, 2000) and Shannon Etheridge, *Every Woman's Battle* (Colorado Springs: Waterbrook Press, 2003).

[18] See Jim Egli, *Encounter God: Leader's Guide* (Houston: TOUCH® Publications, 2000).

Chapter 10

[1] C. S. Lewis, *The Screwtape Letters* (New York: Harper Collins, 2001), 31-32.

[2] Ibid, 81.

[3] Ralph Neighbour, *Where Do We Go From Here?, 10th Anniversary Edition* (Houston: TOUCH® Publications, 2000), 20.

[4] Greg Boyd, *God at War* (Downers Grove, IL: Intervarsity Press, 1997), 290.

[5] Eugene Peterson, *Christ Plays in Ten Thousand Places* (Grand Rapids, Eerdmans, 2005), 243.

[6] Peterson, 244.

[7] See Greg Boyd, *Repenting of Religion* (Grand Rapids: Baker, 2004).

[8] On the existence of demons see: Graham Dow, "The Case for the Existence of Demons," *Churchman* 94 (1980) 1999-208; Edith Turner, "The Reality of Spirits," *ReVision* 15/1 (Summer 1992) 28-32; Phillip Wiebe, *God and Other Spirits* (New York: Oxford University Press, 2004). On the biblical portrayal of Satan, the demonic and spiritual warfare see Gregory A. Boyd, *God at War: The Bible and Spiritual Conflict* (Downers Grove, IL: InterVarsity, 1997).

[9] Walter Wink, *The Powers that Be: Theology for a New Millennium* (New York: Doubleday, 1998), 27. For a thorough analysis of the systemic or structural interpretation of the demonic see his *Naming the Powers: The Language of Power in the New Testament* (Minneapolis: Fortress Press, 1983).

[10] On the "already/not yet" or inaugurated eschatology see Werner G. Kummel, *Promise and*

Fulfillment: The Eschatological Message of Jesus, third edition (London: SCM, 1957).

[11] George Eldon Ladd, *The Presence of the Future* (Grand Rapids: Eerdmans, 1974), 338.

[12] On Daniel 10 as dealing with demonic entities see Boyd, *God at War*, 136-38; John J. Collins, *Daniel* (Minneapolis: Fortress, 1993), 374-76; J. E. Goldingay, *Daniel* (Dallas: Word, 1989), 291-92, 312-14.

[13] On Jesus' approach to the demonic see Boyd, *God at War*, 192-327; Graham H. Twelftree, *Jesus the Exorcist: A Contribution to the study of the Historical Jesus* (Tubingen: Mohr-Siebeck, 1993).

[14] On discerning the voice of the Spirit see Dallas Willard, *Hearing God: Developing a Conversational Relationship with God* (Downers Grove, IL: InterVarsity Press, 1999).

[15] R. T. France, *The New International Greek Testament Commentary, The Gospel of Mark* (Grand Rapids: Eerdmans, 2002), 196.

[16] Eugene Peterson, *The Contemplative Pastor* (Grand Rapids: Eerdmans, 1989), 32-33.

Additional Resources by the Author

How Do We Get There From Here?

Navigating the Transformation to Holistic Small Groups
by M. Scott Boren

This resource breaks down the transition process into eight manageable parts. If your church is just beginning its transition, these materials will help you focus on building holistic small groups on a sure foundation. If you are in the midst of developing your groups, it highlights where to focus your energy. No matter where you are with your church, these resources will help you identify your current stage of small group development and articulate a plan to address that stage.

The Navigation Guide for Making Cell Groups Work

by M. Scott Boren, Bill Beckham, Joel Comiskey,
Ralph W. Neighbour, Jr and Randall Neighbour

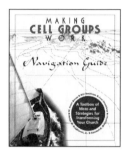

This massive compilation is filled with hundreds of articles by pastors and experts, and includes helpful articles such as shifting your church calendar and budget for a growing cell ministry; how to choose team members to implement the transition; tips on proto-typing groups, and much more! In our opinion, one of the most valuable resources found in this "toolbox" for transitioning churches is a readiness assessment tool. This assessment will help you determine the four key areas of health required for a church to implement groups successfully.

Cell Group Leader Training

Leadership Foundations for Groups that Work
by Scott Boren and Don Tillman

Through the use of teaching, creative activities, small group interaction, and suggested between-the-training exercises, this eight-session training will prepare people for holistic small group group leadership like no other tool. The *Trainer's Guide* provides teaching outlines for all eight sessions and options for organizing the training, including different weekly options and retreat options. The Trainer's Guide also has bonus sections, including teaching outlines for a strategic planning workshop and detailed interview discussion guides for *The Journey Guide for Cell Group Leaders*. This comprehensive training tool will establish your group leaders on a sure foundation.

www.touchusa.org

Visit TOUCH® Outreach Ministries' web site for dozens of free articles by M. Scott Boren. All of the resources on this page can also be purchased from TOUCH® via our web site or by calling our toll-free order line, 1-800-735-5865.